Thomas Garnett

Thomas Garnett

Science, Medicine, Mobility in Eighteenth-Century Britain

Robert Fox

BLOOMSBURY ACADEMIC
LONDON • NEW YORK • OXFORD • NEW DELHI • SYDNEY

BLOOMSBURY ACADEMIC
Bloomsbury Publishing Plc, 50 Bedford Square, London, WC1B 3DP, UK
Bloomsbury Publishing Inc, 1385 Broadway, New York, NY 10018, USA
Bloomsbury Publishing Ireland, 29 Earlsfort Terrace, Dublin 2, D02 AY28, Ireland

BLOOMSBURY, BLOOMSBURY ACADEMIC and the Diana logo
are trademarks of Bloomsbury Publishing Plc

First published in Great Britain 2024
This paperback edition published in 2025

Copyright © Robert Fox, 2024

Robert Fox has asserted his right under the Copyright, Designs and
Patents Act, 1988, to be identified as Author of this work.

Cover image © New Discoveries in Pneumatics. A popular demonstration
at the Royal Institution, London, given by Thomas Garnett (1766–1802).
Cartoon by James Gilray. Photo 12/Alamy Stock Photo.

All rights reserved. No part of this publication may be: i) reproduced or
transmitted in any form, electronic or mechanical, including photocopying,
recording or by means of any information storage or retrieval system without
prior permission in writing from the publishers; or ii) used or reproduced in
any way for the training, development or operation of artificial intelligence (AI)
technologies, including generative AI technologies. The rights holders expressly
reserve this publication from the text and data mining exception as per Article
4(3) of the Digital Single Market Directive (EU) 2019/790.

Bloomsbury Publishing Plc does not have any control over, or responsibility for,
any third-party websites referred to or in this book. All internet addresses given
in this book were correct at the time of going to press. The author and publisher
regret any inconvenience caused if addresses have changed or sites have ceased
to exist, but can accept no responsibility for any such changes.

A catalogue record for this book is available from the British Library.

A catalog record for this book is available from the Library of Congress.

ISBN: HB: 978-1-3502-3929-6
PB: 978-1-3502-3932-6
ePDF: 978-1-3502-3930-2
eBook: 978-1-3502-3931-9

Typeset by Integra Software Services Pvt. Ltd.

For product safety related questions contact productsafety@bloomsbury.com.

To find out more about our authors and books visit www.bloomsbury.com
and sign up for our newsletters.

Contents

List of illustrations	vi
Preface	ix
Note on references and abbreviations	xi
Introduction	1
1 A northern prologue	9
2 Edinburgh: Conformity and dissent in medicine	25
3 Yorkshire: Spa doctor and man of science	49
4 Britain's new north: Lecturer and crusading tourist	77
5 London: Trials and tragedy in Mayfair	107
6 Reputation and legacy	133
Epilogue: The Garnett heritage	147
Bibliography	156
Index	180

Illustrations

0.1 Portrait of Garnett, artist unknown, painted during his time as professor of natural philosophy at the Andersonian Institution, Glasgow, 1796–9. The original, a gift from the nineteenth-century merchant and cultural polymath James Smith of Jordanhill, is in the University of Strathclyde Collections (GLAEX A9). Photograph (GB 249 OP/4/5/2) reproduced courtesy of Archives and Special Collections, University of Strathclyde Library   xv

1.1 Garnett family tree. Source: Author's sketch   11

1.2 High Bank House, Barbon, where Garnett spent his childhood. The property, then known as Bank House, had been built, or rebuilt, by Garnett's grandfather Thomas Garnett in the 1740s, at a time of growing prosperity among better-off yeoman families. It remained a Garnett property until it was finally sold to the Gibson family, owners of the nearby Whelprigg House and Estate, in 1859. Photograph by, and by courtesy of Michael Kingsbury   12

1.3 John Dawson of Sedbergh, standing over a pupil. Mezzotint engraved by William Whiston Burney, and dated June 1809, after an original portrait by Joseph Allen. The portrait is now lost, but the caption to the print identifies its owner in 1809 as Robert Holt Leigh (1762–1843), M.P. for Wigan from 1802 to 1820. The identity of the pupil is unknown, although the name Litterdale is suggested in John Willis Clark and Thomas McKenny Hughes, *Life and Letters of the Reverend Adam Sedgwick*, 2 vols. (Cambridge, 1890), vol. 1, 70. Courtesy of the Wellcome Collection. Public Domain Mark   17

2.1 The Brunonian scale of sickness and health, showing 'Health' at the mid-point between the extremes of sthenic and asthenic disorders. From Garnett, *Popular Lectures on Zoonomia, or the Laws of Animal Life, in Health and Disease* (London, 1804), 221. Adapted from the 'Table of Excitement and Excitability' in John Brown, *Elements of Medicine*, new edn., 2 vols. (Edinburgh, 1795), vol. 1, folding plate facing p. 1. Private collection   33

Illustrations

3.1 Garnett's table of the contents of five of the main Harrogate waters. The water in the first line was the strongest of four sulphur waters known and frequented in Low Harrogate and the only one that was drunk, mainly as a purgative taken (by those who could endure the unpleasant taste and smell) early in the morning. The other sulphur waters were used in warm baths for the treatment of herpes and other cutaneous disorders. The waters of the Tewit Well and Old Spaw contained significant quantities of ferrous carbonate and were classed as mild chalybeates. They were drunk as stimulants to counter debility and what were commonly called 'nervous' disorders, typically manifested as melancholy, hypochondria and listlessness. From Garnett, *A Treatise on the Mineral Waters of Harrogate* (first edition, 1792), 70. Courtesy of the Wellcome Collection. Public Domain Mark. In the second (1794) and subsequent editions of the *Treatise*, Garnett added data for a third chalybeate spring, St George's Well 61

3.2 Dedicatory plate to Alexander Wedderburn, first Baron Loughborough, in the first edition of Garnett's *Treatise on the Mineral Waters of Harrogate* (1792), iii. The plate, engraved by the Manchester-based artist and engraver William Green, incorporates Wedderburn's coat of arms. In the second edition of the *Treatise*, by which time (May 1794) Garnett was living at Wedderburn House in Harrogate, it was replaced with an effusive four-page dedication to Wedderburn, Garnett's 'friend and protector'. Courtesy of the Wellcome Collection. Public Domain Mark 65

3.3 Mezzotint of Garnett seated next to a Nooth apparatus, artist and engraver unknown. The portrait probably dates from the early 1790s, when Garnett, established in Harrogate and 'protected' by Alexander Wedderburn, was working hard to attract patients for his treatments. John Mervin Nooth, physician and army officer, developed his apparatus for producing carbonated water in the 1770s. Although the water was appreciated for its pleasant taste, the vogue it enjoyed in Garnett's time owed more to its supposed medicinal qualities, including treatment for scurvy and the stone. Garnett was a convinced advocate of its use. Courtesy of the Wellcome Collection. Public Domain Mark 66

4.1 The York Cascade, falling into the River Tilt on the Duke of Athol's pleasure grounds at Blair Athol, Perthshire. The wild, broken falls of the Cascade were widely praised by admirers of sublime scenery. But both William Gilpin and Garnett felt that the proximity of the 'greater

viii   *Illustrations*

stream' of the Tilt (below the scene depicted) detracted from the sublimity of the view and a 'simplicity' that was lost through the falls' appearing 'frittered' rather than as a single turbulent gush. Aquatint plate from Garnett, *Observations on a Tour through the Highlands and the Western Isles of Scotland*, 2 vols. (London, 1800), vol. 2, facing p. 47. The plate was one of 52 in the book, all drawn by Walter Henry Watts and engraved by William Green. Private collection   92

5.1 Portrait of Garnett as professor of natural philosophy at the Royal Institution. Stipple engraving by Simon Phillips, after a painting by Thomas Phillips, now lost. Garnett's commanding pose, with one hand holding a book, the other on the receiver of an air pump, conveys the authority associated with a man of learning, though one who also engaged in the active investigation of nature. The engraving is dated 1 May 1801, only a month before Garnett's unhappiness at the RI forced his resignation. His confident appearance suggests an earlier date for the original painting, probably during his first year as professor. Courtesy of the Wellcome Collection. Public Domain Mark   115

5.2 One of two surviving designs for the temporary lecture-theatre at the Royal Institution. The lecturer is shown on a dais in the centre of the room (now part of the library on the first floor of the RI), with ladies seated in the lower rows. Although the designs bear no signature, they are thought to be by Thomas Webster, clerk of works, then clerk, to the RI. The design is in the Drawings & Archives Collection of the Royal Institute of British Architects (SD/55/4/6). Courtesy of RIBA Collections   116

6.1 'Scientific Researches! ... New Discoveries in Pneumaticks ... or, an Experimental Lecture on the Powers of Air'. Coloured etching by James Gillray, published 23 May 1802 by Hannah Humphrey. The cartoon depicts a lecturer at the Royal Institution administering nitrous oxide to Sir John Coxe Hippisley, with embarrassing results. Such an episode, including its consequences, is recorded in the diary of Elizabeth, Lady Holland as occurring in mid-March 1800, when the lecturer was Garnett. Gillray's is an imaginative reconstruction of this true event, which he sets not in the temporary space in which Garnett would have given the lecture (see Figure 5.2) but in the new lecture-theatre, inaugurated a year later. He also portrays Humphry Davy, holding the bellows, as the lecturer's assistant, although it was another year before Davy arrived at the RI. Courtesy of Getty Images   141

Preface

Thomas Garnett has been a companion since I first engaged with him in helping to prepare an exhibition on north-country scientists in the Library of the University of Lancaster in 1983. But it was more recent work for the brief entry about him for the *Oxford Dictionary of National Biography* that convinced me of the potential for an extended study of a figure who had been largely lost from view after a brief period of national celebrity as the founding professor of natural philosophy and chemistry in two institutions: first at the Andersonian Institution (now the University of Strathclyde) and then at the Royal Institution. As was soon evident, the significance and interest of Garnett's career extended far beyond his professorial activities in Glasgow and London, important though these were. By the time of these high-profile appointments in the last years of his short life, he had moved from the obscurity of a yeoman childhood in rural Westmorland to prominence as an Edinburgh-trained spa doctor in Harrogate and recognition in the vibrant scientific network that flourished in the English provinces, especially in the industrial North and Midlands, in the later eighteenth century. The way he navigated through these distinct but adjacent worlds provides a core theme of my book.

A life of such varied achievements has consequences for a biographer, and the debts I have incurred reflect the diversity of Garnett's own experiences. Among the many librarians and archivists on whose knowledge and skills I have drawn, it is a pleasure to record my particular thanks to Charlotte New at the Royal Institution, Anne Cameron in the Andersonian Library, University of Strathclyde, Enid Gardner at the Royal Society of Medicine in Edinburgh, Scout Noffke in the Rauner Special Collections Library, Dartmouth College, and Lauren Alderton and Jonathan Makepeace, who have given essential help with items in the collections of the Royal Institute of British Architects. No acknowledgements would be complete, too, without a mention of the support I have enjoyed day by day in my wonderfully rich and welcoming 'home' library, the Bodleian Library, in Oxford.

Beyond libraries and archives, I owe a special debt to Frank James for many years of encouragement and advice, and an unfaltering belief that this biography would eventually see the light of day. Over the years, as well, I have benefitted from the responses of seminar and other groups in Lancaster, Sedbergh, Penrith, Durham, Oxford and London to talks I have given on Garnett and the broader dimensions of his career and work. In these settings and elsewhere, it has been a privilege to learn from others with often unexpected points of shared interest in a man of rare gifts and the intellectual range of a true son of the Enlightenment. A recent chance encounter with the literary scholar David Duff, currently working on the Royal Institution's publishing press as part of a study of prospectuses, illustrates the value of discussions in unanticipated areas of common ground. Further afield, exchanges with Michael Kingsbury, the owner of the house in Barbon where Garnett spent his childhood, have been a special pleasure since we met more than fifteen years ago through the Sedbergh and District History Society. So too my contact with David and Carol Thomas, who have generously shared the documentary resources on which they have based their deep knowledge of Garnett family history.

In 2020, it was my great good fortune to mention my work on Garnett to Ludmilla Jordanova and, through her, to make a first contact with Frances Arnold and Emily Drewe at Bloomsbury Academic. Since then, the passage from refereeing (by singularly helpful referees) to production has proceeded with exemplary efficiency, aided by the unfailingly judicious and friendly coaxing of Megan Harris since she took over the editorial supervision of the book more than a year ago. In the final stages, Paige Harris at Bloomsbury Academic and Shamli Priya at Integra Software Services have likewise given generously, with support and guidance in seeing the project through to completion. The result has been an association as happy and rewarding as any author could ever hope to have with a publisher.

Oxford
Robert Fox
August 2023

Note on references and abbreviations

Am. Hist. Rev.	*American Historical Review*, Washington, DC
And. MM	Minutes of meetings of managers and trustees, Anderson's Institution. University of Strathclyde Archives and Special Collections, Glasgow
Ann. Phil.	*Annals of Philosophy; or, Magazine of Chemistry, Mineralogy, Mechanics, Natural History, Agriculture, and the Arts*, ed. Thomas Thomson. London
Ann. R. Coll. Surg.	*Annals of the Royal College of Surgeons of England*, London
Ann. Reg.	*Annual Register, or a View of the History, Politics, and Literature*, London
Ann. Sci.	*Annals of Science*, London
APS	American Philosophical Society, Philadelphia
ASC Durham	Archives and Special Collections. Durham University Records, Durham
Asiatic J.	*Asiatic Journal and Monthly Register for British India and Its Dependencies.* London
Athenaeum	*The Athenaeum and Literary Chronicle*, London
BL	British Library, London
Bod.	Bodleian Library, University of Oxford
Brit. Crit.	*The British Critic*, London
Br. J. Hist. Sci.	*The British Journal for the History of Science*, London
Crit. Rev.	*Critical Review; or, Annals of Literature*, London
Edin. Alm.	*Edinburgh Almanack and Scots Register*, Edinburgh
EIC	East India Company

EUA	Edinburgh University Archives
EUL	Edinburgh University Library
Eur. Mag.	*European Magazine, and London Review*, London
Eur. Rom. Rev.	*European Romantic Review*, Los Angeles, CA
Gender Hist.	*Gender & History*
Gent. Mag.	*The Gentleman's Magazine*, London
HWJ	*History Workshop Journal*, Oxford
IMS	Indian Medical Service
J. 18th-Cent. Stud.	*Journal for Eighteenth-Century Studies*, Chichester
J. Hist. Med.	*Journal of the History of Medicine and Allied Sciences*, New York, etc.
J. Med. Biog.	*Journal of Medical Biography*, London
J. Roy. Inst.	*Journals of the Royal Institution of Great Britain*, London
Ladies' Mus.	*The Ladies' Museum*, London
'Life of Garnett'	'An account of the life of the author', in Garnett, *Popular Lectures on Zoonomia, or the Laws of Animal Life, in Health and Medicine* (London, 1804), v-xxii
Lit. Gaz.	*The [London] Literary Gazette and Journal of Belles Lettres, Arts, Sciences, &c*, London
Lonsdale Mag.	*The Lonsdale Magazine, or Provincial Repository*, Kirkby Lonsdale
Med. Comm.	*Medical Commentaries, Collected and Published by Andrew Duncan*. Edinburgh
Med. Hist.	*Medical History*, London
Med. Phil. Comm.	*Medical and Philosophical Commentaries. By a Society of Physicians in Edinburgh*. Edinburgh
Med. Phys. J.	*The Medical and Physical Journal*, London
Med. Reg.	*The Medical Register for the Year ...*, London

Mém. Acad. Sci.	*Mémoires de mathématique et de physique, tirés des registres de l'Académie royale des sciences*, Paris
Mem. Med. Soc. London	*Memoirs of the Medical Society of London*, London
Mem. MLPS	*Memoirs of the Literary and Philosophical Society of Manchester*, Manchester
MLPS	Literary and Philosophical Society of Manchester
Monthly Mag.	*The Monthly Magazine; or, British Register*, London
Monthly Rep.	*The Monthly Repertory of English Literature*, Paris
Munk's Roll	William Munk, et al. (eds), *The Roll of the Royal College of Physicians of London*, 12 vols. to date (London: Royal College of Physicians, 1861-)
NHS papers	Papers of the Natural History Society. Edinburgh University Archives (Da. 67 Nat)
Obs. phys.	*Observations sur la physique, sur l'histoire naturelle et sur les arts ... par M. l'abbé Rozier*, Paris.
ODNB	*Oxford Dictionary of National Biography*, 60 vols. (Oxford: Oxford University Press, 2004)
Oriental Mag.	*Oriental Magazine, and Calcutta Review*, Calcutta
Phil. Mag.	*Philosophical Magazine*, London
Phil. Trans.	*Philosophical Transactions of the Royal Society of London*, London
Phys. Persp.	*Physics in Perspective* Basel
Proc. R. Inst.	*Proceedings of the Royal Institution of Great Britain*, London
RI	Royal Institution of Great Britain, London
RI MM	Minutes of Meetings of Managers, 15 volumes, Royal Institution Archives, London. Reproduced in *The Archives of the Royal Institution of Great Britain in Facsimile. Minutes of Managers' Meetings 1799–1900*, ed. Frank Greenaway, 7 vols. (Ilkley: Scolar Press, 1971–3)

RI MS HBJ	Henry Bence Jones Papers, Archive Collections, Royal Institution of Great Britain, London
RMS	Royal Medical Society, Edinburgh
RMS diss.	Medical Dissertations read before the [Royal] Medical Society of Edinburgh. Transcriptions in Royal Medical Society Library, Edinburgh
RPS	Royal Physical Society, Edinburgh
RPS diss.	Royal Physical Society Dissertations, Edinburgh University Archives (Da. 67 Phys)
RS	Royal Society, London
Sci. Am.	*Scientific American*, New York, etc.
Strathclyde MSS	Papers in the University of Strathclyde Archives and Special Collections, Glasgow
Trans. CWAAS	*Transactions of the Cumberland & Westmorland Antiquarian & Archaeological Society*, Kendal, etc.
Trans. Roy. Soc. Ed.	*Transactions of the Royal Society of Edinburgh*, Edinburgh
Vis. Res.	*Vision Research*, Amsterdam
West Mid. Stud.	*West Midlands Studies*, Wolverhampton
Whelprigg Papers	Papers relating to the Gibson family of Whelprigg House and Estate, Barbon. Cumbria Archive Centre, Kendal

Figure 0.1 Portrait of Garnett, artist unknown, painted during his time as professor of natural philosophy at the Andersonian Institution, Glasgow, 1796–9. The original, a gift from the nineteenth-century merchant and cultural polymath James Smith of Jordanhill, is in the University of Strathclyde Collections (GLAEX A9). Photograph (GB 249 OP/4/5/2) reproduced courtesy of Archives and Special Collections, University of Strathclyde Library.

Introduction

Thomas Garnett's life was one of significant achievement and even greater, though only partially fulfilled promise. It took him from rural obscurity in the small Westmorland village of Barbon in north-west England to the fashionable world of Georgian Mayfair, as the first professor at the Royal Institution, only to be ended by typhus fever in 1802, when he was thirty-six. Before his appointment at the RI, he had had a distinguished student career at Edinburgh, successfully practised medicine in the Yorkshire spa resort of Harrogate and won national recognition as a scientific lecturer at the newly established Anderson's University, more commonly known as the Andersonian, in Glasgow. Along the way, he had pursued active interests across many areas of chemistry, natural philosophy, medicine and the life sciences and established himself as a leading champion of the 'Brunonian' principles of the deviant Scottish physician John Brown, which he expounded in a posthumous volume of medical lectures. Although he died with no law or notable discovery to his credit, his high standing in the eyes of contemporaries is beyond question. That two of the country's most innovative educational institutions, first the Andersonian and then the RI, chose him as their founding professor was itself an accolade, and his analyses of the waters of Harrogate and other northern spas continued to be cited until well into the nineteenth century. His two-volume account of a tour of the Highlands and Western Isles, written with the keen eye of a 'scientific' tourist especially interested in geology and fauna, also had its readers, going through two editions (1800 and 1811) and even being translated into German (1802).

While Garnett's science was plentiful and, in its way, important, the main aim of this biography is not to rehabilitate him as a scientist. It is rather to set his life in the broader context of scientific and medical career-making in late-eighteenth-century Britain and, in doing so, to throw light on both the possibilities and the limitations of ascent to national prominence through science for someone from his intensely provincial background. Garnett's, in fact, was an exemplary trajectory, made possible, though never easy, by a profound transformation in British society during the second half of the century. In these mid-Hanoverian years, as Paul Langford has argued, the main agents of transformation were not the landed gentry or the church but rather the middling classes, the embodiment of a 'polite and commercial people' (Langford's term) who combined heightened prosperity with a growing taste for refined modes of behaviour and forms of consumption.[1]

One such form was an appetite for medical cures of more or less proven efficacy; among these, Garnett's speciality of mineral water treatments was a prime example, and a profitable one for many physicians besides himself. Another taste that he was well placed to satisfy was a vogue for science that reached a peak in his lifetime. This fed the market for scientific books and instruments and made the later eighteenth century a golden age for the kind of authoritative but accessible lecturing in which he excelled. The instrument-maker and public lecturer Benjamin Martin caught the incipient mood as early as the 1740s. In his words, 'knowledge is now become a fashionable Thing, and Philosophy is the Science a la mode'.[2] Half a century on, when Garnett was in his prime as a lecturer, that perception had even greater substance, now reinforced by a recognition of the importance of science for the modern industrial and agricultural economy.

Garnett's rise to a position from which he could respond to the burgeoning eighteenth-century demand for scientific and medical expertise was a tortuous one. With no prescribed career track to follow and few trailblazers to open his eyes to horizons beyond Westmorland, he knew that if he was to strike out from the agricultural world of his childhood and of generations of Garnetts before him, he would have to fashion his own destiny. He had no choice but to become the opportunist he went on to be, watching for openings that he might exploit, seeking out individuals who might help him and adapting, so far as his condition allowed, to favourable and unfavourable turns of fate.

Presentation of Garnett in this way promises something of a rags-to-riches story. The model, though, does not quite fit. His early years, while not privileged, were far from deprived. In many respects, in fact, he was fortunate. Fortunate to be brought up in a region known in the eighteenth century for its high rate of literacy and the number of boys, many of them with scientific and mathematical ability, who went on to distinguished careers far from their rural origins. Fortunate, too, in his family, deeply rooted in the yeoman world of the western Dales but sensitive to the gifts of a son whose studious temperament set him apart from the run of village boys. Above all, he was fortunate in the meeting of minds and eventual close friendship that began when, at the age of fifteen, he moved the few miles from Barbon to the small Yorkshire market-town of Sedbergh. There, he was apprenticed to the surgeon-apothecary and celebrated self-taught teacher of mathematics, John Dawson. Even though Garnett did not leave the area in his four years with Dawson, he was exposed in Sedbergh to the cognate worlds of science and medicine between which he was to move for the rest of his life. By the time he left Dawson's care, to begin his studies at Edinburgh, he did so with his vocation formed and the foundations of his scientific education, as well as his broader world view, firmly laid.

The significance of Garnett's contact with Dawson lies in the fact that his was not an isolated case: over half a century, beginning in the 1750s, Dawson left his mark on an uninterrupted flow of pupils and apprentices, mostly from Sedbergh and nearby but including a number who travelled far to be taught by him, often before going up to Cambridge or while studying there for the Mathematical Tripos. What happened in Sedbergh was part of a broader regional pattern in which schoolmasters, medical practitioners, incumbents of parishes and independent men of science played crucial roles in nurturing the ambitions of boys from the remotest parts and the most unpromising backgrounds. While thinly populated and geographically remote from the traditional centres of learning, the rural north-west was no cultural backwater.

One who knew this was John Dalton, who fashioned his identity as a chemist in much the same way as Garnett, his exact contemporary; both men were born in 1766. Advancing from yeoman roots in the Cumberland hamlet of Eaglesfield and encouraged there by the meteorologist Elihu Robinson, Dalton travelled wherever openings and encouragement beckoned. His first destination was Kendal, forty-four miles away and something of a Westmorland metropolis, where he taught for twelve years in a Quaker school, tried his hand (unsuccessfully) at public lecturing and came under the influence of the blind Kendal naturalist John Gough. In 1793, he moved on to the northern 'shock city' of Manchester.[3] There he found employment as a professor of mathematics and natural philosophy in a recently opened school and, in due course, as an independent teacher and secretary of the Manchester Literary and Philosophical Society. It was a pattern of ascent, part of what Arnold Thackray has identified as 'the Manchester model', that owed its existence to the explosion in population and wealth in Britain's emergent industrial age.[4]

Important though conditions in the area were in facilitating scientific vocations such as Garnett's or Dalton's (or, for that matter, Robinson's or Gough's, which had similar origins), there is no reason to think that social mobility through science was an exclusively northern phenomenon. Here, the parallels between Garnett's career and that of his slightly younger contemporary and rival Humphry Davy are striking. Davy's passage from modest small-town origins in Cornwall to become Garnett's successor at the Royal Institution and, in due course, a knight, baronet and socially accomplished president of the Royal Society was spectacular. But, like Garnett's trajectory, it was neither easy nor preordained. It called for what Jan Golinski has analysed as a lifelong process of self-fashioning.[5] Adopting a variety of often overlapping identities and astutely exploiting key personal encounters (most notably with the radical west-country physician and chemist Thomas Beddoes), Davy made his way in a world in which institutional structures were unhelpful and public support meagre. In Golinski's words, he made himself into a 'scientist', and a highly successful one, 'before there was such a thing'.[6]

In the manner of Golinski's Davy, Garnett too can be seen as adopting and shedding multiple personae as he moulded his own identity as a physician and teacher. Garnett's path, however, was an even more uncertain one. Ambitious though he was, the career-changing decisions that he made tended to be responses to chance and immediate circumstance rather than steps in the fulfilment of a prior vision. Contact with a local family that he came to know during his first brief attempt to establish himself as a doctor in Bradford seems to have been crucial in drawing him to the study of mineral waters; delay in Liverpool as he waited for a vessel as part of a plan to abandon his thriving medical practice in Harrogate for a new life in America in 1795 left him with time to deliver the successful public lectures, first in Liverpool and then in Manchester, that made him an attractive candidate for the unexpected professorial opening at Andersonian; and it was a combination of his wife's death in childbirth on Christmas Day 1798 and the fortuitous timing of the foundation of the Royal Institution soon afterwards that led to his departure from Glasgow and the beginning of his depression-plagued last years in London.

In Garnett's as in any biography, contingency and quirks of temperament have their place. But so too, and with special force in his case, does the wider context of the pivotal two decades of his maturity, the 1780s and 1790s. Here, I come back to contemporary public acceptance of science as the epitome of reliable knowledge and a form of cultural capital appropriate to the modern age. In his quest for patients in Harrogate, it was a belief in the authority of science-based ways of thinking that underlay Garnett's flaunting of his analyses of the waters and the supposedly scientific foundations of Brunonianism, conceived by him and Brown himself as a system analogous in medicine to Newton's in the physical world. Likewise, at the Andersonian and the RI, his perception of the strength and profile of the market for science informed the teaching programmes that he was largely responsible for fashioning. His solution in both institutions was to maintain two distinct strands under the same roof: one in the proven mode of the eighteenth-century public lecture (though with the innovative proviso that women should be encouraged to attend), the other geared to industrial and agricultural employment. Attendances in both Glasgow and London suggest that his judgement of the public taste for the two types of teaching was right.

Although Garnett's differentiation between the lecturing styles appropriate for his diverse audiences brought its successes, the burden it imposed on him, as both institutions' sole professor, was immense. He found himself not only catering for distinct publics but also teaching across the whole range of chemistry and natural philosophy. It left him vulnerable to a crippling workload that he shouldered without complaint and, in his desire to please, did nothing to trim. His Andersonian lectures won unqualified acclaim, and he began strongly at the RI. But from the moment the leading figure at the RI, Benjamin Thompson, Count Rumford, turned against him, as happened early in his time there, Garnett found himself under intolerable pressure. His spirits, never robust since the death of his wife, began to sink, and eventually he became a shadow of the captivating lecturer who had been headhunted from the Andersonian. After only eighteen months in the RI chair, he had no choice but to resign. A year later he was dead, the victim of the illness he contracted while attempting to restore his fortunes yet again, now as a physician to the St Marylebone Dispensary.

A life cut short in such unhappy circumstances has its own tragic quality. That Garnett died so young, with his intellectual potential largely unrealized, has also had consequences for his reputation and (S. G. E. Lythe's excellent study apart) our knowledge of him.[7] Even his medical testament, *Popular Lectures on Zoonomia*, which loyal friends published by subscription in support of his two orphan daughters in 1804, was soon lost from view as the Brunonian principles on which much of it was based fell from favour. Likewise, after the initial tide of interest, his *Tour of the Highlands and Western Isles* was eclipsed in the market for travel literature as the reading public tired of accounts of wild places that became increasingly accessible and familiar to the nineteenth-century tourist. The changes in both medical theory and taste did Garnett a disservice and have left him an unduly neglected figure.

In any reassessment of Garnett, it is important to stress that he was not groundbreaking in all he did. Indeed, it is a particularity of his career, and an instructive one, that many of his actions bore the stamp of the older ways of the eighteenth century alongside new departures that sat more easily with his forward-looking, reforming inclinations. In both Bradford and Harrogate, for example, he wielded the threat of duels, despite their illegality, in his campaign against the conservative or fraudulent physicians he found in his path. In Harrogate, too, he was happy to cultivate the controversial political figure of Alexander Wedderburn, Lord Loughborough, as a patron in the quest for patients for his mineral water treatments. And even his professorships at the Andersonian and the Royal Institution bore marks of the cusp of change on which he found himself. As new posts in new institutions, they foreshadowed the world of institutional employment for men of science that was to transform scientific career-making during the nineteenth century. Yet, especially at the RI, Garnett still encountered the remnants of the dying traditions of aristocratic patronage, exemplified in a body of gentlemanly managers on whose favour he depended but whose society he could never hope to enter on anything like an equal footing.

Quite apart from his unhappy relations with Rumford, the RI was a less than ideal fit for Garnett. Although he had shown ample versatility in his earlier social interactions, notably in his dealings with the moneyed clientele he had treated in Harrogate and the very different urban elite that employed him at the Andersonian, he had little natural affinity with high metropolitan society. In this, his northern roots weighed heavily, to the point that a poignant clause in his Will expressed the wish that, in the event of his death, his daughters should return to Barbon and be brought up there. Despite the convergence of events that drew him to London, his basic inclinations remained provincial. This is not to imply that they were in any way inferior, still less that Garnett saw them in that light. In the cultural hierarchy of his day, the modern-minded intellectual elites of the manufacturing towns of the North and Midlands of England were a respected force, and they formed a dispersed community of peers in which Garnett would have been well placed to rise, and been happy to rise, had his appointments at the Andersonian and the RI not taken him in a different direction. Dedications of two of his works to leaders of the community, Thomas Percival (in Manchester) and Erasmus Darwin (in Derby), and respectful correspondence with Darwin (on a theory of winds) and James Watt (about an abortive plan for a series of lectures in Birmingham) were significant overtures to men he regarded as senior to himself but whose values he instinctively shared. Like them, he was progressive in his attitudes (embracing in his case an involvement of uncertain seriousness in Freemasonry) but fearful of the threats of social disorder posed by the more radical strands of Enlightenment thought.

Despite the fragilities that plagued him at the very end of his life, Garnett's story remains a compelling one. It can be read, at one level, as the individual quest of a man of rare gifts whose hard-won advances in testing circumstances never quite matched his expectations. Whatever his personal disappointments, however, his achievements exemplify professional and social ascent of a kind that even a generation earlier would have been significantly more difficult for someone from his yeoman roots. In that respect, Garnett was very much a man of his time, sensitive to the new possibilities of career-making that proliferated through the last decades of the eighteenth century but aware that the rewards they promised did not come easily. They had to be earned, and earned the hard way, through precisely the determination and ingenuity that he displayed as he pursued his own remarkable trajectory.

Notes

1. Langford, *Polite and Commercial People*. Langford's characterization of the English originated in William Blackstone *Commentaries on the Laws of England* (1765–9).
2. Martin, *Course of Lectures,* unpaginated preface.
3. For Asa Briggs's characterization of Manchester as Britain's 'shock city', see Briggs, *Victorian Cities*, ch. 3.
4. Thackray, 'Natural Knowledge in Cultural Context'.
5. Golinski, *Experimental Self,* esp. 1-17, for a statement of Golinski's thesis.
6. Ibid., 1.
7. Lythe, *Thomas Garnett* remains an essential starting point for any study of Garnett.

1

A northern prologue

Thomas Garnett was born a northerner, and he retained northern loyalties and traits, including a strong trace of regional speech, that marked him throughout his life. His roots were in the few square miles of north-west England, centred on the market-town of Kirkby Lonsdale, where the counties of Westmorland, north Lancashire and the western extremity of Yorkshire meet. The terrain is rugged, and in the eighteenth-century mountainous geography, an often harsh climate and an uncertain rural economy made for hard lives. It was an area calculated to leave its mark on those who were brought up in it, and Garnett was no exception. It was also an area that invited stereotypes. Metropolitan perspectives, then and since, have too often cast it as a remote backwater with little by way of intellectual ambition or knowledge of the wider world of learning and culture. Such an extreme caricature, however, sits uneasily with reality. While the world from which Garnett emerged had few pretensions to elegance or urban sophistication, it was not unchanging or, by the time of his birth, impervious to external influences. As his own life was to show, it offered pathways to intellectual and social advancement, however limited in number and poorly charted, for boys with the ability, determination and energy to make the most of them. And it harboured families increasingly ready to help their children to navigate through such opportunities as existed and strike out in pursuit of better lives, wherever those might take them.

A Garnett childhood

Garnett's was just such a family. While it remained profoundly loyal to its agricultural roots in and around the south Westmorland village of Barbon, its horizons were broader than they would have been even a generation earlier and far broader than those that had bounded the aspirations of Garnett families for centuries before. Garnetts may well have been in the area by the Middle Ages, and they are known to have been there by the reign of Elizabeth. Thereafter, they had shared, unspectacularly but steadily, in an improvement in security and material wellbeing that many of the more prosperous families of their kind in the rural north-west came to enjoy. But yeomen they remained, sometimes known locally as 'statesmen', with livelihoods drawn primarily from the modest plots of land they cultivated.

Within the yeoman class, the fortunes of individuals were so uneven that generalization about their condition is risky. Garnett's parents, though, were certainly a cut above the norm, distinguished by their ownership of the family home and the adjacent land that went with it. While ownership in itself was no guarantee of prosperity, as a social marker it set property-owners apart from the run of lesser yeomen who lived as tenants, often with an insecure fixity of tenure. It also offered a measure of stability, and it would be hard to imagine a household stabler than the one into which Garnett was born on 21 April 1766. At the time, his parents, John Garnett (1736–1812) of Barbon and Elizabeth Skyring (1733–1807), one of the six children of Robert Skyring, a farmer and tanner from the nearby village of Lupton, were living in Casterton, a hamlet on the edge of Kirkby Lonsdale (see Figure 1.1). Thomas' birth took place there, probably in a Garnett property, and it was only in the following year that John and Elizabeth moved the two miles to Barbon, where Thomas was to spend the rest of his childhood. There, he enjoyed the support and companionship that came with a large extended family. His father John's ancestors can be traced back with certainty for a further two generations: first to his parents, Thomas Garnett (1702–69) of Barbon and Margaret Harrison (d. 1769), who had four children, and on to this Thomas' parents, Edward Garnett (c. 1675–1713) and Mary Robinson (d. 1745), who had seven.[1] Many of the children, in turn, had large and generally healthy families of their own, and they rarely moved away. All of this helped to make Garnetts and those they married a significant presence in and around Barbon.[2]

The older Thomas' place in the higher reaches of the yeoman class was reflected in the part he played in the extensive rebuilding of domestic accommodation that was under way in the region by the mid-eighteenth century. Among the houses he owned or had a substantial interest in was Bank House, a fine-standing property on the edge of Barbon that he built, or more probably rebuilt, in the 1740s. The house, subsequently renamed and known today as High Bank House, bears witness to the improved accommodation to which a family like his was by now coming to aspire (see Figure 1.2). Thomas and Margaret made it their home until 1767, when they moved to another Garnett house in the

A Northern Prologue

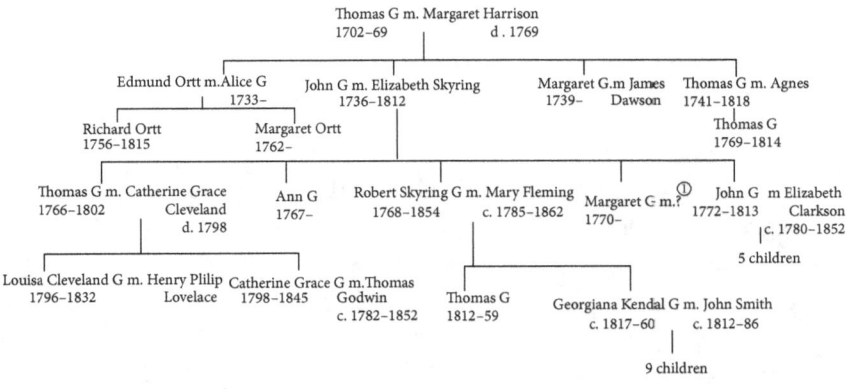

①Margaret Garnett married either Adam Carlisle (1807) or Joseph Sharpe (1808)

Figure 1.1 Garnett family tree. Source: Author's sketch

village, to allow their son John to take it over for his own family, following the move from Casterton. At the time, John and Elizabeth had only Thomas, barely a year old. But, with space to expand, four other children – two sons and two daughters – followed quickly.

The status of a rising family in these years was not an affair of houses and land alone. Tastes bred of widening cultural horizons were also making their mark.[3] One sign was a heightened respect for education, and in this, too, Garnett's grandfather, Thomas, blazed a trail. In 1745, he was elected a trustee (or 'feoffee') of Queen Elizabeth School, a well-endowed grammar school in Kirkby Lonsdale, and was followed by his son John, variously described as a 'yeoman' or 'husbandman', who was serving as a trustee at the time of his death in 1812.[4] Election to such offices betokened a measure of cultivation as well as personal standing, and we know that the older Thomas had received at least some 'school learning', possibly at the school itself, though more probably from the minister of the chapel of ease that had existed in Barbon since the early seventeenth century. It was a significant new departure for a family in which only the most rudimentary education had hitherto been the norm.

In their engagement with the Queen Elizabeth School, Thomas and John were giving material expression to attitudes to learning noted by D. C. Richmond, an assistant commissioner working on the Schools Inquiry Commission under Lord Taunton in the 1860s. In a special report devoted to what he presented as the exceptional case of Westmorland, Richmond looked back to an eighteenth century in which Latin and, in some cases, Greek had been taught, not only in the

Figure 1.2 High Bank House, Barbon, where Garnett spent his childhood. The property, then known as Bank House, had been built, or rebuilt, by Garnett's grandfather Thomas Garnett in the 1740s, at a time of growing prosperity among better-off yeoman families. It remained a Garnett property until it was finally sold to the Gibson family, owners of the nearby Whelprigg House and Estate, in 1859. Photograph by, and by courtesy of Michael Kingsbury.

county's forty or more grammar schools, including the Queen Elizabeth School, but in many village schools as well.[5] The purpose of Richmond's report was to contrast the low demand for classical instruction in his own day with the more adventurous linguistic tastes he believed to have been common in Westmorland in the previous century, and hence to argue for the rationalization of an excessively generous provision for a now outmoded curriculum. Although his depiction of old Westmorland has to be read with caution, supporting evidence for it does exist. Writing in the 1820s, the eminent antiquary and clergyman John Hodgson looked back on his own childhood in the county thirty years earlier, when 'the yeoman and the shepherd could enliven their employment or festivities, with recitations from the beauties of Virgil, idylls of Theocritus, or wars of Troy'.[6] Even discounting the distortions of nostalgia and literary gloss, there is enough in the recollection to reinforce Richmond's point, the more so as Hodgson, a stonemason's son, had himself gone through twelve years of a classically based curriculum at the grammar school in the tiny Westmorland village of Bampton in the 1780s and 1790s.[7]

It is beyond question that educational opportunity of the kind that Hodgson recalled did not extend to every corner of the county; still less did it extend equally across the social scale. Yet, in the accessibility of mathematical instruction and at least the linguistic foundations of classical culture, Westmorland does seem to have outstripped even the adjacent county of Cumberland and the rural North Riding of Yorkshire, where grammar schools and academically strong village schools were plentiful too. Also, and by a far larger margin, it outstripped the southern counties of England, where such schools were more thinly spread. One notable contemporary who saw the products of the northern schools at first hand was the controversial champion of political and religious nonconformity, Gilbert Wakefield. Reflecting in later life on his time as an undergraduate and fellow of his Cambridge college, Jesus, in the 1770s, Wakefield identified schooling as the key to the qualities that distinguished the 'hardy progeny of the North, from Cumberland, Westmoreland, and the remoter parts of Yorkshire'.[8] It was this that set them apart from 'their polished brethren from the public seminaries of the South' and made them 'the profoundest proficients in mathematics and philosophy'. The accolade is striking, and the more persuasive as it came from someone who knew the northern mind well and recognized the particular form of excellence that was rewarded in Cambridge's fiercely competitive mathematical Tripos. The trial was one in which Wakefield himself had excelled, as the second mathematician, or second Wrangler, of his year, 1776.

Beyond the minority of boys with their eyes set on a university education, schooling had a more diffused effect in fostering the high levels of general literacy found across the rural north-west.[9] How this impinged on Garnett's own childhood is unclear. It seems that the teachers he encountered at the village school in Barbon, in all probability (as in his grandfather's day) a succession of chaplains or perpetual curates serving the chapel of ease, changed as many as three times in his seven or eight years as a pupil.[10] But even this disrupted pattern of schooling left him with a grounding in mathematics, Latin, French and English grammar that went far beyond the bare necessities of country life. For Garnett, though, it did not go far enough. Such fragmentary accounts of his childhood as survive point to a diffidence of character, aggravated by a delicate physique, that distanced him from the more boisterous activities of other boys and served to bolster his reflective side. By temperament, he had all the makings of a loner, anxious to please his teachers but more interested in mechanical contrivances that he enjoyed devising at home.[11] The simple quadrant he used, at the age of eleven, to measure the height of the hills behind Bank House conveys something of his introspective and probably frustrated ingenuity.[12]

Garnett was plainly cut out for more studious pursuits than were possible in Barbon, and shortly before his fifteenth birthday he moved to Sedbergh, seven miles away and just over the county boundary with Yorkshire. There he began four years of what was to be a transformative apprenticeship with the charismatic John Dawson, long celebrated in the area as a surgeon and apothecary though by now far better-known nationally as a mathematician and teacher of mathematics.

John Dawson: Model, mentor, friend

In Sedbergh, a community of some 1,600 people at the time, Garnett encountered a world larger and more cosmopolitan than Barbon, with its population of fewer than 250.[13] A striking presence in the town was the grammar school, a sixteenth-century foundation like the Queen Elizabeth School in Kirkby Lonsdale. Garnett's name appears in the register of admissions to the school, though without a date and with no further evidence of his attendance.[14] It is likely that he was no more than an occasional pupil attending classes in parallel with his apprenticeship, and he probably did not stay long. But even a short stay would have opened his eyes to a new world of academic attainment. The two headmasters who served during his time in Sedbergh were men whose deep roots in the town went hand in hand with intellectual distinction of more than local significance. Dr Wynne Bateman, in post since 1746, and Christopher Hull, his successor from 1782, had been at the school themselves and gone on to successful undergraduate careers in Cambridge and fellowships of their college, St John's, which in turn appointed them to their headships.[15] Back in Sedbergh, their university accomplishments – Bateman's as a distinguished classical scholar and university preacher and Hull's as the third Wrangler of his year – were rather wasted.[16] But the experience and contacts that both men brought with them served in helping a regular flow of boys who aspired to enter Cambridge (less commonly the more arts-oriented Oxford) themselves. In Bateman's thirty-six years as head, eighty-nine Sedbergh boys went on to Cambridge (many of them benefitting from the school's closed scholarship at St John's), and sixteen more followed under Hull (1782–99).[17] It was an avenue that made Sedbergh, as viewed from Cambridge, anything but an irrelevant cultural outpost.

Despite the academic cast of the grammar school, much about Sedbergh remained profoundly rural. The lives and values of many of the families there differed little from those Garnett had known in Barbon, and their familiarity helped to ease the transition to his new life. It also helped that Dawson and he, though a generation apart in age, were cut from the same cloth, socially and culturally. Dawson's yeoman origins, in the secluded valley of Garsdale, rising out of Sedbergh, had much in common with Garnett's, though with a lesser leavening of material comfort.[18] In later life, the future geologist Adam Sedgwick, who studied with Dawson before going up to Cambridge in 1804, dwelt on the family's particular hardships: his description of Dawson as 'the son of a very poor statesman in Garsdale, with perhaps not more than £10 or £12 a year' sat well in a story cast as an heroic rise from impoverished obscurity.[19] The fact remains, however, that Dawsons counted for something in their community, as Garnetts did in Barbon. They were among the older, more established families of the Dale and had a substantial home and farm, Raygill, to match.

As model, mentor and in due course friend, Dawson did more than anyone to fashion Garnett's twin vocation as both physician and man of science. The way in which Dawson had constructed his own dual career was a lesson in itself. His starting point, like Garnett's, had been education, in his case the elementary schooling that he and an elder brother, James, received under Garsdale's minister and legendarily strict schoolmaster, the Revd Charles Udal. James went on to become an exciseman with responsibility for collecting duties and enforcing excise laws in the port of Lancaster: for the son of an aspirational yeoman family with a gift for figures and a taste for middle-level urban employment, it was a prized position and a recognized step on the path of upward mobility.[20] Dawson himself turned initially to mathematics, which he learned using books borrowed from his brother or bought with money earned, in good Dales fashion, from the sale of stockings that he knitted while working as a hillside shepherd on the family farm. By the mid-1750s, now in his early twenties, he was confident enough to begin taking mathematical pupils, often travelling to their homes and even staying with them for lengthy periods. But occasional tutoring promised a meagre living, and it was economic necessity as much as heightened ambition that directed his thoughts to medicine, another favoured trajectory for the ablest products of the yeoman world.

Preparation for the kind of medical career that Dawson had in mind, as a surgeon and apothecary, was lengthy and by no means cost-free. Yet it did not entail the expense of prolonged full-time study that was required for formal qualification as a physician, and the rewards, in income and status, could still be substantial. Outside London and the large towns, in fact, members of the Royal College of Physicians were rare. There, as in Sedbergh, an academic degree carried less weight than skills learned on the job, and it was in search of experience that Dawson followed his brother to Lancaster, to become an assistant and pupil to the prominent surgeon and writer on farriery Henry Bracken. Even someone as successful as Bracken (the son of a Lancaster innkeeper) had had to improvise his medical career, in his case through stays in London, Paris and Leiden (though never a degree) and lessons learned in a failed attempt to establish himself in London.[21] As Dawson knew, he too would have to fashion his future in much the same way. After Bracken and a year of unlicensed practice in Sedbergh, he used £100 of family savings to pay for time in Edinburgh (making his way there on foot, to save money), then London, where he attended private surgical courses, witnessed public dissections and walked such hospital wards as would admit him. The diploma he received, probably from the Corporation of Surgeons, bestowed no rights and left him with a professional standing far below that of a full member of the Corporation. But back in the world that Dawson knew best and showed no inclination to leave, the knowhow he had accumulated was quite enough for the practice he established from his large house in the main street of Sedbergh.

With the advantage of his Garsdale roots and the integration that came with his marriage to the daughter of a local family similar to his own, Dawson quickly became a much-loved figure across Yorkshire's western Dales. His stock in trade was a typically rural one, and Garnett learned much from accompanying him in the daily routines of births, bone-setting, minor operations and the prescription of traditional remedies. It was a strenuous life but profitable, to the point that by the time Garnett arrived, Dawson was beginning to review his priorities, in particular to find more time for teaching. For some years, he had enlarged his core clientele of local boys with a steady flow of pupils from beyond Sedbergh, who lodged with him or in accommodation in the town. Among them were some of the ablest young mathematicians of the day, attracted by his fame as a coach both for boys seeking entry to Cambridge and for advanced undergraduates preparing for the formidable exercises of the mathematical Tripos. And his reputation was still growing. His record over the next quarter of a century, in fact, was extraordinary: between 1781 and 1807, no fewer than twelve of Cambridge's 27 Senior Wranglers, the top mathematicians of the year, had been tutored by him either before or during their time at the university.[22]

Garnett's encounters with such young men, from a world and with ambitions and career-prospects far removed from his own, opened new vistas. In circumstances that made him effectively a member of the household, he would have witnessed at first hand the impact that a great teacher could have on a young mind. As an apprentice rather than a mathematical pupil, he was probably not subjected to Dawson's 'peripatetic' style of instruction, which

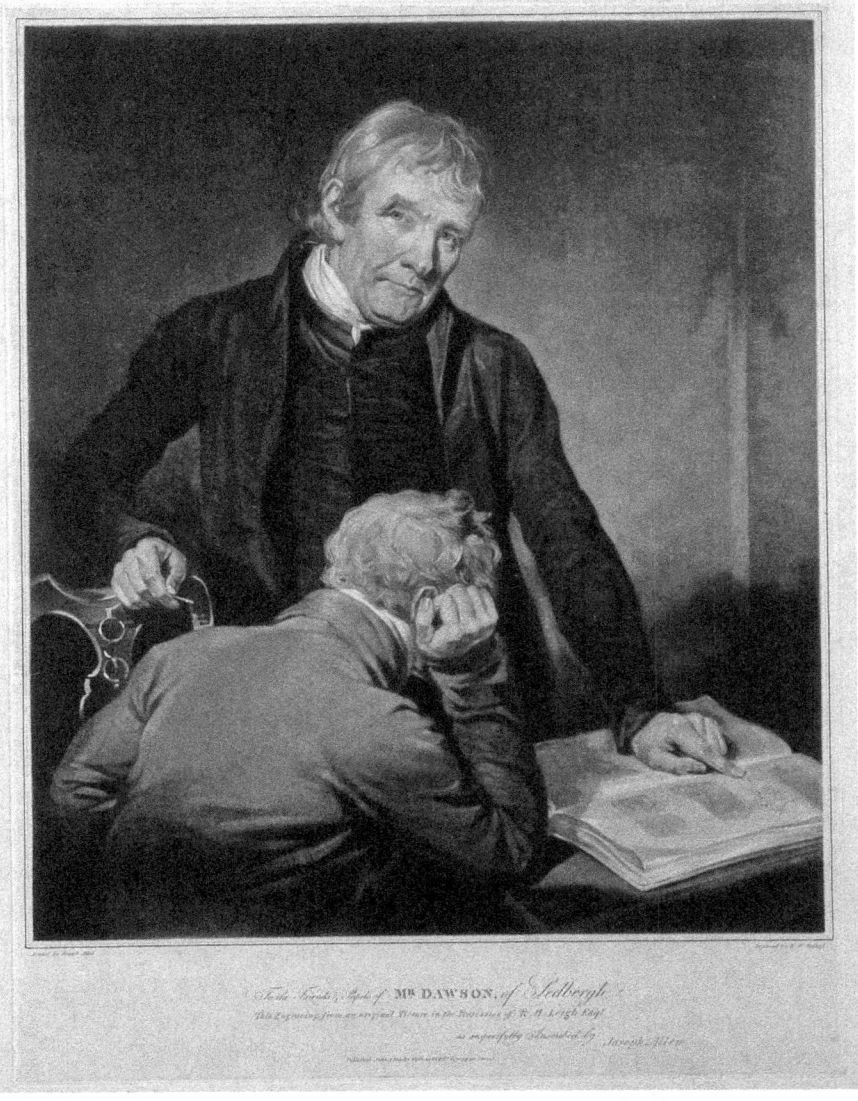

Figure 1.3 John Dawson of Sedbergh, standing over a pupil. Mezzotint engraved by William Whiston Burney, and dated June 1809, after an original portrait by Joseph Allen. The portrait is now lost, but the caption to the print identifies its owner in 1809 as Robert Holt Leigh (1762–1843), M.P. for Wigan from 1802 to 1820. The identity of the pupil is unknown, although the name Litterdale is suggested in John Willis Clark and Thomas McKenny Hughes, *Life and Letters of the Reverend Adam Sedgwick*, 2 vols. (Cambridge, 1890), vol. 1, 70. Courtesy of the Wellcome Collection. Public Domain Mark.

entailed his simultaneously supervising pupils distributed at different places in his house (see Figure 1.3). Nevertheless, he would have assimilated something of Dawson's achievements in mathematics. In the most notable of these, in the 1760s, Dawson had demonstrated the error of Matthew Stewart's overestimate, by a quarter, of the distance between the earth and the sun.[23] His criticism of Stewart, a distinguished professor of mathematics at Edinburgh, had been bold, and it had created a stir, confirming his standing as a serious mathematician and aligning him with the view, soon to be vindicated, that the transit of Venus method offered the only way to a viable solution.

Despite the pedagogical successes and distinction of so many pupils proud to identify themselves as Dawsonians, Garnett would have recognized that the highpoints of Dawson's own mathematical career lay a decade or more in the past. The Dawson that Garnett encountered in Sedbergh in 1781 had adopted new intellectual priorities that were diverting him from cutting-edge mathematics towards moral questions, in particular the challenge of Joseph Priestley's doctrine of philosophical necessity. Priestley had elaborated his position most fully four years earlier in two of a series of works in which he made the case for materialism and determinism while arguing that the consequent denial of free will and the existence of the soul was consistent with Christian theism.[24] The issues he raised touched on the very foundations of faith in an age when, in his words, 'the rational use of the human faculties' promised 'a freedom from vulgar and debasing prejudices'.[25] In subsequent exchanges, Priestley defended his radical position and the values it embodied against some of the leading philosophers and theologians of the day.[26] The resulting literature was imposing, to the point that by the time Dawson came out against Priestley, in an unsigned twenty-four-page book in 1781, there was little more to be said.[27] Dawson had entered the debate too late, and his laboured discussion of the logical implications of supposing the 'necessarian principle' to be true and his rejection of them as incompatible with Christian belief passed virtually unnoticed.

Garnett's, though, was a receptive ear. Pertinent to his still malleable personal morality was the concluding appeal of Dawson's book that wherever the niceties of philosophical debate might lead, we should trust our 'feelings and common sense' and not allow ourselves to be 'imposed upon by the mere force of metaphysical subtilty and ingenuity'.[28] It was only by making that choice, as Dawson maintained, that we could sustain our belief in the freedom we know instinctively to be ours as moral beings able to choose between good and evil. They were the words of the 'good sober practical Christian of the old school' that his loyal former pupil Adam Sedgwick knew Dawson to be.[29] And they were to have discernible echoes in what Garnett subsequently revealed of his own quietly conformist religious position and adherence to the 'common sense' philosophy of Priestley's adversary on the necessitarian question, Thomas Reid (see Chapter 2).

Dawson's thoughtful but unyielding Anglican piety and mistrust of the deterministic strands in rational religion were just one facet of a wider profile of values, knowledge and experience that Garnett assimilated from him in Sedbergh. While we know nothing of Garnett's day-to-day encounters with Dawson, the broad conformity of their views on morality and the foundations of knowledge suggests a relation of rare intimacy between master and pupil. So too the mutual respect: Dawson for abilities that raised Garnett well above the normal run of apprentices, Garnett for the man he was to praise feelingly, in the dedication of his Edinburgh M.D. thesis in 1788, as both his mentor in science and a friend of unblemished virtue.[30] Over his four years in Sedbergh, Garnett was drawn to the heart of Dawson's world. His closeness to a man so fashioned by geography, personal circumstance and a strong dose of Yorkshire stubbornness left its mark. In that respect, if not as a mathematician, Garnett was a true Dawsonian.

A provincial dilemma

One thing that would not have escaped Garnett was that Dawson's tastes and temperament were deeply provincial. In mathematics, his natural place was not in the traditional centres of academic life but in the corresponding network of largely self-taught mathematicians of which he was a leading member. It was a network, dispersed through the English provinces though with a strikingly solid base in the North and Midlands, in which intense rivalry and an appetite for puzzle-setting and solving tended to find expression in general magazines and almanacks rather than in traditional learned journals.[31] Contributions sometimes bore on major mathematical issues. This had been the case with Dawson's criticism of Stewart or when, a few years later, his endorsement of Thomas Simpson's identification of an error in Newton's treatment of the precession of the equinoxes brought him into conflict with William Emerson, a prolific and testy autodidact in County Durham.[32] More characteristic of the genre, however, was a protracted dispute between Dawson and the Nottinghamshire clergyman and schoolmaster Charles Wildbore, said to have refused election to the Royal Society on the grounds that he preferred the retired life of a 'humble village pastor' far from the 'busy hum of men'.[33] In this debate the homespun nature of the problem (the velocity of water emerging from a hole in the bottom of a vessel in motion) was as typical as the acerbic tone of the exchanges and the vehicle in which they were conducted. Dawson (signing himself 'Wadson') and Wildbore put their arguments, with spirit verging on acrimony, in one of their community's favoured locations: *Miscellanea Mathematica*, a widely circulated compendium of mathematical correspondence edited by another informally educated provincial mathematician, Charles Hutton.[34]

Dawson's pattern of publication did not mean that he went unrecognized beyond his mathematical correspondents. Grateful former pupils subscribed for the fine portrait of him by Joseph Allen (see Figure 1.3) and, after his death in 1820, for the bust that stands high in the nave of St Andrew's Church, Sedbergh. And the Edinburgh professor of mathematics John Playfair, a declared admirer from the time of Dawson's exchange with Stewart, displayed his esteem by visiting Dawson in Sedbergh. But the recognition that Dawson enjoyed was patchy. The only institutional distinction he received was his election to corresponding membership of the Literary and Philosophical Society of Manchester in December 1791, when he was in his late fifties.[35] And even that honour was bestowed several months after the election of his much younger *protégé* Garnett, possibly even at Garnett's instigation.

Playfair's judgement was that Dawson's taste for a retired existence in the Dales had set limits to his achievements and reputation; as he put it, Dawson 'might have enjoyed more of the fame, had he been less satisfied with the possession of knowledge'.[36] Similar thoughts must also have crossed Garnett's mind and contributed to the decision about his future that he had to make as his time in Sedbergh came to a close. Was he to settle for a life like Dawson's, as a respected figure in a close-knit but remote community, perhaps as a country surgeon and apothecary or a teacher, with time to pursue intellectual interests on the side? Or should he exploit the new opportunities for educational advancement and career-making that were multiplying as industrialization and urbanization began to change the face of England? As polite tastes and middle-class prosperity fed an unprecedented tide of consumption, the opportunities were tempting, and for Garnett, single-mindedly ambitious now as he was to be throughout his life, there could in the end be only one choice. Much as he admired Dawson, and despite the depth of his roots in the area, he knew that he had to leave.

A Dawsonian path that was effectively closed to him was the mathematical one. Garnett does not appear to have been particularly gifted mathematically, and he may well have felt unsuited to the cultural norms he would have associated with the ancient universities. In this respect, he was no Adam Sedgwick, whose father, the incumbent of Dent, close to Sedbergh, was himself a Cambridge graduate as well as an early Dawsonian. Faced with the other of Dawson's vocations, in medicine, Garnett could look to more realistic role models from the Dawson stable. A giant among them was John Haygarth, whose medical reputation had made him something of a Sedbergh legend: one of Dawson's first mathematical pupils and a childhood neighbour in Garsdale in the 1750s, Haygarth had gone on via Cambridge to study medicine in Edinburgh and was now, while still in touch with Dawson, a leading champion of inoculation in the battle against smallpox mortality in Chester. Closer to Garnett in age by almost a generation was Robert Willan, the member of a long-established Quaker family in Marthwaite near Sedbergh. Willan was a favourite of Dawson's and someone Dawson must have talked about with Garnett. Also, perhaps decisively for the career path that Garnett was about to take, Willan had benefitted from the regularization of medical training that had gathered pace since the mid-century. His father had been an informally trained male midwife and apothecary in the Dawson mould. But Willan himself had gone on to take an Edinburgh M.D. shortly before Garnett's arrival in Sedbergh. And now, after a move to London in 1783, he was building a distinguished career as a pioneer of dermatology.[37] It was an example of inter-generational ascent calculated to fire Garnett's sense of vocation, should reinforcement still be needed, and to help to make Edinburgh his natural goal.

With the die cast in favour of full-time study, Garnett set out for Edinburgh in the early autumn of 1785. The hands-on medical experience and knowledge of chemistry and other sciences that he had acquired under Dawson left him better equipped than most beginning students. And he went with the blessing of his family, also with the promise of the material support needed to see him through the tough three years that lay ahead. The two-day journey, probably by stagecoach via Lancaster or Kendal, must have been exhilarating for a nineteen-year-old with no experience of the world beyond Sedbergh. With exhilaration, though, went anxiety. Garnett was on his way to a place where he had neither family nor, so far as we know, friends. And he was about to cross a cultural divide that would distance him from his roots. If he succeeded in his medical ambitions and followed the route of a Haygarth or a Willan, there could be no return, however tender his feelings for the people and places he was leaving behind.

Notes

1. Little is known of the family backgrounds of the wives of the elder Thomas and Edward, though both were from nearby villages: Margaret Harrison from Middleton, Mary Robinson probably from Old Hutton.
2. For information about the Garnetts and help with the information summarized in the family tree in Figure 1.1, I am indebted to the present owner of High Bank House Michael Kingsbury and to David and Carol Thomas of Manchester, who have generously shared their research with me. On Garnett's childhood, as on all aspects of his life, I draw heavily on 'An account of the life of the author', published anonymously in Garnett's *Popular Lectures on Zoonomia*, v-xxii, cited hereafter as 'Life of Garnett'.
3. On changing yeoman fortunes in the area, see Marshall, *Old Lakeland*, 32-60.
4. I am grateful to Sarah Rose for a discussion of the role of 'feoffees' in the management of the school.
5. Richmond, 'Proposed System of Grouping Schools', 902-5.
6. Hodgson, 'Westmorland as It Was', 210.
7. Raine, *Memoir of the Rev. John Hodgson*, vol. 1, 4-11.
8. Wakefield, *Memoirs of Gilbert Wakefield*, 1792 edn., 80-1; 1804 edn., vol. 1, 83-4.
9. On the regional pattern in literacy, see Marshall, 'Migration and Literacy'.
10. 'Life of Garnett', v. The list of incumbents at the chapel of ease is incomplete for the period of Garnett's childhood; see cumbriacountyhistorytrust.org.uk, with a link to Emmeline Garnett's draft history of Barbon. The entry on Barbon is now being revised for publication in the forthcoming Victoria County History of Westmorland: Edmonds and Rose, eds., *History of the County of Westmorland*.
11. 'Life of Garnett', v-vi.
12. Ibid., vi.
13. Figures estimated from the returns for the first national census, in 1801, where the populations are recorded as respectively 1639 and 242. See entries for Sedbergh and Barbon in the website of the Cumbria County History Trust: cumbriacountyhistory.org.uk.
14. See *Sedbergh School Register 1546 to 1909*, 196, in a register of entrances between 1770 and 1782.
15. Although the school had prospered during the first quarter of a century of Bateman's headmastership, Garnett encountered it in a period of difficulty resulting from signs of approaching old age and negligence during Bateman's last decade in the post. See Clarke and Weech, *Sedbergh School 1525-1925*, 67-75.
16. Bateman, *Philosophorum veterum et sapientum*, his 'Concio ad clerum' sermon delivered at the Great St Mary's, the University Church, Cambridge in 1746.
17. *Sedbergh School Register 1546 to 1909*, 173-203 and Platt, *Parish and Grammar School of Sedbergh*, 155-6. It is striking that only eight boys went to Oxford under

Bateman, and just one under Hull, despite the school's access to the Hastings Exhibitions at The Queen's College, Oxford. The bonds with St John's College, Cambridge, which appointed the school's headmasters, were far stronger.

18 On Dawson, see Clark and Hughes, *Life and Letters of Sedgwick*, vol. 1, 60–70, an account that draws on a letter from Sedgwick to Charles Lyell and Sedgwick's *Supplement to the Memorial of the Trustees of Cowgill Chapel*, 50–4. Also Thompson, *Sedbergh, Garsdale, and Dent*, 233–40. An informative contemporary account is the unsigned 'Mr. Dawson, of Sedbergh', in *Public Characters of 1801–1802*.
19 Clark and Hughes, *Life and Letters of Sedgwick*, vol. 1, 61.
20 Hodgson, 'Westmorland as It Was', 210.
21 Harley, 'Ethics and Dispute Behavior in the Career of Henry Bracken'.
22 For the names and years of 'Dawsonian' Senior Wranglers, see Clark and Hughes, *Life and Letters of Sedgwick*, vol. 1, 65n.
23 For the initial exchanges, see Stewart, *Distance of the Sun from the Earth* (1763) and [Dawson], *Four Propositions* (1769).
24 Priestley, *Disquisitions Relating to Matter and Spirit* and *The Doctrine of Philosophical Necessity Illustrated*, both published in 1777.
25 Words from the unpaginated dedication to the prominent lawyer and religious dissenter John Lee, in Priestley and Price, *A Free Discussion of the Doctrines of Materialism, and Philosophical Necessity*.
26 Including, most notably (though with conspicuous civility), Richard Price, his fellow nonconformist minister and champion of radical causes. See Priestley and Price, *A Free Discussion* (1778).
27 [Dawson], *Doctrine of Philosophical Necessity Briefly Invalidated*. Dawson acknowledged authorship by putting his name to a second edition (1803), otherwise unchanged from the first apart from the addition of his response to a notice that had appeared in the *Monthly Review* in 1781. Dawson's conservative piety emerges strongly in his correspondence with the Lancashire schoolmaster and clergyman Thomas Wilson in the 1770s; see Wilson, *Miscellanies*, 105–23.
28 [Dawson], *Philosophical Necessity* (1781), 24; 2nd edn. (1803), 28.
29 Clark and Hughes, *Life and Letters of Sedgwick*, vol. 1, 68.
30 Garnett, *De visu*. Garnett also dedicated the thesis to his student contemporary and fellow-northerner William Allanby of Flimby on the Cumberland coast.
31 The community is vividly evoked in Hutton, *Correspondence of Charles Hutton* and Wardhaugh, *Gunpowder and Geometry*.
32 Dawson to the editor ('Mr. Urban'), 22 November 1771 and 9 May 1772, in *Gent. Mag.*, 41 (November 1771), 597–9 and 42 (May 1772), 207–8; and Emerson to the Editor, ibid., 42 (March 1772), 118. Dawson was joining a debate between Emerson and an unidentified ΑΣΤΡΟΝΟΜΙΚΟΣ that had been running in the magazine since March, following the recent dismissal of Simpson's position in Emerson, *Short*

Comment on Sir I. Newton's Principia, esp. 100 and 125. The editor declined to print part of Dawson's last letter on the grounds that the content had become 'rather personal than illustrative'.

33 'Wildbore (Charles)', in Chalmers, *General Biographical Dictionary*, vol. 32, 54–6.
34 Hutton, *Miscellanea Mathematica* (1775), 3–19, 42–50, 67–71, 120–3, 166–8, 222–5, and 267–8. Hutton had been an independent teacher of mathematics in Newcastle until his recent appointment as professor of mathematics at the Royal Military Academy in Woolwich.
35 Despite my point here, in the dedication of his M.D. thesis, *De visu*, Garnett does refer to Dawson as an honorary member of the Royal Medical Society and Royal Physical Society in Edinburgh, though there is no mention of his election in the records of the societies.
36 Playfair, 'Account of Matthew Stewart', 68–9.
37 See, in addition to Deborah Brunton's *ODNB* article, the account of Willan's complicated family background in Booth, 'Robert Willan and his kinsmen'.

2

Edinburgh
Conformity and dissent in medicine

We know nothing of where Garnett chose to live in Edinburgh or of the first contacts he made there. But after matriculating at the University, ready for the start of lectures in October, he settled quickly. His regime was relentless. Even if, in reality, he allowed himself more than the four hours' sleep a night that is said to have been his upper limit, he set to working with the seriousness of a student, convinced that his future course in life depended on his making a success of an opportunity of which earlier generations of Garnetts could never have dreamed.[1] The timing of his exposure to Edinburgh was crucial. He can only have been dazzled by a university at the height of its reputation for intellectual brilliance. And he would have seen ample evidence of the prosperity and civic pride that, for a quarter of a century, had driven the city's expansion from the confines of the overcrowded Old Town of the mid-eighteenth century to embrace the elegance of James Craig's 'New Town' taking shape on virgin land north of the now drained North Loch.[2] It was an encounter to captivate any receptive mind. Added to the haunting memory of how, a generation earlier, a full-time course of medical study had been beyond Dawson's reach, it can only have added to Garnett's determination to succeed.

The curriculum and beyond

The University's matriculation registers show Garnett enrolling, over his three years, for lectures across the whole range of medicine: anatomy and surgery, the practice of physic, obstetrics, medical theory (known more formally as institutes of medicine, essentially physiology), chemistry, materia medica (the theory and prescription of medicines), and botany and medicine.[3] On these subjects, all of which were required for graduation, and in the popular elective course on midwifery, he would have heard some of the world's greatest authorities at a time when the Edinburgh Faculty of Medicine was arguably rivalled only by Leiden.[4] Of his professors, William Cullen, whose lectures on the practice of physic he attended in his first year, was in failing health and showing signs of age. John Hope, in the chair of botany, was elderly too, and he died in 1786. But among other chair-holders, Joseph Black (chemistry), Alexander Munro secundus (anatomy and surgery), Francis Home (materia medica), James Gregory (institutes of medicine), Alexander Hamilton (a pioneer of midwifery) and Daniel Rutherford, who replaced Hope, were in their prime, with international reputations to match.

To be taught by men of such distinction was a privilege, and Garnett appears to have attended their courses assiduously. Edinburgh, though, had more to offer than the lectures of its formally appointed professors, and a tradition of loose supervision left students with great freedom to fashion their own programme of work. One extra-curricular world that Garnett entered with enthusiasm was that of the medical societies. These had long been an important part of the experience of ambitious students. And in the 1780s they were flourishing as never before.[5] Their immediate function was to provide members with an antidote to the solitariness of prolonged study and an opportunity of broadening their scientific knowledge and honing a skill in argument that would pay dividends in the examination for their degree, the all-important M.D. Thereafter, in their careers, the mixture of social and intellectual qualities that societies helped students to cultivate would be expected to bear fruit in a profession that prized confidence and elegance of expression, in particular oral expression, as complements to the core activities of clinical practice. James Ford, the son of a former physician extraordinary to Queen Charlotte and a student not long before Garnett, may have been unusually sensitive to the importance of broader cultural attainments. But he was expressing a commonly held view when he insisted that the physician who wished to be more than a 'mere mechanic' should seek to 'act in a literary character'. To that end, the physician should study the sciences not just for their immediate applicability to medical procedures but also as the foundation for the higher qualities of a 'metaphysician', someone whose interests extended beyond medicine to philosophy and mathematics.[6] Failure to cultivate such interests, with their corollaries in a good written and spoken style, would 'denote Indolence or want of genius'.

Garnett set out to be far more than one of Ford's 'mere mechanics'. It was an aspiration that drew him into an active involvement in at least three societies. Since entry to all societies was by election, membership in itself betokened a certain standing in the student community. But what did most for a future career was not just belonging to a society but holding a position of leadership within it. In two of the societies – the Royal Physical Society (RPS) and the Natural History Society (NHS) – Garnett rose to the top, becoming in both cases one of the Society's annual presidents, a number of whom, usually four, were elected to serve each year. It has to be said that he assumed his presidencies as the replacement for presidents, both of them Americans who resigned in mid-year and left without taking a degree.[7] Even so, there was no greater honour for a student than the title of president, whatever the circumstances.

Garnett's achievement in securing his two presidencies was a notable one. This was especially so in the RPS. Devoted to 'physic', and newly designated 'Royal' in 1788, the RPS was the largest of the societies with medical interests, with 440 members.[8] Prominence in it, as in all societies, was earned mainly through the presentation of papers, or 'dissertations' as they were usually called, and Garnett did not hold back. The dissertations that he read to the RPS and NHS (two in each case) towards the end of his student career would not only have allowed him to exercise his dexterity in debate and impress his student peers. They would also have brought him to the attention of professors, a number of whom took an interest in the societies and even, in some cases, attended and occasionally presented their own work.

Exposure to the University's medical elite promised even richer dividends in the third of Garnett's three societies, the Royal Medical Society of Edinburgh. Founded in 1737 and granted a Royal Charter by George III in 1778, the RMS was the senior student society in every way. It was not just the oldest but also the best-endowed, and during Garnett's student years it was at the peak of its reputation and influence.[9] Although it was not alone in having its own premises (the RPS too had a house and library), its 'Medical Hall', built in 1776 on land in Surgeons' Square granted by the College of Surgeons, was especially imposing.[10] So too was its fine library, to which student members had privileged access (thereby relieving them of the need to compete for books in the university library). From 1785, the Society even provided a modest laboratory for private dissection and chemical experiments. The RMS, though, offered more than superior facilities. Everything about it was geared to the higher mission of fashioning the gentleman physicians that the medical school regarded as its finest and most distinctive products. Essential to the goal was the preservation of the Society's elite status, and to that end it remained determinedly small, with a core of roughly eighty resident members, drawn from the several hundred students attending medical classes at any time.[11] The core was augmented by any professors who cared to be involved and a non-resident membership of about three hundred, all Edinburgh graduates engaged in medical careers throughout the world. But the conduct of meetings and other regular business remained the jealously guarded preserve of the student members.

An elaborate process of election, involving a sequence of proposal, endorsement by between six and twelve members, and a vote, epitomized the Society's exclusiveness, and it is a measure of Garnett's qualities and standing that his candidature for membership went through quickly.[12] On 8 April 1786, after the stipulated minimum of six months as a student, he was one of three new ordinary members who were invited to pay the not inconsiderable first year's fee of five guineas.[13] Election gave him access to the Society's meetings, held weekly through the winter session from the last Saturday but one in October to the following spring: twenty-four in all. With membership came explicit obligations. Regular attendance was enforced through a system of fines for unauthorized absences, and the conduct of meetings followed a strict protocol. These were to begin at 6 pm, with up to an hour of 'private business' devoted to the Society's affairs, and they lasted until the end of 'public business', essentially the reading and discussion of dissertations, which could go on until midnight, even beyond. Under no circumstances could those attending leave before 10 pm, and between 10 and midnight they could only do so with the express permission of the president for the evening.[14]

In their time at the University, members were expected to deliver a total of three dissertations, normally in their last year, on subjects allocated by lot, though with room for marginal negotiation. The subject of one dissertation would be taken from a list of general 'medical or philosophical' questions proposed by members themselves; another would be a discussion of the diagnosis and treatment of a particular case; and a third, delivered in Latin, would be a commentary on a Hippocratic or more recent medical aphorism. A dissertation of each kind was presented at every meeting, in a cycle determined by seniority, with members of longest standing heading the rota. In keeping with the seriousness of the occasion, three copies of the evening's dissertations were deposited three weeks before the meeting in which they were to be read. This allowed time for their transcription in the Society's registers and the preparation of a number of copies for circulation to members, who were allowed six hours in which to read them.[15] Like everyone in the Society, Garnett would have found the writing and presentation of the three dissertations that we know he read before the RMS, all towards the end of 1787, an ordeal. The fellow-students who composed the greater part of the audience were competitive, and the mixture of recent graduates, occasional professors and invited extra-academical practitioners who made up the rest were knowledgeable and potentially severe critics. It was, and was intended to be, a formidable exercise, involving rituals of style and presentation in which, to judge by the two dissertations by him that have survived, Garnett excelled.

Another important resource for a student of Garnett's ability and commitment was the system of extramural lecturing that had functioned on the fringes of the University since the sixteenth century. Extramural lectures were conducted in ways that promoted closer interactions between teacher and pupil than were usual in the Faculty's official courses, and through the 1770s and 1780s, in particular, they drew large audiences. An attraction of the lectures was that they often treated areas patchily covered in the normal, rather fragmented curriculum. One such area was surgery, and it is probable that Garnett learned much of what he knew of the subject from John Aitken, a prolific writer on surgical practice and, from the late 1770s until his death in 1790, a prominent independent lecturer.[16] Although Aitken had matriculated as a medical student in the 1760s and served as the RMS's senior president in 1774–5 and 1775–6, he did not take his M.D. at Edinburgh. In this respect, and without a chair though a member of the Corporation, later Royal College, of Surgeons of Edinburgh from 1770, there was always something of the outsider about him. Even so, he practised successfully as a surgeon at the Royal Infirmary and, despite mixed judgements of his contributions to the medical literature, maintained regular contacts with the academic community. His leading role in founding the Chirurgo-Obstetrical Society (for several years, one of the most successful of Edinburgh's medical societies) in 1786 gave him special prominence and may have been a context in which Garnett met him, although there is no evidence that Garnett was ever enrolled as a member.[17]

Even Aitken, however, could not match the drawing power of the most consistently successful of the extramural lecturers, Andrew Duncan the elder, or senior, a distinguished physician and pioneer of public health who had founded Edinburgh's Public Dispensary, the first of its kind in Scotland.[18] Despite serving for two years as locum professor of institutes of medicine after the death of John Gregory in 1773, Duncan had been disappointed in his application for the chair, to which Gregory's twenty-three-year-old son James was appointed in 1776. Yet he was determined to continue teaching, if only to maintain his income. In a valedictory lecture on his departure as a locum, he announced his intention of delivering a regular 'Independent course of lectures on the Theory and Practice of Medicine outwith the walls of the University'.[19] The course, to which both medical students and the public would be admitted, would cover 'the whole fundamental principles of the healing art ... within the short space of six months'. It was understandably popular and still had a substantial following throughout and after Garnett's time in Edinburgh. Duncan continued to offer it, in many years with a summer course on materia medica as well, until 1790, when he finally succeeded James Gregory in the institutes of medicine chair, following Gregory's appointment to succeed Cullen in the more lucrative chair of the practice of physic.

Although no attendance registers exist, there can be little doubt that Garnett attended Duncan's course, given in the purpose-built premises of his 'medical academy' in Surgeons' Square, close to Surgeons' Hall and the Hall of the Royal Medical Society.[20] Whether through the lectures or through the RMS, of which Duncan served as president for six sessions and as treasurer from 1771 to 1786, Garnett would have had ample opportunity of encountering him personally and been proud to do so. It was the kind of contact that could significantly advance the prospects of an aspiring physician on the threshold of a medical career. The point was not lost on Garnett, and there could be only one destination for his first paper, on the successful treatment of a patient he had attended with Dawson for the effects of an enlarged liver.[21] The paper was published in Duncan's annual *Medical Commentaries* for 1788. To appear in the *Commentaries*, founded as the cutting-edge *Medical and Philosophical Commentaries* in 1773 and edited by Duncan as a private venture on into the 1790s, was an accolade that drew a young author into the most progressive circles of Edinburgh medicine and gave exposure across the world.[22] When the author, as in Garnett's case, was still a student, the accolade was all the greater, and there is evidence that Duncan thought highly of him.[23]

A Brunonian apprenticeship

Among the great extramural spectacles in the years just before Garnett's arrival in Edinburgh were the lectures of the eccentric Dr John Brown. In the late 1770s, a year or two after Duncan, Brown had established himself as a lecturer on the margins of the medical community.[24] His lectures were extravagant performances, delivered at his home in the Old Town or in a chapel nearby and routinely conducted with a bottle of whisky and a phial of laudanum to hand. Whether Garnett was among the students who flocked to hear him is uncertain. By the mid-1780s, Brown was in financial difficulties, to the point of spending periods in the traditional sanctuary for debtors adjacent to the Abbey and Palace of Holyrood and briefly in prison. But he continued to lecture as best he could (even from prison), and it is conceivable that Garnett heard him in the winter of 1785–6, by which time Brown was trying to restore his fortunes with the aid of funds advanced by the eminent judge Francis Gordon, Lord Gardenstone. With Gordon's support, Brown hoped to buy off his creditors. The result, though, was relief rather than a cure, and at some time in 1786, he left Edinburgh for the anonymity and possibility of a new start in London.

Whether or not Garnett attended these last lectures, he would have entered a student community awash with stories of Brown's erratic behaviour and misfortunes. He would also have encountered an intensity of continuing debate that set Brown above the ranks of a flamboyant lecturer with little of substance to say. Brown, in fact, had established himself as a serious opponent of the traditional teachings of the medical school, in particular Cullen's. From the start, the irregularity of his training and career had set him apart. As a student, he had only turned to medicine after abandoning his early studies in philosophy and divinity. And although he was admitted to medical lectures at Edinburgh, he was never formally enrolled and had eventually taken his M.D. at St Andrews, which awarded degrees without serious examination and despite having no medical school of its own. By the time he took the degree, in 1779, he was in his mid-forties, and an initial closeness to Cullen, who had earlier employed him as his Latin secretary and a tutor to his children, had long since soured into mutual animosity. Through the 1770s, the ill feelings had intensified as Brown struggled to win formal recognition, most visibly in 1776 as a candidate for the chair of institutes of medicine, for which both he and Duncan competed unsuccessfully and for which the now hostile Cullen declared him to be quite unsuitable.

From 1780, when he published a 450-page account of his 'Brunonian' system, *Elementa medicinae*, Brown's star as a waspish critic of the medical establishment rose spectacularly.[25] His attacks were fierce, and they meant that Garnett lived his three years at the university amid the excitement of a learned battleground on which the *Elementa* continued to circulate, now in a second, revised edition (1784), though still in Latin; the first English translation, by Brown himself, did not appear until the year of his death, 1788.[26] The confrontations, heightened by Brown's excoriating unsigned attack on 'the old system of physic' in 1787, had a strong element of intergenerational conflict.[27] In the eyes of progressively minded students, Garnett among them, Brown had delivered a timely challenge to the authority of an inflexible professorial establishment. And even if students were not sufficiently convinced to become Brunonians themselves, they enjoyed the spectacle. One young Brunonian who did was William Margetson Heald, a student contemporary of Garnett's embarking on what was to be a short career (before ordination) as a surgeon and apothecary in Yorkshire.[28] Heald's mock-heroic poem, *The Brunoniad*, published under the pseudonym of 'Julius Juniper' in 1789, portrayed Edinburgh's warring factions as Homeric gods exchanging words and missiles of food in a battle between Nestor's (Cullen's) forces and the 'majestic Bruno' and his disciples. Heald's villains were the Senate of identifiable professors who rallied to Nestor. Ranged against them were the heroes in the Brunonian camp, including Garnett himself, who appeared as 'my Garnett', a leader among Brown's supporters.[29]

Lightly though Heald's criticism was cast, it was unforgiving in its portrayal of the grip that Cullen had exercised for so long on Edinburgh medicine. It also conveyed the seriousness of the challenge that Cullen now faced in a clash that went to the heart of medical belief and practice. Whereas Cullen's aim was to establish a taxonomy, or nosology, of diseases of different types, each with a distinct origin and cure, Brown proposed a unitary system. He regarded all disease as the consequence of a single disorder, with symptoms corresponding to the intensity with which the disorder acted on an individual patient or a particular organ of the body. In procedures shot through with explicitly Newtonian overtones of objectivity and measurement, Brown had a clear view of the goal of medicine. It was to discover the laws governing living matter and apply them in maintaining an appropriate level of vital activity, or 'excitement', in a patient's bodily functions.

As a key measure of health, 'excitement' lay at the heart of Brown's therapies, and its monitoring and control were the essence of the physician's art. In a system that treated life as a forced condition, Brown saw excitement as the result of the interaction between 'excitability' (a measure of a body's capacity to respond to stimulus) and the external stimuli, or 'exciting powers', to which the body was constantly subjected. In a healthy body, the level of excitability was such that everyday exciting powers, such as food, alcoholic drink, warmth, light or physical activity, all taken in moderation, would provoke a moderate degree of excitement and so maintain life. It was a system of beguiling, not to say excessive, simplicity, though one with an involved lineage going back to debates that had circulated since the mid-century around Albrecht von Haller's concepts of irritability and sensibility.[30] Brown's excitability, in fact, had much in common with Haller's irritability. But his ideal of an intimate union of theoretical and practical medicine distanced him markedly from Haller, whose investigations

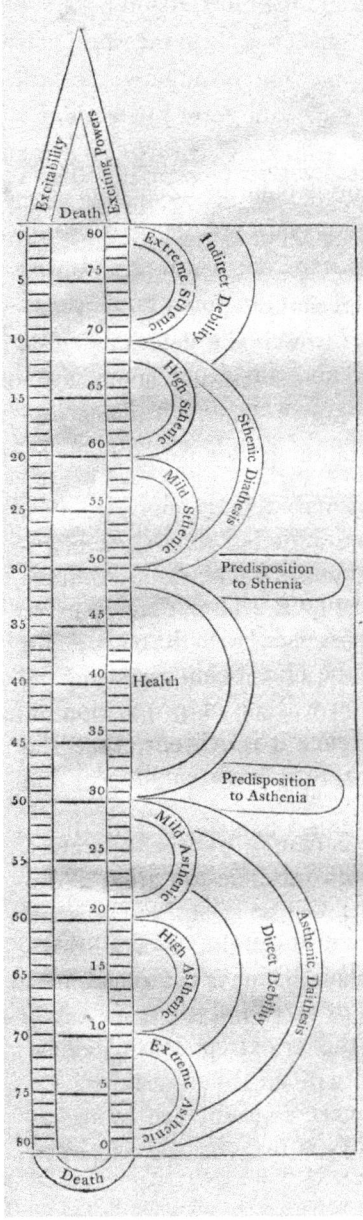

Figure 2.1 The Brunonian scale of sickness and health, showing 'Health' at the midpoint between the extremes of sthenic and asthenic disorders. From Garnett, *Popular Lectures on Zoonomia, or the Laws of Animal Life, in Health and Disease* (London, 1804), 221. Adapted from the 'Table of Excitement and Excitability' in John Brown, *Elements of Medicine*, new edn., 2 vols. (Edinburgh, 1795), vol. 1, folding plate facing p. 1. Private collection.

of physiological processes in the muscles and nerves were of a complexity and abstraction that did not transfer easily to the world of pathological practice.[31]

Both the simplicity and the quantitative aspirations of the Brunonian system are conveyed in schematic form in a scale of sickness and health that first appeared in the 1795 edition of Brown's *Elements* and was then adapted by Garnett in his posthumously published *Zoonomia* (see Figure 2.1). Conditions at the two extremities of the scale were those of disorders which, unless treated, could be the prelude to death. At the lower end, where the patient had been deprived of food and other exciting powers, the result (despite a high level of accumulated excitability) would be a deficiency of excitement, manifested in the 'asthenic' symptoms of weakness and fatigue. In Brown's terminology, such a condition was one of 'direct debility', and typical remedies would include the controlled administration of stimulating cordials or appropriately diluted drafts of alcohol or opium, or simply keeping the patient warm. Conditions towards the top end of the scale were very different. Associated with a surfeit of exciting powers and consequently high levels of excitement, they resulted in the 'sthenic', or 'phlogistic', symptoms of redness or inflammatory swelling, typical of rheumatism, scarlet fever or pleurisy. In the majority of sthenic cases, 'depletives' would be effective: bleeding, a reduced diet, purging and other sedative remedies would normally be enough to ease the inflammation and allow the reduced levels of excitability to be cautiously restored.

Less straightforward, however, were the complications that arose when a sthenic condition went unchecked. In such circumstances, the classic 'high' sthenic symptoms of enhanced excitement and vigour risked becoming 'extreme'. A patient in the advanced stages of inebriation, for example, might fall into a drunken stupor, with the same symptoms of lassitude and unresponsiveness that characterized an advanced asthenic condition at the other end of the scale and bore the same risk of imminent death. Such a reaction was an instance of what Brown called 'indirect debility', in which the body's excitability had been so diminished by excess that normal exciting powers would be ineffective; as the condition worsened and the body became even less responsive, ever-stronger powers would be required if a proper level of excitement was to be restored. Since excess had caused the disorder in the first place, there was something paradoxical about the use of an abnormally powerful stimulus to treat an extreme sthenic condition, and indirect debility remained one of the most contested aspects of the Brunonian system.

We do not know how or when Garnett fell under Brown's spell. His conversion may have occurred early in his time at the University, when the initial Brunonian furore was still at its height. But it was not until the winter of 1787–8 that he came out as a Brunonian. He did so in dissertations on the laws governing living matter that he read before all three of his student societies. The different audiences that he faced in the societies called for different emphases and styles of presentation. Before the RPS, he offered an austerely academic account treating life in both the animal and the vegetable kingdoms, without digressions or criticisms.[32] In accordance with the Society's practices, he wrote in Latin, probably with professional help (though his Latin appears to have been good), and his terminology followed that of the canonical *Elementa medicinae*: hence *incitatio*, *incitabilitas* and *potestates incitantes* for excitement, excitability and exciting powers. Done in a tone of unqualified respect for 'Bruno illustrissimus' and laced with quotations from the *Elementa*, it was the work of a close disciple.

The dissertation he read before the NHS on 17 January 1788 showed the same unqualified commitment. This time, he wrote in English and in a more adventurous style appropriate for an audience whose interests extended beyond the medical technicalities. He began with a presentation of Brown's ideas that reads as an original English version from which his RPS dissertation had been translated. But a sober expository start was the prelude to larger reflexions on a 'scale of life' in which it was 'highly probable' that life extended uninterruptedly not only through the animal and vegetable kingdoms but even to minerals.[33] The idea that life might be characteristic of the mineral creation was far from new; it had been something of a commonplace in the sixteenth and seventeenth centuries, and it still circulated, though less commonly, in the later eighteenth century. In 1761, the French naturalist Jean-Jacques Robinet had given it strong support in a book, *De la nature*, with which Garnett would almost certainly have been familiar.[34] And eight years later Denis Diderot had put the assertion that 'stone must feel' in the mouth of d'Alembert in the imaginary, and as yet unpublished, conversation of *Le Rêve de d'Alembert*.[35]

By the 1780s, however, such beliefs lay firmly outside the scientific mainstream, and Garnett knew that many in his audience would regard his most daring speculations as fanciful. But he did not hold back. Might it be that large rocks were 'the expansion of the parts of a minute grain of sand', the result of a gestation too slow and lengthy for us to comprehend? Might even the earth itself be 'one organized living piece of matter' whose apparently unchanging nature concealed the deeper reality of its immense longevity and the likelihood that it would eventually die and decay? Might the growth of crystals illustrate a form of growth peculiar to the mineral kingdom? The purpose of such questions was, at one level, to impress by a display of learning and imagination. But the questions also complemented his endorsement of Brunonianism by portraying nature as a fount of truths hidden from normal sight but waiting to be laid bare. This, for Garnett, was precisely what Brown had done in illuminating the age-old mystery of the difference between living and non-living matter.

Important though his dissertations before the RPS and NHS were, it was the RMS that Garnett chose as the setting for his major Brunonian set piece, 'In what does life consist?' He knew that there he would face an audience particularly attuned to the sensitivities on both sides and familiar with the controversy's history. Brown himself had served as an annual president of the RMS on two occasions in the 1770s and left a coterie of dedicated supporters thirsting to pursue their rhetorical attacks on the Cullenian establishment. In 1781, tensions engendered by the confrontational attitude of a newly elected student with Brunonian sympathies had culminated in talk of a duel and the expulsion of the student concerned.[36] In the same year, too, Andrew Duncan's closeness to the RMS had led to the Society's indirect involvement in a dispute between him and a recent graduate and follower of Brown, Robert Jones, who had contributed, with Duncan, to the treatment of a student. The clash between the claims of traditional and Brunonian therapeutic procedures to be responsible for the patient's recovery had occasioned the taking of depositions on oath and an exchange of accusatory pamphlets that exposed the familiar animosities at their most intense.[37] Other, equally disruptive episodes had followed, fanned by leaks to the press about debates in the RMS that should, in principle, have remained confidential. Shortly before Garnett's arrival in Edinburgh, these had even provoked a lawsuit that set the Society in open conflict with the Brunonian-inclined *Edinburgh Evening Post*.[38]

In these various spats, the Cullenian leadership of the RMS had done its best to trim the extreme Brunonian tendencies within the Society, while maintaining its commitment to free speech and stopping short of a total ban. It had had some success, to the point that by the mid-1780s, as Lisa Rosner's findings suggest, there were probably no more than between ten and fifteen thoroughgoing Brunonians among the eighty or so resident members.[39] But the hard core remained vociferous and loyal to the cause, and those of them who heard Garnett's RMS dissertation knew him to be one of their own. He appears to have shown his hand in earlier, informal exchanges among members.[40] And in case any doubted where his sympathies lay, he topped and tailed the written version of the dissertation with the trappings of Brunonian loyalty: an initial Latin epigram from the *Elementa medicinae* to begin with and the tag 'Alumnus Brunonis' after his concluding signature.

He began the dissertation cautiously. Declaring himself to be 'not in the least prejudiced' in favour of Brown's ideas, he was ready to yield to his fellow-members if they could demonstrate the system's absurdity. But deference was an artful cover for the unyielding defence of Brunonian principles that followed. From a summary of them, drawn largely from his dissertations before the RPS and NHS, he moved on to a more specifically medical discussion of diseases and their cure. His diagnostic starting point was a classic Brunonian statement that 'every power which produces universal disease, must do it by increasing or diminishing the excitement'. On that, he built a superstructure that Brown himself could not have presented with greater conviction or more telling case-histories. By a cruel irony, Garnett's illustration of indirect debility dwelt particularly on typhus fever, to which he was himself to fall victim almost fifteen years later. In Brunonian terms, he described the advanced symptoms of the fever as brought on by the violent exciting power of the contagion and the consequent exhaustion of the body's excitability. As this happened, a patient's initial high level of excitement would pass, over a day or two, to lassitude, then vertigo, delirium and chronic nausea. At this stage, if death was to be avoided, the condition called for cautious intervention that would nurture the restoration of a measure of excitability sufficient to allow the excitement in the patient's body gradually to accumulate again.

Despite Garnett's boldness and pride in presenting himself as a Brunonian, his use of the term was never intended to apply to the whole range of medical practice. Brown's system, limited to 'universal' diseases (his term for conditions arising from a deficiency or excess of excitement affecting the whole body), left many areas of medicine that a Brunonian physician could pursue without reference to the unorthodox principles underlying his therapies. In these non-Brunonian areas, Garnett was critical but not dismissive of medical school teaching. The discussion of the case of a nine-year-old boy with whooping cough that he presented as one of his two dissertations before the RMS makes the point. In it, Garnett used the terms 'exciting causes' and 'debility' in ways that flagged his debt to Brown.[41] But there was little in his citation of existing authors, discussion of symptoms or recommendation of possible remedies that marked him as a rebel. The treatments he reviewed, including blisters, emetics, opium and mild electric shocks, were part of the armoury of any physician, so too the use of Peruvian bark (Cinchona) as a tonic once the patient's worst symptoms had passed.

It was in his studies of vision that Garnett stepped most decisively, and perhaps with some relief, into aspects of medicine untouched by Brown's teachings. His priority in the dissertations on the subject that he read before the NHS in April 1787 (on animal vision) and before the RPS (in Latin, on squinting) later in the year was to display a command of the literature and a capacity for informed reflexion on current beliefs and treatments. He did both. And he went on to do so where it mattered most of all, in his M.D. thesis *De visu*, a wide-ranging discussion of the anatomy and functions of the eye and the surrounding muscles that he defended publicly, in his last act as a student, on 12 September 1788.[42]

In the thesis as in his dissertations, Garnett laid no claim to originality. As he knew, a thesis such as Joseph Black's on magnesia alba (1754), for which Black carried out ground-breaking original work, was the exception.[43] By the academic criteria of the day, in fact, his handling of squinting, to which he devoted a substantial part of *De visu*, was a model. It entailed not only finding a way through the thickets of a scholarly literature going back to the seventeenth century but also taking a view on what remained a perplexing condition. Interpretations had essentially coalesced around the competing hypotheses of the French mathematician and astronomer Philippe de la Hire and the English Newtonian Jean Jurin. For de la Hire, followed by Hermann Boerhaave, the defect arose from a slight displacement of the most sensitive part of the retina, which caused the distorted eye to realign itself in such a way that the image would be formed where it would be best perceived. Jurin's explanation rested rather on an inequality between the eyes, with the consequence, as he supposed, that in cases of significant disparity the weaker eye would turn inwards to avoid confusing the image received by the better one. In the absence of decisive evidence, observations by Georges Buffon in France, the Edinburgh physician William Porterfield and the philosopher Thomas Reid had tipped the balance in favour of Jurin.[44] And subsequent endorsements by Joseph Priestley and Erasmus Darwin had reinforced the rather shaky consensus, at least in Britain.[45] So when, in *De visu*, Garnett declared in favour of the majority view, he was playing safe, and he played even safer by buttressing his argument with an examination of more than forty cases that lent support to Jurin's conclusion. In the context of an M.D. thesis, there was little chance of his observations having any other outcome.

With learning rather than originality so overwhelmingly the norm, the bookish style of the final doctoral exercise and its conduct in Latin can too easily suggest that the later stages of the passage to the M.D. were a formality. By the time of the defence, however, Garnett had had to face a sequence of sterner tests that had been imposed as part of a tightening of the University's regulations for medicine since 1770.[46] The process would have begun at least three months before he wanted to graduate with an interview with the dean of the medical school, whose task was to receive candidates' certificates of attendance at the required lecture-courses, check the adequacy of their Latin and take a £10 graduation fee. What followed had both oral and written elements. A private *viva voce* examination before a group of the medical professors in one of their homes would have been a tough ordeal, as would a second oral examination, held in the university library before two professors. The written part of the examination called for commentaries on a Hippocratic aphorism, a general medical question and two case histories. These closely mirrored the exercises of the RMS, and Garnett would have been well up to the task, the more so as the answers were written at home and with access to notes and books.

As he fulfilled the successive requirements, Garnett would have felt the mounting pressure of the thesis, which had to be submitted at least six weeks before the defence. The text that he produced was polished, written in a correct, even elegant Latin that again suggests his access to one of the coaches or 'grinders' who helped students with their preparations. It delivered all that was expected of it. On the day of the defence, he would have gathered with the other candidates for the degree, to be examined individually in the University's Public Hall. He would then have retired, while the professors deliberated, and returned, wearing his black doctor's gown, to take the assertively protestant oath that was required of all medical graduates and sign the historic register of Laureation and Degrees.[47] He was one of twelve admitted on the same day *Doctoratus in arte medica*.

Physician, philosopher, Freemason

With the ceremony and three years of intense study behind him, Garnett could look back on a well-conducted student career. Quite apart from his thesis and degree, he had earned solid credentials in the science and pathology of vision, assumed a position of leadership among his generation's young Brunonians and achieved a prominence in student societies that set him among the elite of his year. In a total cohort of twenty-eight who took their M.D. in the two graduation ceremonies in 1788 (an average class size for the 1780s), he would have been known not only to his peers and the professors who examined him but also to other senior figures in Edinburgh medicine, most importantly Andrew Duncan, who was still taking an interest in his career several years after graduation.[48] The copy of *De visu* that Garnett inscribed for Duncan conveys both his genuine debt and an astute perception of possible future support.[49]

But Garnett's time at the University had done more than confirm his vocation as a physician. He had also matured from the raw nineteen-year-old who had arrived from his secluded upbringing in Barbon and Sedbergh. Reconstruction of the transition is difficult, and such sources as we have are fragmentary. With maturity, though, had come a worldview and personal morality rooted in the ideals of the Scottish Enlightenment. In the dichotomy that has done so much to colour recent historiography in the wake of the exchanges between Margaret Jacob, Jonathan Israel and others since the 1980s, Garnett's Enlightenment was 'moderate' rather than 'radical'.[50] It was an Enlightenment supportive of the goals of justice and controlled improvement but fearful of political doctrines that threatened to subvert rather than reform society. As such, it had far more in common with the principles of moderation and social harmony professed by America's founding fathers than with the forms of political activism that fomented civic disorder in Britain throughout the 1780s and 1790s and were soon to make Joseph Priestley and Thomas Beddoes vulnerable to public attack. It is significant that, despite their overlapping scientific interests, Garnett's mentions of both men were respectful rather than warm. Their world, though close, was never quite his.

Underlying Garnett's moderation was a sense of a divine plan for both nature and society that humanity would upset at its peril. This made its first appearance in the dissertations he wrote for the student societies. Incorporated in texts whose main purpose was the presentation of medical principles, discussion of such wider issues was dispersed and incidental. Yet it conveyed a sensitivity to 'the infinite wisdom of the Author of Nature' (Garnett's words) that went beyond the providentialism he would have imbibed in what appears to have been his easy-going Anglican upbringing. In the study of animal vision that he presented to the NHS in April 1787, something of a routine eighteenth-century sense of God's providence can be read into his wonder at structures that allowed the chameleon to perceive the world through two eyes moving independently of each other, and the spider and dragonfly to see in almost any direction by using their multiple or multifaceted eyes to overcome an inability to move their heads.[51] But his reverence for the divine was informed by more than individual commonplaces about God as a master-craftsman. The wonder of creation, for Garnett, lay less in its parts than in its comprehensiveness as a harmonious cosmic machine obeying universal laws that it was the mission of the true man of science to study.

Such were precisely the laws that Brown had uncovered and thereby given medicine, for the first time, a foundation of theory that could boast 'a title to be called philosophical'; the words again are Garnett's.[52] It was in seeing more profoundly than the established practitioners of medicine that Brown had shown himself a philosopher, just as Newton had done with his insights into heavenly motion. And it was that superior status to which, as a true Brunonian, Garnett himself aspired. As he put it, in a spirit of deliberate provocation, to the members of the NHS, just as philosophy that had allowed 'the illustrious Bruno' to fashion his insights, so the time had come to raise the pursuit of natural history as well above 'mere Classification' and the study of the appearances alone.[53] This was not to despise natural history but to insist on the insufficiency of its current practices; 'without a view of Philosophy', Garnett told the Society, an activity that did not venture beyond methodical arrangement remained 'a tedious unprofitable labour … unworthy the attention of a rational being'.

The link between Garnett's conception of providence and his advocacy of a broader philosophical perspective in science and medicine found expression in his adoption, in *De visu* as in the posthumous *Zoonomia*, of Thomas Reid's ideas on some of the most commonly debated aspects of human vision. A focus for Garnett's endorsement of Reid was Reid's view that the parallel motion, or conjugacy, of human eyes was 'the work of nature' rather than a 'habit' acquired in childhood.[54] As an innate property, conjugacy belonged among what Reid called 'the original powers and principles of the human mind' and was not, as Robert Smith and William Porterfield, following Bishop Berkeley, had argued, the fruit of 'custom', or learned.[55] In taking this position, Reid was affirming notions of perception that deliberately distanced him from David Hume and the broader Lockean tradition, with its emphasis on objective knowledge of the world as a product of sense impressions alone. By clear implication, Garnett's support for Reid set him too in the anti-Humean camp. And it was a support that extended beyond conjugacy. On such age-old questions as how images from our two eyes result in a single image in the brain and why an inverted image on the retina allows us to see things correctly oriented, Garnett followed Reid closely, to the point of weaving passages from Reid's *Inquiry into the Human Mind* into his own discussion.[56] For him, as for Reid, the 'fixed and immutable laws of nature' held the key to any understanding of vision, and their very existence pointed to the reality of a divinely executed creative act.[57]

There was little in such opinions that could not have been accommodated within a broadly cast Anglican faith. But Garnett's conception of a creator God, allied to his conviction that science, and science alone, was capable of penetrating the hidden nature of things, points to a mind receptive to strains of thought beyond the strictly Christian tradition. This may well have been what drew him to Freemasonry, possibly while he was still a student. He had certainly been admitted a Freemason by the mid-1790s, when members of the masonic 'Lodge of Lights' in Warrington invited him, as 'Brother Thomas Garnett', to lecture to them on astronomy.[58] While nothing more is known about Garnett's masonic affiliation, the absence of his name from the archives of the United Grand Lodge of England suggests that he may have become a Freemason in Scotland and that he could have been one of the small but steady flow of medical students who are known to have joined lodges in Edinburgh from the mid-eighteenth century.[59] During his student years, he certainly did not want for masonic models, even personal influences. Among his teachers, Andrew Duncan was prominent in the Lodge Canongate Kilwinning, No. 2, the oldest and most prestigious of the Edinburgh lodges.[60] Another possible contact was through Brown, who moved from his home Lodge St Andrews to become the founder and master of the Lodge Roman Eagle a few months before Garnett began his studies.[61] It is known that at least two student members of the RMS joined Brown's new lodge early in its history, and Garnett may well have followed, although there is no mention of him in such imperfect lists as have survived.

Whatever the circumstances of Garnett's admission as a Freemason, we have no way of knowing how seriously he took his masonic commitment or how far he progressed in the grades. Apart from the approach from the 'Lodge of Lights' in 1796, all that can be said with certainty is that the worldview on which he lifted a rare veil in his NHS dissertation on 'the principal laws by which living matter is regulated' was one with which any Freemason would have felt at ease.[62] Also, in citing lines from James Thomson's *Poem Sacred to the Memory of Sir Isaac Newton* and his long blank-verse poem *The Seasons*, as he did in the dissertation and elsewhere, Garnett gave what can be read as an additional hint. While he may simply have been adding a literary embellishment bestowed by a poet still immensely popular forty years after his death, contemporaries with the antennae to perceive a more meaningful affiliation would have recognized the signs of kinship with one of the leading figures in the early British masonic movement. Though a good generation apart, Garnett and Thomson shared a sense of the cosmic whole made compelling by providentialist convictions rooted in, but not bound by, their Christian upbringings. For both of them, an emotional sensitivity to the beauties and abundance of the natural world went hand in hand with a boundless admiration of Newton, 'our philosophic sun', whose laws had demonstrated the presence of the 'secret hand' at work in the world.[63] With non-doctrinal faith, sensibility and reason working together, the underlying divine order, which it was our human duty to uncover, would be revealed. In that understanding of God's plan and the need for watchfulness against the forces of disorder threatening to disrupt it there lay the foundations of political and moral principles that were to guide many of Garnett's actions in later life.

Despite his hard work and success as a student, Garnett left Edinburgh in the autumn of 1788, with his preparation incomplete. Above all, he lacked significant exposure to patients, other than those he had encountered through a continuing contact with Dawson during vacation visits to Sedbergh. This was a common deficiency, aggravated by the generally rather low attendance at the twice-weekly clinical lectures that were offered at the Royal Infirmary.[64] Hence it was with a view to filling an obvious gap that Garnett settled in London, attending lectures and frequenting hospitals in search of clinical experience. Somehow, he survived in the capital for several months. But seriousness of intent was not enough, and the constraint of limited material resources eventually prevailed. He retreated, as he was so often to do, to the refuge of his parents' home in Barbon. There, it became a matter of urgency to determine his next course of action.

A persistent myth has it that Garnett used his time in Westmorland to revise the unsatisfactory article 'Optics' that had appeared in the second edition of the *Encyclopaedia Britannica*, ready for the third edition then in preparation.[65] Given his age and limited command of the subject, it is an improbable story, and certainly false; the revised article that eventually appeared was unquestionably the work of John Robison, and Robison, as professor of natural philosophy at Edinburgh, was a natural choice for the task.[66] What does appear plausible, however, is that, as he reflected on his future, Garnett may already have had thoughts of trying to make a living as a lecturer and writer on natural philosophy, perhaps in parallel with medical practice.

Lecturing, though, would have been a risky venture calling for a significant initial investment in demonstration apparatus and an astute eye for potential audiences, and if Garnett did contemplate such a course, he soon abandoned it. For a young Edinburgh M.D. on the threshold of adult life and with a strong student record, medicine was a far safer option. That decision made, one immediate reality he had to face was that the most elevated medical careers, leading to election to the Royal College of Physicians via a lengthy metropolitan presence and normally a degree at Oxford or Cambridge, were effectively closed to him. This was partly a matter of cost but also of a temperament and inclinations bred of his upbringing. Other paths to medical practice, however, remained realistic options. One might have led to a future like Dawson's, with the material comfort that Dawson enjoyed and the security of integration in a rural community in which he would have felt immediately at home. But the ongoing transformation of British society now promised a would-be physician greater opportunities and richer rewards than Dawson could ever have dreamed of. As Garnett recognized, his best hopes lay in this new Britain, with its expanding market for medical care and cautious loosening of traditional hierarchies of status and class.

Notes

1. 'Life of Garnett', vii, on the austerity of Garnett's life as a student.
2. Youngson, *Making of Classical Edinburgh*, 111–32 brings out the exceptional rapidity of the urban expansion in the 1780s.
3. The annual matriculation registers are bound as 'Matriculation register for medicine, 1783–1790', EUA IN1/ADS/STA/2.
4. Although midwifery was not required, its practical value meant that most students enrolled for the course. See Rosner, *Medical Education*, 44–61.
5. McElroy, *Scotland's Age of Improvement*, 128–42 and Jenkinson, *Scottish Medical Societies*, 8-67 and 205–21.
6. Ford, 'What is the best method of studying medicine?' RMS diss., 11 (1778): ff. 152-9 (156). On Ford and his views, see Rosner, *Medical Education*, 120.
7. Garnett's presidencies followed the resignations of George Buchanan and Benjamin Smith Barton, respectively presidents of the RPS for 1786–7 and the NHS for 1787–8. See *Laws and Regulations of the Royal Physical Society* (1788), 91 and *Laws of the Society … for the Investigation of Natural History* (1788), 33.
8. Hume, *Learned Societies and Printing Clubs*, 173. Cf. the approximately 100 members of the Natural History Society at the time.
9. The standard history of the RMS remains Gray, *Royal Medical Society*; see pp. 65–83 on the Society in Garnett's time. New insights on the same period are in Risse, *New Medical Challenges*, 67–132. Both of these accounts draw on William Stroud's earlier 'History of the Medical Society of Edinburgh', printed as a prefatory text in *List of Members, Laws, and Library Catalogue of the Medical Society* (1820), iii-ci. Important among more focused studies are Rosner, *Medical Education*, 119–34; Christie, '"The most perfect liberty"', esp. 89–96; and Gray, 'Royal Medical and Medico-Chirurgical Societies', esp. 134–45.
10. The Hall is illustrated in Shepherd, *Modern Athens!*, facing p. 10. Reproduced in Gray, *Royal Medical Society*, facing p. 120.
11. *Edin. Alm.*, 1788, 58. Cf. Lisa Rosner's estimate that fewer than 13 per cent of students at any one time were members; Rosner, *Medical Education*, 126.
12. *Laws and List of the Members of the Royal Medical Society of Edinburgh* (1788), 13–15.

13 Ibid., 96.
14 Ibid., 1–3.
15 Ibid., 34–9.
16 Kaufman, 'John Aitken' and, more generally on the context of Aitken's activities in Edinburgh, Rosner, *Medical Education*, 101 and 119–25.
17 Aitken, *Address to the Chirurgo-Obstetrical Society*.
18 On the many facets of Duncan's life, see the essays in John Chalmers, ed., *Andrew Duncan Senior*, esp. Chalmers's 'Biographical overview', 1–35. Also the briefer accounts in Chambers, ed., *Biographical Dictionary of Eminent Scotsmen*, vol. 1, 497–9 and Rosner, *Andrew Duncan*.
19 Duncan, 'Conclusion of the clinical lectures', 105.
20 The premises appear in the illustration cited above, note 10.
21 Garnett, 'Account of a suppuration of the liver'.
22 On the prestige of the journal, see Iain Chalmers, et al., '*Medical and Philosophical Commentaries and Its Successors*'.
23 See ch. 4, 84.
24 On Brown and his system, see Thomas Beddoes's 'Observations on the character and writings of John Brown', a perceptive prefatory essay published in the 1795 edition (though not in the 1788 edition) of the English translation of Brown's *Elements*. Writing as a convinced but critical Brunonian, Beddoes offers a valuable contemporary perspective, including a vivid account of Brown's lectures (ibid., lxxxv-lxxxvii). In the modern literature, see the essays in Bynum and Porter, eds., *Brunonianism in Britain and Europe* and Guenter Risse's biography and study of Brown, 'Explaining Brunonianism'.
25 Brown, *Elementa medicinæ* (1780).
26 On the English translations of 1788 and 1795, see notes 24; also ch. 3, note 78, on the American editions in the 1790s.
27 [Brown], *Old System of Physic*. On both the immediate technicalities and the wider debate, see, in addition to Bynum and Porter, eds., *Brunonianism in Britain and Europe*, the detailed but highly critical discussion of Brown in Thomson, *Life of Cullen*, vol. 2, esp. 222–489, where Thomson argues that Brown exaggerated the originality of his ideas and systematically played down his debt to Cullen.
28 After briefly practising in Wakefield, Heald went on to become a prominent Yorkshire clergyman, well known to the Bronte family.
29 [Heald], alias 'Julius Juniper', *The Brunoniad*, 4.
30 On these antecedents, see Steinke, *Irritating Experiments*.
31 As Hubert Steinke has put it, 'Haller's physiology was too complicated and Brown's too simple'. See Steinke, *Irritating Experiments*, 251.
32 'Pauca de legibus quibus gubernantur corpora viventia', RPS diss., vol. 10 (1785–88), ff. 494–501.

33 'Short view of some of the principal laws by which living matter is regulated', NHS papers, vol. 7 (1787–88), dissertation no. 84.
34 Robinet, *De la nature*. On the tradition of speculation about mineral vivency, see Wolfe, 'Gorgonick spirits'. I am grateful to Jessica Wolfe and Pietro Corsi for advice and leads on early modern debates on the subject.
35 Diderot, *Rêve de d'Alembert*, ed. Jean Varloot, 3. The work remained unpublished until 1830.
36 Beddoes, 'Character and writings of John Brown', lxvii–lxxiv and Risse, *New Medical Challenges*, 110–11.
37 Chalmers, 'Duncan and the Brunonian Society', in Chalmers, ed., *Andrew Duncan Senior*, 181–6.
38 Risse, *New Medical Challenges*, 111–22.
39 Rosner, *Medical Education*, 132–3.
40 Garnett, 'In what does life consist? How are those variations from health, called diseases, produced? And how shall we best cure them?', RMS diss., vol. 21 (1787–88), dissertation no. XI, ff. 365–87, f. 366. On the contemporary state of the debate, see Gray, *Royal Medical Society*, 56–61 and Risse, *New Medical Challenges*, 122–5.
41 'A. B. (aetat. 9) has ... laboured under symptoms similar to those of a common catarrh', dated December 1787, RMS diss., vol. 22 ('Cases'), ff. 1–15.
42 Garnett, *De visu*. The text of *De visu* appeared in English as the chapter 'Vision' in Garnett, *Zoonomia*, 130–68, with a diagram of the eye added, the opening paragraph and all footnote references omitted, and minor changes made to the last two pages.
43 A point well made in Rosner, 'Eighteenth-Century Medical Education'.
44 Buffon, 'Dissertation sur la cause du strabisme'; Porterfield, *Treatise on the Eye*, vol. 2, 318–28; Reid, *Inquiry into the Human Mind*, 2nd edn. (1765), 252–7. Garnett's references show that he used this second edition of the *Inquiry*.
45 Priestley, *Vision, Light, and Colours*, 652–60 and Darwin, 'New case in squinting', 90.
46 On the examination procedures, see Rosner, *Medical Education*, 72–85.
47 Garnett's signature appears on p. 127 of the register covering the years 1587–1809, EUA IN1/ADS/STA/1/1; see the University of Edinburgh's 'Archives online' site. The text of the oath is in *List of the Graduates in Medicine from MDCCV to MDLCCCVI*, v; also in *Nomina eorum, qui gradum medicinae doctoris adepti sunt*, v. Candidates swore 'in veritate et puritate Religionis Christianae ab omnibus Pontificiorum erroribus repurgatae'.
48 In addition to the twelve students who graduated on 12 September 1788 were sixteen who had graduated in June. See (from the previous note) *List of Graduates*, 21 and *Nomina eorum*, 187.
49 See ch. 3, note 70.

50 For different perspectives in an extensive secondary literature, see Jacob, *Radical Enlightenment. Pantheists, Freemasons, and Republicans* and Israel, *Radical Enlightenment. Philosophy and the Making of Modernity*.
51 Garnett, 'On the organs of vision in different animals', NHS papers, vol. 6 (1786–7), dissertation 235, unpaginated.
52 Garnett, *Zoonomia*, 214.
53 Garnett, 'Short view of the principal laws', cited in note 34.
54 Reid, *Inquiry into the Human Mind*, 2nd edn. (1765), 185–9. For Garnett's endorsement of Reid, see *De visu*, 43–5; also *Zoonomia*, 155–7.
55 Reid, *Inquiry into the Human Mind*, 2nd edn. (1765), 258–68. For the views of Smith and Porterfield, see Smith, *Compleat System of Opticks*, vol. 1, 46–9 and Porterfield, *Treatise on the Eye*, vol. 1, 114–15.
56 Reid, *Inquiry into the Human Mind*, 2nd edn. (1765), 190–232; Garnett, *De visu*, 37–47 and *Zoonomia*, 152–8. For a comment on Reid's significance, see Westheimer, 'Law of equal innervation'.
57 Reid, *Inquiry into the Human Mind*, 2nd edn. (1765), 268.
58 Harrison, 'Lodge of Lights.'
59 See, for example, the striking number of medical students who joined the Lodge Canongate Kilwinning, No. 2 in the period 1735–65, for which records are available at sites.google.com › canongate-kilwinning-lodge-no-2.
60 On the history of the lodge and its place in the Edinburgh Enlightenment, see Mackenzie, *Lodge Canongate Kilwinning, No. 2*.
61 Risse, 'Explaining Brunonianism', 42–8 and Beddoes, 'Character and writings of John Brown', lxxxv.
62 Garnett, 'Short view of the principal laws', cited in note 33.
63 The phrases are Thomson's, in 'A poem sacred to the memory of Sir Isaac Newton', published in *The Seasons* (1730), 241–52, lines 15 and 90.
64 Rosner, *Medical Education*, 53–4.
65 Both 'Life of Garnett', viii and Anon., 'Memoir of Thomas Garnett', 480 refer to Garnett's having used his time in Barbon to revise the article.
66 Robison is identified as the author of the article (one that he revised but was far from happy with) by George Gleig, the editor of the third edition's later volumes, in a letter to the editor of *The British Critic*, 29 (1807), 219–20. See also Playfair, 'Biographical account of the late John Robison', 520–1.

3

Yorkshire

Spa doctor and man of science

Someone with Garnett's profoundly northern roots and loyalties might not have been expected to look further afield than the North for the first move in his medical career. But his decision to start in Yorkshire, first in Bradford and then in Harrogate, was not an emotional one alone. The North, like the industrial Midlands, was rich in opportunities and a magnet for the professional classes as well as for those who found work in and around mills and factories. Arnold Thackray has made the point in a classic study of late-eighteenth-century Manchester, where a booming urban economy attracted large numbers of modern-minded 'new' men, mostly of provincial origin and many of them physicians and surgeons, whose family origins, education and social position distanced them both from working-class culture and from the traditional 'high' culture of the capital and the ancient English universities.[1]

Thackray's 'Manchester model' is applicable to any number of expanding manufacturing towns, large and small, in the later eighteenth century. Bradford was just such a town. Still modest in size but already launched on its rise to dominance of the English worsted industry and on a phase of spectacular growth, it was a setting in which a young man with Garnett's drive and high qualifications could hope to rise quickly. But opportunity and growth were inseparable from the harshness that went with a raw, unformed community, and his subsequent move to Harrogate reflected the pull of the more refined society and different clientele of an emerging spa town. Yet Harrogate, too, had many of the characteristics that went with rapid expansion; as Garnett was to find, it offered its own profile of opportunities but also its own impediments to social integration.

Bradford and Harrogate, in fact, exemplified the diversity of ways in which changes on the national scale took concrete shape in specific local contexts. Even in the narrow confines of two Yorkshire towns only twenty miles apart, Garnett witnessed a microcosm of social and economic adjustment as profound as any in

England's history. His perspective, of course, was overwhelmingly provincial. But it was provincial at the high point in a cultural flowering of the English provinces that had been gathering strength since the middle decades of the eighteenth century. It is that which gives Garnett's experiences in Yorkshire their significance as windows on an age in which 'province' played its full part with 'metropolis' in fashioning the nation's intellectual life, especially in the sciences.[2] In these years, in fact, the English provinces were far more than the distant witnesses of a wider European Enlightenment; in key areas, they were founts of distinctive enlightenments of their own. Studies by Peter Jones (of the 'Industrial enlightenment' of Birmingham and the West Midlands) and Jon Mee and Jennifer Wilkes (of a 'Transpennine enlightenment', with its poles in Manchester and Newcastle) make the point compellingly and draw welcome attention to seats of provincial vigour of precisely the kind that mattered most to Garnett.[3]

Yorkshire's two faces: Bradford and Harrogate

Why Garnett's choice fell on Bradford among the many options open to him is unclear. Entry into any new medical community would normally require introductions, and we can only suppose that he received help of this kind. It is an easier matter to identify those who welcomed and encouraged him on his arrival. Prominent among his early friends was the Bradford surgeon and apothecary William Maud, the son of Timothy Maud, also a surgeon, both of them Quakers. Here, a Sedbergh connexion may well have played its part in easing Garnett's initial contact with the family: the elder Maud had been a friend of the Quaker physician and botanist John Fothergill, who had been educated at the grammar school in Sedbergh and would have been known to Dawson (although Dawson was more than twenty years his junior). But there was much else that made the Mauds congenial companions. Timothy Maud was soon to collaborate with another Quaker, William Tuke, in founding the Retreat, an innovative asylum in York for the treatment of mental illness, and to become the institution's first superintendent. The Mauds' world of charitable improvement was one in which Garnett would have felt entirely at home.[4]

If any further bond was required, this lay in a shared interest in science. Before his arrival in Bradford, Garnett's mind may already have been attuned to the study of mineral waters through the work of the Dawsonian protégé (and Quaker) Robert Willan, whose analyses of the sulphureous Yorkshire springs of Croft and Harrogate were published during Garnett's apprenticeship years in Sedbergh.[5] But it was probably William Maud who introduced him to the experimental technicalities involved. We know, at least, that Maud accompanied him on an early visit to Redmire Spaw on Rombalds Moor, near the Mauds' family home in Bingley, and then collaborated with him on the examination of the water back in Bradford.[6] The tone of Garnett's account of what appears to have been his first exercise in analysis suggests that the friendship was close, and it evidently extended well beyond the initial excursion.

Such friendships mattered. And Garnett worked hard, and quickly, to establish the network of support that he needed as an unproven newcomer to Bradford's medical community. Another influential figure whom he courted was James Crowther, physician and surgeon at nearby Leeds General Infirmary, the leading hospital in the area and something of a showpiece, less than twenty years old. Garnett's dedication of his first volume of analyses to Crowther, 'as a small token of respect and gratitude', suggests both conventional deference and a measure of collegiality; though the younger man by a generation, Garnett was reaching out to a fellow Edinburgh graduate and member of the Royal Medical Society.[7] Friendship with Crowther and the Mauds, however, could only do so much, and from the start Garnett found Bradford a far from comfortable place. It was not just a matter of insalubrity. A town that was rich in opportunity for the adventurous was also a haven for tricksters and mountebanks. Medical care, in particular, was notoriously open to dubious claims and practices that left reputable practitioners in a state of relentless vigilance in defence of their interests.

Garnett was as watchful as anyone, and he was soon involved in the public unmasking of George Mossman, a Scot of uncertain origins who had set up as a physician in Bradford about a year earlier.[8] Mossman presented himself as an Edinburgh M.D. who had studied at the university between 1780 and 1787. But everything about him was obscure, and Garnett, who may have known, or known of, Mossman in his own student days, openly denounced his claim to the degree as fraudulent. At best, according to Garnett, Mossman had 'bought' his M.D. from St Andrews on the basis of some experience as a 'journeyman apothecary' in the Yorkshire town of Beverley. In such an encounter, the combative side of Garnett's personality made him a tenacious adversary, and the matter would have ended in a duel if Mossman had not backed down. Even Mossman's last-ditch assertion that he had only been denied his Edinburgh degree because of his espousal of Brunonian principles rang hollow. Set against Garnett's experience as a declared Brunonian who had graduated without difficulty, it convinced no one. And it lost all plausibility when it emerged that Mossman had spent only two winters as a student in Edinburgh and that, in reality, even his easily won St Andrews qualification was no more than a licentiateship.

The support that Garnett received in his attack on Mossman is evidence of his success in establishing alliances with Bradford's social and cultural elite beyond the medical community. Prominent among his non-medical allies in the Mossman affair was the lawyer Samuel Hailstone, in age an almost exact contemporary and in every respect, including their shared botanical interests, a kindred spirit. In a brisk pamphlet war, Hailstone came out in warm support of Garnett's role in an exposure that had left Mossman 'the Object of Laughter and Contempt in every Quarter of the Town and Country' (not that the unmasking seems to have significantly impeded Mossman's rather successful medical career).[9] Garnett, for his part, revelled in his victory over a duplicitous rival and is said to have delightedly shown a confession signed by Mossman wherever he went.[10]

No sense of personal satisfaction, however, could efface other day-to-day realities of life in Bradford. A tradition of riotous protest had begun in 1770 with agitation in support of the radical supporter of the American Revolution John Wilkes, and this continued through the 1780s and 1790s, along with a pattern of unrest extending to demonstrations against the high price of corn and in support of the revolutionary writings of Thomas Paine. Even if the opening of a subscription for the relief of the distressed poor in 1789 proffered reassurance that something was being done to ease tensions, it also reminded employers and the professional classes of the fragility of their position. Widely shared fears of disorder certainly weighed heavily in Hailstone's animosity towards Mossman, whose sympathies lay openly and unequivocally with Paine, and we can be sure that Garnett's political inclinations, combining as they did an openness to reform with a fear of social disruption, were aligned with Hailstone's.[11]

With so much to disturb him and medical practice in Bradford evidently not matching his expectations, Garnett began to look further afield. The springboard for his next move lay in the analyses of mineral waters that he had begun with Mead, allied to a keen eye for the potential of the accelerating vogue for spa treatments. As a foundation for future study and exploitation, his most promising target was Horley Green Spa, a short ride away near Halifax. Over the preceding decade, James Drake, the landowner and member of a notable Halifax family, had constructed a spa house at Horley Green and even begun building accommodation for patients; he had also planned a landscaped walk and gardens that would make the most of a scenic 'little paradise' embellished with 'a most grand and romantic prospect down the valley towards Wakefield'.[12] Drake had been encouraged in his venture by evidence of the remarkable cures that the water had effected, either when applied externally to skin eruptions or, more commonly, drunk in controlled doses; patients suffering (in Brunonian terms) from the diseases of debility and a diminished level of excitement had derived particular benefit.[13] The prospects for the water seemed bright, and Garnett's account of its abnormally high iron content, which accounted for its qualities as a tonic, gave it a powerful boost among England's many chalybeate (literally, 'iron-bearing') springs.[14] For a while, in the fevered atmosphere of claims and counter-claims about the efficacy of rival waters, the demand from sufferers from digestive complaints, circulatory problems and diabetes was brisk. But the early success did not last. Access by road from Halifax was not easy, and the spa's popularity waned quickly, only to be briefly restored in the 1840s, though never very successfully.[15]

Despite his advocacy, Garnett would have recognized that, in both practicality and therapeutic potential, other sources in the area might have the edge on Horley Green, and alternatives were readily at hand. By the summer of 1790, he was at work on another spring, this time on marshy land in Harrogate, twenty miles north of Bradford. The spring, discovered as recently as 1783, was in the still largely undeveloped area of Low Harrogate, a mile or so from the Old Spaw and Tewit Well (or English Spaw), two chalybeate wells in High Harrogate that had been known and used since the sixteenth century. As Garnett's examination showed, the new Crescent water, so called because of the Crescent Inn, on whose grounds it had been found, had an unusual chemical character in that it combined sulphureous and chalybeate properties, usually thought to be antithetical in their effects.[16] Since many spa treatments involved taking both types of water, in carefully measured quantities and a controlled sequence (usually sulphureous before breakfast, followed soon afterwards and later in the day by chalybeate), the new water held out interesting possibilities for treatment. Most commonly used for drinking though sometimes also as a warm bath, it promised a middle way between the cooling, purgative qualities of a sulphur-rich water (which, again to use the Brunonian categories in which Garnett presented his treatments, diminished the inflammatory symptoms of sthenic disease) and chalybeate water (whose tonic effect was good for asthenic conditions).

Garnett was soon recommending Crescent water as beneficial in chronic illnesses that called for lengthy treatments (always profitable for physicians), including persistent indigestion and intestinal disorders, both common conditions of visitors to spas. As the number of case-histories of patients who had been successfully treated with the water grew, there followed a concerted campaign. Garnett's recommendation, the testimony of a rising surgeon-apothecary and loyal ally John Jacques, and the installation of a pump and cistern by the knowing owner of the site all played their part, and soon the Crescent water was 'advancing in reputation'.[17] Garnett's reputation, too, was advancing and encouraging him to see the potential of a new life as a spa doctor. With a prominence heightened by his substantial pamphlets on the Horley Green spa and now the Crescent water, he threw in his lot with the mineral water movement and left Bradford for Knaresborough, three miles from Harrogate.

For a physician with an interest in waters, Knaresborough was a natural destination. The town had long been known for St Robert's Well (reputed as a healing well) and its 'Dropping Well' (a spring of limestone water that petrified objects over which it ran). But it was only since the late seventeenth century, when the Leeds antiquary Ralph Thoresby had visited both sites while taking the waters, that Knaresborough had begun to acquire a reputation beyond the local.[18] For the reputation to grow, it mattered that there was more to Knaresborough than its waters alone. Crucial in making that point were successive and ever larger editions of a promotional guide to the area, first published in 1769.[19] The author and publisher of the guide was an entrepreneurial bookseller, printer and local antiquarian, Ely Hargrove, who had moved from Halifax to settle in Knaresborough in 1762. The attractions of the town and its surroundings could not have had a more energetic advocate. Knaresborough's 'very pleasant romantic situation', with its historic castle finely set above the River Nidd, helped to create a scene 'as truly Romantic as any the Chinese ever yet devised'.[20] And there was much else to interest the visitor. This included the medieval St Robert's Chapel, the blatantly touristic installation of Fort Montague (a house newly constructed in the rock and presided over by its eccentric self-styled 'governor' Thomas Hill, a former weaver) and an association with the still active builder of turnpike roads, Blind Jack Metcalf, whose largely ungrammatical recollections Garnett was instrumental in editing and seeing through to publication.[21]

By the time Garnett arrived, the development of Knaresborough, exemplified in the recent promotion of St Robert's Well as a cold bath, was proceeding apace.[22] But he would have been aware that the nearby star of Harrogate was rising too, and more dramatically. As a much smaller community with little by way of civic structure, Harrogate offered no challenge to Knaresborough's status as an administrative and commercial centre. Its reputation and future lay rather in its springs, though by comparison with other, better-known resorts, these had been slow to win recognition. A rehearsal of the virtues of the Tewit Well and other sources in Edmund Deane's early-seventeenth-century classic on the waters of the area had presented them as worthy rivals to anything the 'German' spas could offer.[23] But then and for long afterwards they struggled against the disadvantages of remoteness and a reputation for amenities so primitive that a contemporary of Deane's, Mary Villiers, Countess of Buckingham, had erected her own tent from which to drink at the Old Spaw.[24]

There was no denying that the first gestures to comfort were modest. In Tobias Smollett's *Expedition of Humphry Clinker,* the dyspeptic, gout-ridden Welsh squire Matthew Bramble described the place in unflattering terms that probably convey Smollett's own judgement following a visit in 1766:

> Harrowgate [Bramble had it] is a wild common, bare and bleak, without tree or shrub, or the least signs of cultivation; and the people who come to drink the water, are crowded together in paltry inns, where the few tolerable rooms are monopolized by the friends and favourites of the house, and all the rest of the lodgers are obliged to put up with dirty holes, where there is neither space, air, nor convenience.[25]

And that was to say nothing of the nauseating smell of the sulphur waters, which cured Bramble of any wish to repeat the treatment. It was only by holding his nose that he managed to drink, and then with dire effects: 'sickness, griping, and insurmountable disgust – I can hardly mention it without puking'.[26]

By now, though, not everyone was put off. The writer and clergyman Lawrence Sterne, who made the twenty-mile journey from his home in the village of Coxwold on at least two occasions in the mid-1760s, saw a visit to Harrogate as a social occasion, independently of the health benefit of the waters. His favourite haunt was the Dragon in High Harrogate, a prominent and relatively elegant inn that had come to be favoured by northern nobility and gentry in search of alternatives to the more fashionable, and expensive, resorts further south. There, he met friends, among them the colourful Yorkshire wit John Hall-Stevenson, often said to have been immortalized as Eugenius in Sterne's *Tristram Shandy* and *A Sentimental Journey through France and Italy*. Encounters between Sterne and the hard-riding, heavy-drinking Hall-Stevenson epitomized the boisterous, predominantly male tone of the place. Harrogate in the 1760s offered little by way of genteel refinement.

Three decades later, the town had not entirely shaken off its rough and ready image. The writer and entertainer George Saville Carey could still describe Harrogate as little more than 'a few scattered houses on a dreary common', with nothing to match 'the numerous beauties and elegances' of Bath and little to see in the surrounding area.[27] But by the time he wrote, in 1799, Carey's judgement was unfairly disparaging. Through the 1780s and 1790s, a wave of improvements had helped to set Harrogate on the path to acceptance as a major spa.[28] A new theatre was built in 1788, followed by a race-course on the 200-acre unenclosed public space in High Harrogate later known as the Stray (1793), and better roads encouraged the growth of stagecoach and post-coach services to the larger northern towns, as well as Edinburgh and London.[29] Accommodation too improved, to the point that in the fifth edition of his guide (1798) Hargrove could report the presence of 'eight very good inns'.[30] With new amenities came new and more discerning visitors. The company may still have been less sophisticated than in the more established watering places. But, as even Carey had to concede, it was good-humoured, decorous and, at least in the three months or so of the season, plentiful.[31]

Hargrove and the two sons who worked with him in his later years faithfully chronicled Harrogate's transformation. Successive editions of the Hargrove guide recorded the signs of growing refinement: the popularity of his own circulating libraries (one now in Harrogate as well as in Knaresborough), the regular public balls (on Mondays and Fridays, with an entry fee of a shilling) and the custom for ladies to offer tea in the afternoons all bore witness to changing tastes.[32] Hargrove, though, was realistic enough to admit that a situation on high ground roughly equidistant between the Irish and the North Seas came with its challenges. While High Harrogate's elevation of 200 m offered the prize of a rare distant view of York Minster twenty miles away, it also meant exposure to tempests from both west and east.[33] But in his characteristic promotional style, Hargrove put the best possible gloss on the invigorating climate. As he insisted, and as Garnett would certainly have agreed, Harrogate's 'keen' air was 'as salubrious as in any part of England' and a benefit 'calculated to promote longevity'.[34]

Hargrove's advocacy played its part in the rise in the number of arrivals in the spa season from 1,551 in 1781 to 2,458 fourteen years later.[35] Growth on that scale confirmed Harrogate as very much a going concern, and Garnett's move, at the peak of the expansion, could not have been better-timed. As a young doctor in search of custom, he saw commercial opportunity in a spa that offered its often desperate visitors a rare variety of waters with which to treat ailments barely touched by mainstream medicine. Among such ailments, gout reigned supreme. As what Roy Porter and George Rousseau have called the 'patrician malady', it had the added and, for a physician, attractive characteristic of fashionability in precisely the affluent circles that were beginning to flock to the leading spa towns.[36] While Bath had been especially successful in exploiting this convergence of medical and social interests, it was by no means the only mecca for gout specialists and their ever-hopeful patients. Nor was gout the only condition for which natural springs virtually everywhere promised relief. By 1790, when Garnett first turned his attention to the Yorkshire waters, Harrogate was poised to follow precisely where Bath and, among the newer spas, Buxton in Derbyshire had gone and to do so in ways that exploited the unusual diversity of its wells and the exceptional range of conditions for which, as a result, it could offer treatment. Amid the enthusiasm, suspicions that the drinking of the Harrogate speciality of strongly purgative sulphurous water might induce symptoms rather than alleviate them were easily overlooked.[37]

Science versus empiricism

Garnett, of course, was not the only physician to perceive the market potential of practice in Harrogate. Far from being a lone pioneer, in fact, he found himself entering an intensely competitive medical world with settled interests and practices. The prevailing tone of advice to patients was firmly, even aggressively, empirical. It was exemplified in William Alexander's *Plain and Easy Directions for the Use of Harrogate Waters* (1773, and later editions), a compendium of common-sense recommendations about the internal and external use of the waters, exercise, diet and sleeping arrangements. Although Alexander was ready to flaunt his Edinburgh M.D. (taken in 1764, a generation before Garnett), he addressed his work explicitly to 'the unlearned solicitor of health and the relief of distress' rather than to 'the learned investigator of principles'.[38] It was a calculated position, founded on the virtues of empirical knowledge and experience. His sideswipe at treatises that began with 'a pompous parade of learning' of little use to the 'unlearned drinker' was directed at science-based sources of advice and their more or less explicit claims to superior authority.

A typical target for Alexander would have been Joshua Walker, who went through the Edinburgh medical school a few years after him and was now physician to the Leeds Infirmary. Benefitting from local knowledge as the son of a Quaker apothecary in Bradford, Walker had devoted his doctoral dissertation at Edinburgh in 1770 to the sulphur springs of Harrogate and published on them and the waters of Thorp Arch, thirteen miles away, near Wetherby in 1784.[39] Walker's approach was rooted in a style of systematic qualitative analysis exemplified, among his contemporaries, in the work of Bath's leading spa doctor William Falconer since the early 1770s.[40] For Walker, as for Falconer, an understanding of the correlation between the therapeutic power of the waters he prescribed and their chemical composition was essential to good medical practice. Only in that way, in Walker's words, could the virtues of a water be established 'upon a reasonable foundation' and the soundness of any treatment be guaranteed.[41]

In declaring in favour of scientific medicine, Garnett knew that he was running a risk. The still uncompromisingly empirical tone of the third edition of Alexander's *Plain and Easy Directions*, published in 1787, suggests why from the start many of the established doctors of Harrogate and Knaresborough regarded Garnett with suspicion, amounting in some cases to unconcealed animosity. Garnett's precept, voiced in successive editions of his *Treatise on the Mineral Waters of Harrogate* from 1792, that 'mere experience will never make a physician' was directed at them, and they knew it.[42] But he never wavered, encouraged by signs that on a broader stage the tide of opinion was beginning to run in his favour. His call for the alliance of practice with science was precisely the one to which Erasmus Darwin gave powerful expression in the years when Garnett was making his way in Harrogate. In the preface to his great medical work *Zoonomia; or, the Laws of Organic Life* in 1794, Darwin was uncompromising. Deploring contemporary deficiencies in the 'art of healing' without theoretical underpinnings, he wrote:

> There are some modern practitioners, who declaim against medical theory in general, not considering that to think is to theorize; and that no one can direct a method of cure to a person labouring under disease without thinking, that is, without theorizing; and happy therefore is the patient, whose physician possesses the best theory.[43]

No one could have come closer than Garnett to Darwin's model of the enlightened physician working to 'distinguish the genuine disciples of medicine from those of boastful effrontery'.

Garnett's alignment with the Darwinian ideal was part of a considered strategy in pursuit of the high profile and strong patient base on which success depended. What mattered for that purpose was the establishment of an authority that set him above his competitors, and Garnett was astute in associating his campaign not only with Darwin ('The Ornament of Science, and the Friend of Mankind') but also with other leaders in science whose names would add lustre to his cause.[44] Frequent allusions to the system that Antoine Lavoisier and other French chemists had elaborated since the mid-1780s achieved just such an aim, with the added aura of openness to a world of science beyond the local or even the national. Garnett, in fact, was an early convert to the new system and its associated nomenclature: after using the language of the old chemistry in his earliest writings, on Horley Green (1790) and the Crescent water (1791), he showed himself an enthusiastic Lavoisierian in the first and subsequent editions of the *Treatise* from 1792.[45]

Important though the new chemistry was to him, it was in his speciality of water analysis that Garnett staked his most distinctive claim to a place at the cutting edges of science. Here, his special debt was to the *Opuscula physica et chemica* by the Swedish chemist Torbern Bergman. The first volume of the *Opusula*, largely devoted to essays on the properties of Scandinavian waters and recently translated from the original Latin of 1779, had established Bergman as the internationally acknowledged master of both quantitative and qualitative techniques.[46] Citing such a work could only reflect favourably on Garnett's own credentials, and he did so liberally. Learned references, though, had to be backed by performance, and on that front too Garnett knew he had to work hard. His goal, without precedent in its scope, was an exhaustive analysis of the composition and properties of all of Harrogate's many waters. It was a task that called for determination and experimental dexterity rather than fundamental new departures. Garnett's core techniques, in fact, had been in common use (though rarely deployed with comparable skill or single-mindedness) since the work of Robert Boyle and the German physician Friedrich Hoffmann a century earlier.[47]

Where Bergman left his most decisive mark, with strong support from Antoine-François de Fourcroy, Jean-Antoine Chaptal and other French chemists, was in the codification of what had hitherto been rather disparate practices. Essentially, a complete analysis in the Bergman manner was conducted in four parts.[48] The first was a physical examination of such qualities as taste, smell, appearance, temperature and specific gravity. The second was a series of qualitative tests by the addition of precipitants, such as a tincture of galls (a test for compounds of iron) or of turnsole (an indicator of acidity). The third entailed a notoriously difficult process of evaporation to dryness, followed by a separation and examination of the salts in the solid residue. And a fourth, often conducted simultaneously with the third, involved the collection of dissolved gases. This was the most uncertain of all the procedures, though one to which Garnett attached particular importance, not only for the bearing of gas content on the medicinal properties of different waters but also for the light it might throw on the elusive question of how the waters held gases in solution.[49]

Typical of Garnett's parade of his scientific credentials was his pride in the device for the collection of gases he developed for his examination of the Crescent water.⁵⁰ The device, presented as an improvement on Bergman's, lent itself to the quantitative aspects of analyses that were, for the most part, qualitative. Despite the carefulness of Garnett's measurements, whether of the gases or the solid residues after evaporation, the notorious difficulty of the analytical procedures cast doubt on his results from the start. Nevertheless, the table reproduced as Figure 3.1, with its display of improbable exactness, appeared in an eighth edition of the *Treatise* as late as 1829. In fact, it was only when A. W. Hofmann applied significantly improved techniques in his laboratory at the Royal College of Chemistry in the 1850s that the analyses, both qualitative and quantitative, were finally superseded and what Bergman regarded as 'one of the most difficult Problems in Chymistry' was satisfactorily resolved.[51]

The analysis-based authority around which Garnett built his offer to patients and the Brunonian-inspired scientism of his treatments stimulated a predictable reaction in Harrogate's established medical community. Seen as an opinionated novice with ideas and ambitions at odds with existing interests, he soon became a target for hostile attention. Stories about him had been circulating for a year by the time he engaged in his first public confrontation, with an innkeeper at the Queen's Head, William Thackwray. In taking on Thackwray, the nephew of the owner of the prestigious Crown Hotel, Garnett was challenging a local family of some consequence. But his response to an insult that he believed Thackwray to have been responsible for circulating took no account of the risk of engaging with such a prominent adversary. As Garnett recounted the episode, in a printed 'short statement' of his exchanges with Thackwray published on 20 July 1792, only three days earlier Thackwray had spoken dismissively about him to an unnamed 'gentleman from London'.[52] Asked by the visitor whether there was a physician by the name of Garnett in Harrogate, Thackwray had replied evasively: 'I believe there is such a person'. He had then compounded his deviousness by adding (in his Yorkshire accent) that Garnett 'is a varry young man, and has hed no experience in our watters'; hence 'we always recommend Dr. Hutchinson, who has been here a long time, and is much better judge of the watters'. Garnett's response, as reported in the 'short statement', brushed Thackwray aside: the 'sordid and interested views of an innkeeper' were beneath contempt. As such, they would not have merited a response had it not been for Garnett's conviction that behind Thackwray's disparagement of him there lay the more substantial threat of the 'false and malicious insinuations' that had been put about since the previous summer, and put about, as he now believed, by the same Dr Hutchinson to whom Thackwray referred.

A TABLE

exhibiting the contents, in a wine gallon, of each of the Harrogate waters.

NAMES of the WATERS.	Specific gravity.	Cubic inches.			Grains.							
		Carbonic acid gas.	Azotic gas.	Hepatic or sulphurated hydrogen gas.	Muriat of soda.	Muriat of lime.	Muriat of magnesia.	Carbonat of lime.	Carbonat of magnesia.	Carbonat of iron.	Sulphat of magnesia.	Sulphat of soda.	Sulphat of lime.
Sulphur Water.	1,0064	8	7	19	615,5	13	91	18,5	5,5	—	10,5	—	—
Crescent Water.	1,002	20,8	—	13,6	137	—	45	3,1	—	2	8	—	—
Tewit Well.	1,00017	16	5	—	—	—	—	—	—	2,5	—	—	4
Old Spaw.	1,00014	15,75	4,25	—	—	—	—	—	—	2	—	3	1,5

Figure 3.1 Garnett's table of the contents of five of the main Harrogate waters. The water in the first line was the strongest of four sulphur waters known and frequented in Low Harrogate and the only one that was drunk, mainly as a purgative taken (by those who could endure the unpleasant taste and smell) early in the morning. The other sulphur waters were used in warm baths for the treatment of herpes and other cutaneous disorders. The waters of the Tewit Well and Old Spaw contained significant quantities of ferrous carbonate and were classed as mild chalybeates. They were drunk as stimulants to counter debility and what were commonly called 'nervous' disorders, typically manifested as melancholy, hypochondria and listlessness. From Garnett, *A Treatise on the Mineral Waters of Harrogate* (first edition, 1792), 70. Courtesy of the Wellcome Collection. Public Domain Mark. In the second (1794) and subsequent editions of the *Treatise*, Garnett added data for a third chalybeate spring, St George's Well.

In redirecting his fire towards Hutchinson, Garnett revealed his true intention of discountenancing the man he perceived as his main rival. It was another bold move. To a degree that he may not have fully recognized, Thomas Hutchinson was a formidable opponent. In addition to the following he had as a practising physician, he was appreciated in cultivated circles as a 'man of taste and literature', a friend of the Wordsworths, the owner of almost a thousand prints and portraits, and a collector whose museum of natural history and antiquities in Knaresborough, including as a prime exhibit the skull of the philologist and murderer Eugene Aram, was 'ever open to the Virtuoso and Antiquary'.[53] Viewed by Garnett, though, Hutchinson was simply a physician of the old school with a reputation as something of a charlatan (notably for a worm powder that had recently been derided as no more effective than traditional home remedies[54]). Predictably, Garnett's attack went straight to the matter of qualifications, as it had done in his assault on Mossman in Bradford. He portrayed Hutchinson (to whom he pointedly referred as 'Mr.') as in reality 'only an apothecary'; his diploma (if he had one) was from St Andrews or Aberdeen, 'which any man may procure without going there, and which every candid medical man will acknowledge is a disgrace instead of an honour to the person who possesses it'.[55]

What impact such an accusation may have had is unclear. The suspect status of the medical degrees from St Andrews and Aberdeen was no secret, and the listing in the annual *Medical Register* of 'Hutchinson M.D. (Aberdeen)' as one of Knaresborough's two 'physicians' (hence a clear notch above the town's three 'surgeons and apothecaries') had passed for years without objection.[56] Nevertheless, Hutchinson considered the attack serious enough to warrant a reply. In a printed broadside nominally authored, under a pseudonym, by a close friend, Hutchinson cast his response to Garnett as a defence of Thackwray.[57] But the real purpose was to cut Garnett down to size. As Thackwray had asserted in speaking to the visitor from London and as Hutchinson's unnamed champion now reaffirmed, Garnett was indeed inexperienced in the Harrogate waters:

> You may have analized those and other waters, but chemical knowledge alone, however great, will never raise your name as a Physician, nor will a diploma from any college stand in competition with medical skill acquired by real practice.

It was a withering assault on 'an unfledged doctor (imberbis puer)' who had yet to learn that theories and paper qualifications were no match for experience. A week later, the already low tone of the exchange descended further, in a twelve-page response, addressed to Hutchinson and published on Garnett's behalf. The author, an unidentified 'M.', rehearsed the charges against Hutchinson once again.⁵⁸ What merit was there in the long experience of a 'dunce', a 'man of no science' who had merely 'brandished a pestle twenty or thirty or even forty years'? Was Hutchinson's chief merit perhaps that he recommended bathing and lengthy stays to all his patients, with beneficial consequences to the hotel trade, including of course Thackwray? It was fierce but inconclusive stuff.

Garnett's inability to leave any slight unanswered had its bizarre sequel in the following spring in his pursuit of another adversary, William Tindall, a surgeon and apothecary practising in Knaresborough. The source of the dispute seems to have been the insinuation, originating with or more probably propagated by Tindall (with the connivance of Hutchinson), that Garnett had had an improper assignation with a lady at a lodging house in Harrogate. The exchange of letters between Tindall and Garnett and of messages conveyed by groups of friends on both sides continued with increasing acrimony over four days in early April 1793, all charted in correspondence that Garnett again arranged to be printed and circulated.⁵⁹ With attempts at a conciliatory meeting coming to nothing, reciprocal demands for an apology unanswered and the ultimate challenge accepted, Tindall and his supporters let it be known that a duel would take place in a secluded spot on the banks of the River Nidd between Knaresborough and Harrogate. Garnett sent his two seconds to attend at the appointed time: 11 am on 4 April. The seconds waited for over an hour (in the presence of a constable, who would in any case have enforced the law by preventing the duel from taking place). But Tindall did not appear, and the matter ended, leaving both parties and their champions proclaiming their honour to be intact and their adversary's in tatters. Only the small crowd that assembled to witness the duel would have been disappointed.⁶⁰

Patronage and marriage

Garnett appears to have revelled in his battles with those he saw as working to deny him his rightful place in Harrogate's medical hierarchy. But his particular *bête noire*, Hutchinson, emerged unscathed and continued to practise as the town's leading physician until his death in 1797. Garnett, for his part, remained the opinionated, brash newcomer that Hutchinson and his allies thought him to be. In an atmosphere of rumbling antagonism that he had done nothing to calm and much to foment, the future promised only conflict and sniping. That at least was so until substantial new support suddenly allowed him to rise above the local struggle. The support came through an act of patronage in the old style by Alexander Wedderburn, first Baron Loughborough. Wedderburn, then at the summit of his political power and influence, was the most visible patron Harrogate could offer. Edinburgh-born and educated but a long-serving chief justice of the court of Common Pleas in England, he was a legendarily ambitious and shifting parliamentarian. On his appointment as Lord Chancellor in January 1793, about the time when Garnett would have known him, he abandoned his former Whig allegiances, entered the Tory cabinet of William Pitt the Younger and remained there until Pitt resigned eight years later, following the failure of his plans for Catholic emancipation.[61]

Wedderburn's backing of Garnett seems to have had little to do with politics: although Garnett's sympathies probably lay somewhere on the reformist Whig spectrum, his career interests prioritized caution and flexibility over allegiance to party or faction. What mattered far more in the relation was the severe gout from which Wedderburn suffered in later life. In search of relief, he had long been a regular taker of the waters, especially since 1786, when he had remodelled and enlarged a farmhouse in High Harrogate to create the elegant Wedderburn House. Attractively situated on the edge of the Stray, the house became his residence during the spa season. But an association between patron and client that can be assumed to have begun with medical consultations also had a personal dimension, reinforced by a shared experience of the Scottish Enlightenment and by science. Though no scientist himself, Wedderburn was a Fellow of the Royal Society and would have respected, even if he did not fully understand, Garnett's scientific attainments.

Wedderburn's interest in the town and the house and adjacent estate he had now accumulated made him someone to be courted, and Garnett seized the opportunity in dedicating his *Treatise on the Mineral Waters of Harrogate* to him in 1792 (see Figure 3.2). Wedderburn had been drawn to invest in Harrogate following the Act of Parliament of 1770 for the enclosure of open pasture and woodland in the vast royal Forest of Knaresborough, most of it belonging to the Duchy of Lancaster. Since the wells lay in the area that became subject to enclosure and the resulting regularization of ownership and occupancy, the Act and the distribution of lands under the definitive Award of 1778 were crucial in shaping the town's economic and social profile.[62] A combination of Wedderburn's personal fortune and that of his first wife, an heiress from Morley, near Leeds, did much to fuel the process by allowing him to exploit the opportunities that came with the passage of common land into private hands. Already in the mid-1770s he had begun acquiring parts of his estate, mainly from the powerful Lascelles family at nearby Harewood House, and on through

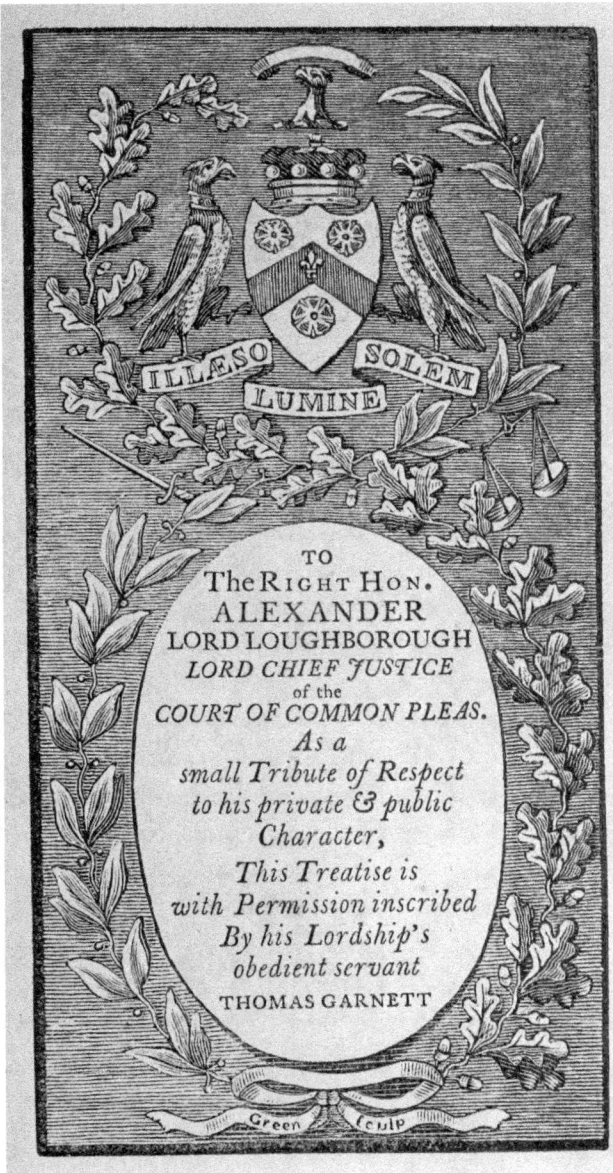

Figure 3.2 Dedicatory plate to Alexander Wedderburn, first Baron Loughborough, in the first edition of Garnett's *Treatise on the Mineral Waters of Harrogate* (1792), iii. The plate, engraved by the Manchester-based artist and engraver William Green, incorporates Wedderburn's coat of arms. In the second edition of the *Treatise*, by which time (May 1794) Garnett was living at Wedderburn House in Harrogate, it was replaced with an effusive four-page dedication to Wedderburn, Garnett's 'friend and protector'. Courtesy of the Wellcome Collection. Public Domain Mark.

Figure 3.3 Mezzotint of Garnett seated next to a Nooth apparatus, artist and engraver unknown. The portrait probably dates from the early 1790s, when Garnett, established in Harrogate and 'protected' by Alexander Wedderburn, was working hard to attract patients for his treatments. John Mervin Nooth, physician and army officer, developed his apparatus for producing carbonated water in the 1770s. Although the water was appreciated for its pleasant taste, the vogue it enjoyed in Garnett's time owed more to its supposed medicinal qualities, including treatment for scurvy and the stone. Garnett was a convinced advocate of its use. Courtesy of the Wellcome Collection. Public Domain Mark.

the 1780s he showed himself to be at once an astute landowner and a committed public benefactor.[63] He was responsible for a small pump room over the Old Spaw, a chalybeate spring on the Stray (also known as St John's Well or the Sweet Spa) in 1786.[64] Two years later the new theatre, of which he and his second wife became major patrons, was largely his doing, and visitors taking the waters particularly appreciated a shady two-mile woodland walk that he planted on his land, close to Wedderburn House. In Ely Hargrove's admiring words, the walk was 'one of the greatest and most useful amenities ever yet made at this place'.[65]

The convergence of Garnett's career ambitions and Wedderburn's aspirations for Harrogate bore richer fruit than Garnett could ever have expected. By the spring of 1794, Wedderburn had provided him with accommodation in or adjacent to his house. With that degree of support and Wedderburn House as his address, Garnett could take a loftier view of the hostility that he had encountered (see Figure 3.3).[66] There was now no reason for him to engage in public confrontations or to hold back in proclaiming either the scientific foundations of his reputation as a physician or the Brunonian principles that his more knowing patients would have recognized in his diagnoses and treatments. The move to the prestigious setting of Wedderburn House had the additional advantage of allowing him to extend his business by housing some of the patients under his care and doing so for the longer periods that he always insisted were necessary for spa treatments to have their full effect. It was an astute new departure. Ladies, in particular, welcomed the more personal form of hospitality that accommodation in private lodgings provided, if only as an escape from the enforced conviviality of the inns and meals taken in common.[67] With an eye to this clientele and as decorum required, Garnett now engaged a chaperone and hostess, in the person of his younger, unmarried sister Margaret, to whom he was particularly close.

The combination of elegant accommodation and a thoughtfully prepared welcome proved attractive. And visitors soon came. Among the first of them was one who was to change the course of Garnett's life: Catherine Grace Cleveland, who arrived in late July 1794 with her companion Mary Worboys. Cleveland, the daughter of a successful London coal merchant, the late John Claveland (a name that the family changed, in the next generation, to Cleveland), and Guglielma Maria Grace Parsons, had come to take the waters on medical advice, in all probability the advice of her older brother, William Cleveland, a 'yeoman' (i.e. regular) member of the Society of Apothecaries who may well have known, or at least known of, Garnett.[68] The 'nervous' complaints, bilious appearance and 'feverish heat' of which Catherine had complained in a letter to her brother a year earlier were common enough manifestations of the state of general lethargy and low spirits that brought many patients to spa towns.⁶⁹ As Garnett would have insisted, such ailments were not easily cured, and Catherine and Worboys settled in for a lengthy stay.

Over five months, Garnett's vivacity and striking appearance appealed to Catherine, just as her sprightly wit and resolute personality (both evident in her surviving letters) appealed to him. On 16 March 1795, she and Garnett were married at St Mary's Church in Wargrave, Berkshire, a village on the Thames, close to where her mother now lived. For Garnett, marriage into the Cleveland family opened cultural and material vistas far removed from his rural northern roots. Along with the patronage of Wedderburn and the continued success of his practice, it gave him every prospect of stability and happiness. Yet now as so often in his life, contentment vied with restlessness. While he sparkled in the sophisticated company that gathered in Harrogate during the summer months, he had always found the winters tedious.

His still driving ambition, too, had an unsettling effect and made him easily dispirited. As an anonymous writer put it many years later, material comforts and local celebrity were never enough for him: 'He did not seek to be accounted a good physician, but one of the first physicians in the kingdom. His ambition was not to appear in the ranks of learning, but at the head.'⁷⁰ It was a revealing remark, and one that helps to explain much in Garnett's career strategy. It also squares with his determination, throughout his time in Harrogate, to retain his visibility in the wider world of science and medicine. The *Treatise* was crucial to that end, as were the communications on medical and other topics that he was careful to send back to Andrew Duncan in Edinburgh and for publication by the Medical Society of London, the Royal Irish Academy and the Literary and Philosophical Society of Manchester.⁷¹

Equally prominent among those whose favour he sought in his Harrogate years was Darwin. When the second edition of the *Treatise* appeared in 1794, he sent Darwin a respectfully inscribed copy.⁷² Later in the year, he wrote again, this time about a compilation of meteorological observations that he had been gathering for presentation before the Manchester Lit. and Phil.⁷³ It is not hard to imagine his gratification on receiving a four-page response in which Darwin urged him to pursue the systematic collation of readings of wind direction and force.⁷⁴ In this, Darwin was offering more than encouragement of a promising younger colleague. He was drawing Garnett, almost as an equal, into the testing of a theory – of the prime importance of winds as a cause, rather than a consequence, of other meteorological phenomena – that he had advanced, untried, in an extended note in his poem *The Botanic Garden*. The accolade was as great as any Garnett could have hoped for. He responded with praise for the theory of the winds and by the immediate performance, at Darwin's suggestion, of experiments on the thawing of ice in the vacuum above the mercury in a barometer.[75]

Even encouragement from Darwin, though, was not enough, and Garnett's relentless quest for success was soon to have its consequences. For some time before his marriage, he had been contemplating a new life in America, primarily as a lecturer in chemistry and natural philosophy, though ideally with medical practice as an auxiliary source of income. Ambition and an ineradicably restless streak converged with his maturing worldview to make the venture attractive. He would have found much to admire in the ideals of the American Revolution and understood the aspirations that drew some notable scientific contemporaries, most famously Joseph Priestley, to embark for the New World in the 1790s. Another model may well have been Henry Moyes, the blind lecturer who had enjoyed spectacular success on an extended lecture-tour of America some years earlier.[76]

Crucially, too, Garnett would not have seen America as a wholly unknown quantity. Among his immediate peers at Edinburgh, where students from the New World had been a significant presence in the medical school since the mid-century, three of the twenty-eight who graduated with an M.D. in his year were American. And he would have encountered others through the student societies. He must have known, or known of, the most prominent of them, Caspar Wistar, a future professor at the University of Pennsylvania in Philadelphia who served as one of the annual presidents of both the Royal Medical Society and the Natural History Society for 1785–6, Garnett's first year. A closer and probably more enduring contact may well have been Benjamin Smith Barton, who spent two years as a student in Edinburgh before returning to America and beginning medical practice and a distinguished academic career in medicine and natural history, also at the University of Pennsylvania, in 1789. It was Barton's term as president of the Natural History Society for the 1787–8 session that Garnett was elected to complete when financial difficulties and a disagreement with two professors led Barton to resign and leave without a degree.[77]

The connexions of Wistar and Barton with the University of Pennsylvania are among several pointers suggesting that Garnett's destination was in all probability Philadelphia, America's temporary capital from 1790 until the move to Washington ten years later. A phase of urban growth that saw the city's population increase by half, from 54,391 to 81,009, between 1790 and 1800, promised an unprecedented demand for knowledge-based skills. Politically, too, Philadelphia had special attractions as the setting for the key events leading from the declaration of independence in 1776 to the Treaty of Paris of 1783, by which the British finally recognized the United States as a sovereign independent nation. Since then, the 'Athens of America' had emerged unrivalled as a cultural capital, as well as America's biggest city.[78] Since the 1740s, it had been the home not only of the University of Pennsylvania but also of the American Philosophical Society, the nation's first learned society. And to all this, it could now add a formidable reputation in medicine, with a medical community that bore comparison with those of leading European cities. More specifically, and perhaps decisively for Garnett, in the 1790s Philadelphia was being swept by a vogue for Brunonian medicine, led by the most celebrated of Philadelphia's doctors, Benjamin Rush (Edinburgh M.D., 1768), and reflected in the four English-language editions of the *Elementa medicinae* that appeared in the city between 1790 and 1795.[79]

The pull of America was strong, and marriage in March 1795 left the plan intact. Within two weeks of the ceremony, Garnett was back in Harrogate to dispose of his furniture and arrange for leaving Wedderburn House. His resolve was such that the plans would in all probability have come to fruition had it not been for a painful turn of events that transformed the fortunes of Catherine's mother later in the year. In 1790, five years after her husband's death, Mrs Cleveland had married the seventy-six-year-old widower William Girdler, the member of an eminent legal family, and moved with her two daughters, Catherine and Mary, into Girdler's Berkshire home, Hare Hatch House. The house, recently constructed in an imposing Georgian style in extensive grounds near Wargrave, provided the elegant setting from which Catherine was married. But when Girdler died on 25 September 1795, ownership passed to his nephew and (in the absence of a direct descendent) heir presumptive. As it became apparent that Girdler had made no provision of any kind for his widow, already uneasy relations between the Cleveland children and the Girdlers turned to unconcealed hostility.

Shortly after Girdler's death, Catherine unburdened herself in a letter to her brother William's wife, Sarah. Never happy about her mother's remarriage from the start, she described the 'distressing situation' that had left her mother trapped in 'the clutches of that wretch'.[80] The 'wretch' in question was unmistakably Girdler's nephew, a lawyer like his uncle and known as someone who harboured contempt for commercial activity. He can have had little time for a family that had made its money in, of all things, the coal trade, and he refused to help. This left Catherine's mother with no alternative but to vacate Hare Hatch House and return in haste to London. There, with the help of William and another doctor-son of her first marriage, she began the painful task of re-establishing a family network to which Catherine and Garnett were increasingly drawn by sympathy for her misfortune. Two years on, the animosity between the Clevelands and Girdler's nephew had still not subsided.[81] In the circumstances, any thought of emigration was unrealistic. So too, by now, was going back to Harrogate. Suddenly and through circumstances beyond his control, Garnett faced the formidable challenge of fashioning a new and uncharted future in an England that a few months earlier he had definitively resolved to leave.

Notes

1. Thackray, 'Natural knowledge in cultural context'.
2. Here I draw on the ground-breaking collection of essays edited by Ian Inkster and Jack Morrell: *Metropolis and Province*. Still valuable forty years on is the introductory essay by Inkster and Morrell, 'Aspects of the history of science and science culture in Britain, 1780–1850 and beyond', 11–54.
3. Jones, *Industrial Enlightenment*; Mee and Wilkes, 'Transpennine Enlightenment'; and Wilkes, 'Transpennine Enlightenment'.
4. On the Mauds in Bradford, see Hodgson, *Society of Friends in Bradford*, 46 and 56.
5. Willan, *Sulphur-Water, at Croft and Harrowgate* (1782; 2nd edn., 1786). On Willan as a Dawsonian, see ch. 1, 21.
6. The only record of the collaboration is in Garnett, *Horley-Green Spaw*, 82–4.
7. Ibid., 2. For Crowther's position at the Leeds Infirmary, see *Med. Reg. 1783*, 121.
8. Garnett's role is recounted in Samuel Hailstone's separately paginated preface 'To the physicians of Leeds, Halifax, and York', in Hailstone, *The Dose Repeated*, 3–8. For an account of the episode, see Alvin, 'Title Acquired without labour'.
9. Hailstone, *A Dose for the Doctor*, 21–2.
10. Ibid., 22.
11. James, *History and Topography of Bradford*, 155–60.
12. Garnett, *Horley-Green Spaw*, 7–9.
13. Ibid., 51–6.
14. Ibid., 39, where Garnett identifies the water as 'the strongest chalybeate known'.
15. Alexander, *Horley Green Mineral Water*, esp. v–ix on the efforts of the author, a physician to the Halifax Infirmary and General Dispensary, to restore the spring.
16. Garnett, *Crescent Water*, esp. 4–6.
17. Ibid., 9.
18. On Thoresby's and other early visits, see Grainge, *History and Topography of Harrogate*, 107–50.

19 Hargrove, *History of the Castle and Town of Knaresbrough* (Knaresborough, 1769). Later editions were published through to a sixth, in 1809. Cited hereafter as Hargrove, *History*.
20 Hargrove, *History*, 2nd edn. (York, 1775), 16.
21 Garnett's role in the publication of *The Life of John Metcalf* at York in 1795 is intimated in the book's preface (iii-vi) and referred to in 'Life of Garnett', x.
22 Simpson, *Cold Bathing*, vi, where Simpson, a 'surgeon at Knaresbro' and a friend of Garnett's, refers to his own recent involvement in erecting a 'public bathing house'.
23 Deane, *Spadacrene Anglica*. In both title and tone, the book was a patriotic response to Henri de Heer's account of the waters of Spa in his *Spadacrene* (Liège, 1614).
24 Hargrove, *History*, 3rd edn. (York, 1782), 82-3; 4th edn. (York, 1789), 97.
25 Smollett, *Humphry Clinker*, 2nd edn. (1771), vol. 2, 99-100.
26 Ibid., vol. 2, 101.
27 Carey, *The Balnea*, 117 and 183.
28 Jennings, ed., *History of Harrogate and Knaresborough*, 221-38 and Neesam, *Harrogate Great Chronicle*, 195-223.
29 Under the Forest of Knaresborough Enclosure Act of 1770 (see below, pp. 64-7), the Stray was reserved in perpetuity for public use.
30 Hargrove, *History*, 5th edn. (York, 1798), 98.
31 Carey's condescension towards spa society in Harrogate contrasts not only with Hargrove's promotional literature but also with the more favourable view in *A Companion to the Watering and Bathing Places of England*, (1800), 57-71.
32 See, for example, Hargrove, *History*, 5th edn. (York, 1798), 98-9.
33 Ibid., 100.
34 Hargrove, *History*, 2nd edn. (York, 1775), 45. Cf. Garnett, *Treatise on the Mineral Waters of Harrogate* (1792 and later editions), 85: 'No place in the kingdom can boast of a better or purer air than Harrogate'. Cited hereafter as Garnett, *Treatise*.
35 Hargrove, *History*, 5th edn. (York, 1798), 101.
36 Porter and Rousseau, *Gout. The Patrician Malady*, esp. ch. 5-9.
37 Suspicions echoed, for example, in Alexander, *Plain and Easy Directions*, 2nd edn. (1780), 89-92.
38 Ibid., 3-4.
39 Joshua Walker, *De aqua sulphurea Harrowgatensi* and *Essay on the Waters of Harrogate and Thorp-Arch*.
40 In a succession of publications, beginning with Falconer, *Essay on the Bath Waters* (1772).
41 Walker, *Waters of Harrogate and Thorp-Arch*, 3.
42 Garnett, *Treatise* (1792), viii; 2nd edn., 1794, x; 3rd edn., 1799, xii.
43 Darwin, *Zoonomia*, vol. 1, 2.
44 The description of Darwin is from the dedication to him in Garnett, *Lecture on the Preservation of Health* (1797), replaced in the second edition (1800) with a fulsome

letter expressing the 'high gratification and instruction' that Garnett had received from reading Darwin's works.

45 Garnett, *Treatise*, 1792, ix-x (preface dated 1 May 1792); 1794, xii (preface dated 1 May 1794).

46 The English translation of the first, second and fourth volumes of the *Opuscula* (originally published in six volumes between 1779 and 1790) had appeared in three volumes as Bergman, *Physical and Chemical Essays* (1784–91). See especially 'Of the analysis of waters', vol. 1, 91–192.

47 Coley, 'Physicians and the chemical analysis of mineral waters' and 'Physicians, chemists and the analysis of mineral waters'.

48 On the procedures and the importance of Bergman, see Christopher Hamlin's excellent account, *Science of Impurity*, esp. 22–30.

49 Garnett's observations on the collection of gases and their medical efficacy appear in all the editions of the *Treatise*. See, for example, *Treatise*, 2nd edn. (1794), 71–81.

50 Garnett, *Crescent Water*, 18–24.

51 Hofmann, *Harrogate and Its Resources*. For Bergman's comment, see his *Physical and Chemical Essays*, vol. 1, 109.

52 Garnett, *Short Statement of Facts*.

53 Nichols, *Literary History of the Eighteenth Century*, vol. 1, 459–60. Hutchinson had been a corresponding member of the Society of Antiquaries of Scotland since 1783 and was to be elected a Fellow of the Society of Antiquaries in London in 1793. He had extricated the skull for phrenological examination from the gibbet in the Forest of Knaresborough, where Aram's body had been suspended, following his execution in 1759. On the Aram case and his skull, which survives in the Stories of Lynn Museum, King's Lynn, see Nancy Jane Tyson's article on Aram in the ODNB and Dobson, 'College criminals: 2. Eugene Aram'.

54 The most unforgiving attack had come from James Makittrick Adair, a notoriously disputatious and now elderly physician, writing as 'Benjamin Goosequill'. No doubt encouraged by Garnett, Adair (a frequent visitor to Harrogate in these, his last years) challenged Hutchinson on his medical qualifications as well as on the efficacy of the worm powder. Adair's challenge has not survived. But the nature of it is evident from Hutchinson's reply, printed as 'A letter from T. H-CH-NS-N to Benjamin Goosequill in answer to his complimentary letter'; BL CUP.21.g.44/72. See also the verse satire on the powder, dated 5 December 1791 and addressed by 'Peter Paragraph' (another of Adair's pseudonyms) to Benjamin Goosequill; copy at BL HS.74/1041 (32).

55 Garnett, *Short Statement of Facts*, 2.

56 See, for example, *Med. Reg. 1783*, 121. In fact, Hutchinson claimed that his degree was from St Andrews. But on the Aberdeen M.D. as an 'irregular' degree, see Johnston, 'All Honourable Men?'

57 'Trim the second', dated Harrogate, 3 September 1792. The text is known only through a hand-written copy; BL CUP.21.g.44/71 (d-e).
58 M., 'To Mr. Hutchinson', dated 10 September 1792; copies at BL RB 23a. 11083 and 11084.
59 Garnett published the correspondence in four closely printed pages, headed 'An accurate detail of the circumstances, respecting some illiberal and injurious insinuations, lately made by Mr. TINDALL of KNARESBROUGH, against Dr. GARNETT, together with an exact copy of the correspondence thereon'; copies at BL CUP.21.g.44/71(a-b) and 44/76(a-b).
60 Although duelling was illegal in England from the late sixteenth century, the practice continued. By the later eighteenth century, however, it was becoming far less common. The last duel on English soil was fought (between two Frenchmen) in 1852.
61 Campbell, *Lives of the Lord Chancellors*, vol. 5, 1–366. For a contemporary account, see Anon., 'Lord Loughborough'.
62 On the enclosure and its impact on Harrogate, see Grainge, *History and Topography of Harrogate*, 82–90; Jennings, ed., *History of Harrogate and Knaresborough*, 239–62; and Neesam, *Harrogate Great Chronicle*, 124–76.
63 Neesam, *Harrogate Great Chronicle*, 293–7.
64 I am grateful to May Catt and Karen Southworth, North Yorkshire Council, Culture, Arts and Leisure, for their help in unravelling the often confused names of the town's wells.
65 Hargrove, *History*, 5th edn. (1798), 91; 6th edn. (1809), 110–11.
66 Garnett gave his address as 'Wedderburne House', with the date 1 May 1794, in the four-page dedication to Wedderburn of his *Treatise*, 2nd edn. (1794), vi; also in the 3rd edn. (1794), viii. In the first edition (1792), the dedication had taken the form of an illuminated escutcheon (see Figure 3.2).
67 Hargrove, *History*, 5th edn. (1798), 98.
68 *Med. Reg., 1783*, p. 29.
69 Catherine Cleveland to William Cleveland, 17 May 1793, in Hardy, ed., *Benenden Letters*, 230–2.
70 Anon., 'Memoir of Thomas Garnett, M.D.' (1820), 481.
71 See the several items dating from his Harrogate years in the Bibliography. Duncan was also the recipient of a copy of *De visu*, inscribed 'Dr. Duncan with respectful comps. from his obedt. and obliged servt. Thos. Garnett'; Centre for Research Collections, EUL, Special Collections, E.B. 61284 Gar.
72 See the copy in Eighteenth Century Collections Online (Gale Primary Sources).
73 See ch. 4, 79.
74 Darwin to Garnett, 14 December 1794, APS Miscellaneous Manuscripts Collection, 1668–1996", reproduced as letter, 463–5.

75 Within days, Garnett had performed the experiments, which disproved Darwin's conjecture that air might be released during the thawing of ice, as recorded in notes that Garnett wrote on the letter cited in note 73. For the praise, see Garnett, 'Meteorological observations' (1796), 519: 'as Dr. Darwin observes, in a letter which I lately received from him, the variation of the course of the wind seems to be the cause of, or key to, the other phenomena of frost or rain'.
76 See ch. 4, 81.
77 Ewan, *Benjamin Smith Barton*, 79–136. On the circumstances of Garnett's presidency of the NHS, see ch. 2, 27.
78 On this characterization of Philadelphia, which had circulated as early as 1783 and continued to be used on into the nineteenth century, see Richardson, 'The Athens of America 1800–1825'.
79 Brown, *Elements of Medicine* (1790). Three subsequent editions followed in 1791, 1793 and 1795.
80 Catherine to Sarah Cleveland, 5 October 1795, in Hardy, ed., *Benenden Letters*, 243–6 (245).
81 See correspondence of July 1797, ibid., 249–52.

4

Britain's new north
Lecturer and crusading tourist

With Harrogate behind him and his plans for emigration in disarray, Garnett found himself relaunching his career in one of the most troubled and uncertain decades in modern British history. The war against France that Britain had conducted, with its principal ally Austria, since 1793 had extracted a heavy toll in rising prices and unemployment, and, with it, mounting levels of unrest in town and country. At the same time, industrialization and urbanization had proceeded apace and created their own tensions. To someone as wedded as Garnett to the ideals of moderate reform within an orderly society, such developments were disturbing, and they may already have contributed to his now abandoned decision to emigrate. Within his immediate experience, he had experienced the challenges at first hand in Bradford. Yet he had seen enough of the new order to know that it was also a source of opportunities, and it was to these that he now looked, as always with a keen eye on the market.

Two decades earlier, Samuel Johnson had captured the emerging mood and its commercial possibilities when he observed that 'learning itself is a trade', one that had come to be addressed to 'the multitude' and was no longer an affair of the fortunate beneficiaries of patronage.[1] Since then, the trade to which Johnson referred had expanded dramatically. The resulting demand for knowledge of all kinds was broad. But no beneficiaries stood to gain more than those whose learned credentials lay in precisely the areas in which Garnett excelled. As a progressively minded physician and, as was soon to become apparent, a man of science with the gifts of a compelling lecturer, he could scarcely have been better equipped to exploit the openings that were beginning to transform the prospects for many besides himself. They were the foundations for what now had to be a hastily improvised new start.

The marketplace for knowledge

Garnett's preparations for America had brought him and his possessions to Liverpool at some time in the spring or early summer of 1795, to begin the wait for a suitable passage. His wife's continuing anxiety had clearly not been enough to dissuade him, and it was only when the affairs of the Cleveland family came to a head in the autumn that his hopes of emigration faded. By now, however, other experiences too had had a disorienting effect. As Bradford had done earlier, Liverpool too exposed him to the realities of late-eighteenth-century urban society, in this case in a community whose population had grown from 6,000 to 80,000 since 1700. The scale was larger than in Bradford, but the tensions were the same. Over the last quarter of the century in particular, the expansion had engendered conflicts of class and culture, and inevitable unease among the professional classes that the demand for skills had drawn to the town. In response, the local educated elite had worked resolutely to bring refinement to a community dominated by Liverpool's status as both a major port and a burgeoning centre of Lancashire industry. Prominent in the elite were 'medical gentlemen' who prevailed on Garnett to unpack his instruments and offer a course of public lectures on natural philosophy. Among the 'gentlemen' was Liverpool's leading physician, James Currie, a Glasgow M.D. and advocate of water treatments for fever who had spent several years in America in pursuit of an unsuccessful business venture in the 1770s. Another welcoming figure would certainly have been Currie's fellow anti-slavery campaigner William Roscoe, a lawyer, banker and man of letters, soon to become a founder-member of the Liverpool Athenaeum, a prominent gentleman's club and library.[2]

It was a circle well suited to Garnett's tastes, and he agreed to give the lectures. By late July, they were advertised, and they began: twice weekly on Thursday and Saturday evenings at a fee of 2s 6d per lecture or a guinea for the complete course of ten.[3] They were an immediate success, to the point that they continued into the autumn. Catherine, at home in an audience that included women (as Garnett would earnestly have wished) and relieved to see an alternative to emigration materializing, wrote excitedly from Liverpool to her sister-in-law Sarah Cleveland in October: 'We were wonderfully gay Saturday evening. The lecture room was quite crowded with beaus and belles.'[4] An invitation to repeat the lectures in Manchester followed. By the time Garnett gave his first lecture there, on 29 January 1796, his aspirations had grown. The plan was now for two courses: one of twelve evening lectures on natural philosophy (one a week, at one guinea for the course) and one of thirty lectures on chemistry (twice a week, for two guineas).[5] It was what became his trademark offering as a lecturer: coverage of both pure and applied aspects of the sciences, especially of chemistry, and all at a level, and with demonstrations, that would afford both 'Pleasure and Instruction'. As in Liverpool, women would be especially welcome: by way of inducement, single tickets would be transferable to a lady and gentleman or to two ladies. The courses were an immediate success. They got under way with sixty subscribers, and as they progressed, numbers grew.[6] The room that Garnett had secured, in a town house at 3 Portland Place, was soon inadequate, and he moved on three times in search of larger premises.

Garnett's commitment to a programme extending over three months suggests that he had perceived the even greater potential of Manchester as a place where he might realize his ambitions without the risk and pain of emigration. Manchester had resembled Liverpool in its growth, also to a population of 80,000 (from some 10,000 a century earlier).[7] But it offered readier access to the intellectual company that he craved throughout his life. An outstanding resource was the town's Literary and Philosophical Society, a focus for gentlemanly high culture since its foundation in 1781. Garnett was already known there and had been elected among the Society's first cohort of corresponding members in February 1791. Initially recognized for his work on the Harrogate waters, he had gone on to attract attention for two digests of meteorological observations made by some of the most prominent figures in provincial science, including the blind naturalist John Gough in Kendal and the Dumfries physician Alexander Copland.[8]

Presentation of the digests, at meetings of the Society in March 1793 and March 1795, had been part of Garnett's quest for intellectual and professional recognition during his time in Harrogate.[9] But with his move to Manchester, the digests and their publication in the Society's *Memoirs* paid more immediate dividends in the local cultural hierarchy in which he now had to make his way. The contact they facilitated with Thomas Percival, the MLPS's main founder and for many years its president, was one that he would particularly have valued; it was Percival, in fact, who had asked him to prepare the digests in the first place. In the same circle, Garnett would also have encountered such eminent members as the apothecary and manufacturer of sparkling mineral waters Thomas Henry and the Edinburgh-trained physician Alexander Eason; both were of the same older generation as Percival and with similar interests embracing medicine and scientific enquiry. These were precisely the kind of men that a northern physician and man of science still in search of a vocation would wish to cultivate.

By the spring of 1796, things were going well. In May, James Watt spoke highly of a lecture that Garnett had given in Birmingham;[10] lectures by him in Warrington and Lancaster appear to have been well received;[11] and a local subscription raised sufficient funds for him to be invited to Dublin, where a short paper on ways of improving the design of rain gauges had been instrumental in his election as the Royal Irish Academy's first and only corresponding member in 1794.[12] Recognition also brought with it a measure of material comfort. The Garnetts' address, 4 Levers Row, close to the Infirmary, was among the best in Manchester: as the *Manchester Guide* of 1804 had it, Levers Row was 'perhaps the most pleasant location absolutely in the town'.[13] And it was while living there that Catherine gave birth to their first daughter, Louisa Cleveland, on 24 February 1796. If the couple needed any further reminder of the comfort that came with established local roots, the baptism that followed at St Mary's Church, Radcliffe, a few miles north of Manchester, on 1 May, can only have confirmed the wisdom of their decision to stay in Britain. Conducted by the Revd Richard Ortt, Garnett's cousin (the son of his aunt, Alice Garnett) and a long-serving usher at Bury Grammar School in Lancashire, it would have been a true family occasion.

The fact remained, however, that Garnett was still at a crossroads. It was not just that he lacked a stable position. He had also to fix on the career he wished to follow. Did his future lie in medical practice, for which Edinburgh had prepared him, or in lecturing, in which his recent successes must have surpassed his expectations? Or might he try to combine the two? The market for both activities was enticing. In the industrial towns as everywhere, the demand for cures, both fraudulent and legitimate, had grown and shown medicine to be an eminently saleable commodity. At the same time and in the same urban context, lecturing too proffered a comfortable future for someone with the right combination of scientific knowledge, business flair and skill in performance. The choice was not easy. But through the winter of 1795–6 lecturing seems to have edged ahead of medicine as Garnett's career choice.

A first question was what sort of lecturer he should become. The success stories were seductive. And some were spectacular. One was that of Adam Walker, a fellow native of Westmorland who had used Manchester as his base while earning fame and prosperity as a travelling lecturer in the northern counties from the late 1760s and then continued his enterprise on a national scale from London. Walker's offering rested on his being equally at home with the audiences of working men with which he began and the aristocratic clientele he increasingly cultivated in his later years.[14] Marrying his presentational skills to the public he was addressing was crucial to his success. But so too was an underpinning of publicity and publication ranging from sketchy outline syllabuses to the luxury of his magisterial *System of Familiar Philosophy* (1799), with its fine paper and plates and almost three hundred subscribers. While Walker's career exemplified the heights to which a lecturing career could lead, Garnett knew that he had to begin more modestly and that other models were more realistically within his reach. Two with special resonance for him were John Warltire and Henry Moyes, honorary members of the Lit and Phil and familiar names in the circles that he now frequented in Manchester. Warltire (a friend of Erasmus Darwin and others in the Lunar Society) and Moyes (a blind lecturer particularly admired by Joseph Priestley) had achieved celebrity through the courses they offered in the same urban settings that Garnett would have to target.[15] In Moyes' case, the settings extended even to the towns he visited in America on an eighteen-month lecture-tour in the 1780s. As I suggest in Chapter 3, it may well be, in fact, that his success there had contributed to Garnett's own thoughts of emigration.

Plentiful though the models were, Garnett would also have recognized lecturing's precarious side. It had more than its share of failures. And there was something unnerving about the streak of political radicalism that had come to be associated with certain leading lecturers, including all three of Walker, Warltire and Moyes, whose profiles were more or less distantly marked by an association with the incendiary figure of Priestley.[16] For a moderate reformer like Garnett, with ideals predicated on the maintenance of social stability, theirs was dangerous territory. By now, too, he was a family man, with responsibilities that would have to be reconciled with long periods on the road. Such thoughts can only have played into his quandary. The pressure to take concrete action was intense, and it was at its height when chance intervened, in the form of a notice in the English and Scottish press in June inviting applications for a professorship in natural philosophy at the new Anderson's Institution in Glasgow.

The Andersonian

The Institution had been founded in accordance with the Will of John Anderson, professor at the University of Glasgow, initially and briefly of oriental languages and then, for thirty-nine years until his death on 13 January 1796, of natural philosophy.[17] The roots of Anderson's plan were embedded in his strongly held personal convictions and more broadly in eighteenth-century civic politics. Since the mid-century, two varieties of the Enlightenment had co-existed uneasily in the city.[18] In university circles, the prevailing values were those of moderation in religious and intellectual matters, in the manner of Francis Hutcheson, professor of moral philosophy from 1729 until his death in 1746, and his distinguished successors in the chair, most notably from 1752 Adam Smith and Thomas Reid. Ranged against this humanistic conception of enlightenment was a body of opinion, vehemently articulated from the 1760s by the Revd William Thom, Minister of Govan at the heart of industrial Glasgow. Thom's was a powerful voice, and for many his insistence on the essentially commercial character of the city and the irrelevance of the intellectualist tone that prevailed at the University rang true.[19] In the ongoing clash between academic and mercantile interests, Anderson sided with Thom, using his following among the city's industrial classes and the success of his practically inclined lectures and experimental course in natural philosophy to promote the cause of town against gown.

Anderson's Will and the Codicil he added a few days before his death were extraordinary documents, running in their public, printed form to thirty pages.[20] Apart from some personal bequests, they were largely devoted to the detailed plan for an 'Anderson's University'. Crucially, and in accordance with the position he had taken for so long, Anderson insisted that his university should be quite distinct from the University of Glasgow in the profile of its teaching and in its requirement that no one connected with the ancient university should have any involvement with it: only by maintaining that separation and striking out on a distinctive path could his overriding goal of 'the good of Mankind and the Improvement of Science' be achieved.[21]

To that end, the Will called on nine named executors to take immediate action. As many as eighty-one trustees, also designated by name and given responsibility for implementing the plan, were to meet four times a year, under the oversight of nine visitors, including the Lord Provost of Glasgow and other eminent officeholders in religious and public life. The trustees were to be distributed between nine 'classes'. One of these was composed of Anderson's kinsmen; the others were devoted to specified areas of knowledge, the economy and society, including trade practices, manufacturing and agriculture as well as the learned disciplines of medicine, law, divinity and natural philosophy. Finally, the trustees would be required to appoint from among themselves nine 'ordinary managers' who would meet monthly and be responsible for both day-to-day administration and the fulfilment of Anderson's wishes. Anderson's meticulousness extended even to the naming of the thirty-six persons whom he wanted to occupy the Institution's chairs. These were to be distributed equally, again in groups of nine, between four colleges: Arts, Medicine, Law and Theology.

For all their obsessive precision, the Will and Codicil failed to address the fatal flaw that they specified no financial provision for what promised to be a costly project. Anderson's bequest of his scientific instruments (insured for £500), museum (mainly of natural history) and library of over 2,000 volumes (insured for £300) offered something of an academic foundation.[22] But once his personal debts had been settled, and even after the sale of his furniture and other effects, a deficit of £55 remained.[23] This shaky start makes it all the more remarkable that steps to implement his wishes were embarked upon with such alacrity. Meetings of the nine executors began on the day of his interment, and by 23 March a group of thirty-nine trustees and executors had taken the crucial step of electing the first nine managers.[24] By early July, the 'Andersonian Institution' (as the managers had now agreed to call it) had been formally established, with temporary premises in two unused rooms in Glasgow Grammar School's new buildings in George Street, granted rent-free by the City Council.[25]

It remained to appoint the professors. Here, Anderson attached special importance to the chair in his own discipline, natural philosophy. But even this one appointment, which he believed should be made first, was fraught with difficulties. Among them was the financial shortfall, to which the managers responded with a public subscription that quickly raised £300 in support of the chair, eventually rising to over £405 by June 1797.[26] Another difficulty, affecting all the chairs, was the uncertainty whether the professors whose names Anderson had proposed would accept the positions designated for them. Anderson's choice for the natural philosophy chair was his assistant at the University of Glasgow, William Meikleham, who had taken over his teaching during his final year of declining health and gone on to cover for Anderson's ailing successor, James Brown. Despite his position at the University, Meikleham stood apart from the most conservative factions among his colleagues, though without quite sharing Anderson's crusading zeal either. After prevarication, he finally announced that he would stay at the University of Glasgow, where he went on to become successively professor of astronomy and professor of natural philosophy. He was to hold the post until succeeded by William Thomson half a century later.

It was in response to Meikleham's withdrawal, and in the absence of any other nomination, that advertisements for the chair were prepared and managers were asked to look out for a suitable 'man of Science and Address'.[27] Garnett could scarcely fail to be interested. But with the stability that the professorship offered, there came constraints, and these may explain his initial reluctance to apply. It took encouragement by Alexander Eason, his friend and colleague in the Manchester Lit and Phil, and no doubt Catherine to persuade him, and from the moment he allowed his name to go forward, he was a clear front-runner. By 21 July 1796, the managers had received letters of recommendation in which Andrew Duncan (a supportive mentor from his Edinburgh days) and Thomas Percival (a witness of the recent success of his lectures in Manchester) 'gave a very favourable report of Dr. Garnett's private character and professional abilities'.[28] Erasmus Darwin, too, wrote in support.[29] Even now, though, the negotiations following the managers' immediate and unanimous decision in favour of Garnett as 'the preferable candidate' were far from straightforward. Contacting Garnett, who was thought to be lecturing in Dublin, proved difficult, and subsequent exchanges between him and John Scruton, a surgeon and the manager appointed to discuss terms, advanced falteringly. It was not until 21 September that a meeting of thirty-five of the eighty-one trustees formally endorsed the appointment.[30]

By the time the deal was finalized, late applications from James Headrick, a Church of Scotland minister who had attended Anderson's classes, and James Watt Jnr, whose declared sympathies for the French Revolution and recent residence in Paris would have made him, in most eyes, an unwelcome candidate, had muddied the waters.[31] But the managers stuck by their decision and tabled the applications, pending a suitable agreement with Garnett. In a letter from Barbon on 6 September, Garnett finally stated his conditions. While he agreed to the modest proposed salary of £200 (rather than the riskier alternative of receiving two-thirds of the fees from his lectures), he struck a hard bargain in insisting on a limitation of his teaching duties to the six months between 1 November and 1 May.[32] The all-important months of freedom that this left for the pursuit of his own scientific and medical activities mattered for financial as well as for other reasons. Now as at other times in his life, money weighed heavily with him. One early biographical sketch even affirmed that the income he was beginning to amass as an independent lecturer significantly surpassed the offer from the Andersonian.[33] While the statement smacks of exaggeration, it helps to explain his watchfulness in securing a compromise between the obligations and security that came with a permanent position and the freedom to pursue outside interests and earnings.

With the terms of his appointment agreed, Garnett arrived in Glasgow on 19 October, met the managers and trustees on the following day, and on 26 October delivered a general introductory lecture that alone yielded £36.3s.0d in fees.[34] It was an encouraging start, made the more so for Garnett by the prospect of a settled family life, beginning in a makeshift rented property in Duke Street that also housed materials bequeathed by Anderson. What lay ahead, however, was a punishing workload. Garnett advertised three parallel courses.[35] The most demanding of them, both for him and for his audience, was to be devoted to 'Arts and manufactures connected with natural philosophy and chemistry'. Lectures in the course would be given every weekday at 8.30 am in the Institution's rooms in George Street, and the level would be uncompromising. The mathematics was to be rigorous, and the discussion of industrial processes, illustrated with mechanical models, was to provide a solid grounding in bleaching, dyeing, calico printing, etching, engraving and metallurgy, all subjects that were mentioned in the announcement Garnett prepared for the press. The two other courses – one in natural and experimental philosophy and one in chemistry, with a weekly lecture in each – were to be of a different character. Offering both 'instruction and entertainment', they would be illustrated with 'pleasing and interesting experiments', and any mathematical content would be reduced to a minimum. To distinguish them from the more earnest morning lectures, they would be delivered in the evenings, at 8 p.m., one on Tuesdays, the other on Fridays, in a room rented in the spacious Trades Hall, an imposing building (though somewhat reduced from Adam's original plan) that had been inaugurated two years' earlier in the recently developed Glassford Street.[36]

The gracious setting in Glasgow's 'New Town' was important, since Garnett intended that the evening lectures should be not only 'popular' but also 'particularly interesting to the Ladies'.[37] As in Manchester, lecture-fees were pitched accordingly: the normal charge of a guinea for each of the popular courses (half the course-fee of two guineas for the morning course) would admit either a gentleman or two ladies or a lady and gentleman. It was a provision that fulfilled not only Garnett's but also Anderson's vision for the new institution. In spirit if not in name, the evening lectures met the requirement of the Will that each year the professor of natural philosophy should offer a 'Ladies' course of physical lectures' that would avoid 'pedantic language' and help those attending to become 'the most accomplished Ladies in Europe'.[38] The only difference was that Garnett wanted his audiences to be mixed, with women attending alongside men. In that way he avoided any residual condescension implicit in a provision reserved exclusively for them.

In a programme that aimed to cater for as diverse a public as possible, the formula of lectures pitched with different emphases worked. At the end of his first year as professor, Garnett could report ticket sales admitting a total of 972 for the three courses; of these, over half had attended the popular courses on natural philosophy, with rather fewer subscribing for the course on chemistry, and the smallest number, a hundred, for the morning lectures.[39] But overall numbers, augmented by 'many visiting strangers' admitted on application to the managers, were not the main source of his satisfaction. It mattered more to him that almost half of those present had been women. In his concluding lecture of the session, he made the point with justified pride: the year had marked 'an era in the annals of female education which posterity may contemplate with peculiar pleasure'.[40] Women, he later insisted, had been unfairly disparaged as having a taste only for frivolous pursuits. In reality, they were victims of a lack of educational opportunity, aggravated in the days of chivalry and since by 'a ridiculous attention or gallantry' that was degrading to them as 'rational beings'.[41] Now, however, the Andersonian had broken the mould. It was 'the first regular institution in which the fair sex have been admitted to the temple of knowledge on the same footing with men'.

With this, as with all aspects of the Andersonian's first year, the managers expressed unqualified satisfaction. No less important, in their eyes, was the progress made in fulfilling the other key aspect of Anderson's legacy: the promotion of 'useful knowledge' applied to trade and manufacturing. Their enthusiasm would certainly have been more muted if the income from the lectures had failed to match expectations. But the sale of tickets for the session yielded just over £300. This was sufficient (with other income, mainly from some substantial donations, bank interest and sales of the published outlines of Anderson's lectures, *Institutes of Physics*) to cover Garnett's salary and other expenses, and to leave almost £300 to spare.[42] In the flush of satisfaction and mutual goodwill, the healthy balance-sheet made Garnett's re-engagement a formality. By March 1797, the managers had offered him a salary of £200 for 1797–8, along with accommodation free of rent, the renewal of the contract for his assistant ('operator') John Parsell, and the promise of an additional sum if the profits significantly exceeded those of the past year.[43] Enthusiastic endorsement of the managers' decisions by the trustees and the report that 'several Gentlemen friends' were planning to raise funds for building new premises soon added further encouragement.[44]

Garnett's contribution to the success lay in his consistently skilled performances. In this, the sophistication of his lecture demonstrations, backed by a cabinet of apparatus as fine as any in Britain, played an essential part. So too did an authority that came with his command of the latest science. This is less evident from a sketchy sixteen-page outline of what appears to have been his rather conventional coverage of experimental philosophy than from the more discursive syllabus he published for chemistry.[45] The chemical lectures, clearly based on the thirty-lecture course he had delivered in Manchester, had a studiedly innovatory character. They proclaimed not only the utility of chemistry for agriculture, industry and medicine but also the debt that chemists owed to recent developments in the discipline, especially in France. Garnett's treatment, in fact, was something of a modernizing manifesto. The nomenclature that he now used was French, and Lavoisier's insights informed his discussions of the oxygen theory of combustion and respiration, the properties of the elements and their common compounds, and thermal phenomena (incorporating Black's theory of latent heat and qualified support for the caloric theory).[46]

Despite the managers' and trustees' satisfaction with the 1796–7 session, by Garnett's own demanding lights things were not going well enough, at least financially. Towards the end of the year, he had already asked the managers for permission to mount a course on mathematics 'for his own emolument', on top of his already formidable burden of lecturing.[47] The request was declined, as was the plan for a similar course from the Revd Robert Lothian, an elderly Presbyterian minister and independent teacher of mathematics, astronomy and geography whom Anderson had nominated in his Will for the professorship of mathematics. Garnett's proposal to add two lectures on practical and experimental chemistry to the weekly programme for the coming session, with extra remuneration taken from a share of the profits, got rather further. At first, the managers were sympathetic, but by the autumn anxieties on both sides about the costs involved and the likely impact on a diminishing enrolment for the other courses won out.[48] The lectures were never given.

Frustrated in his attempt to increase his income at the Andersonian, Garnett turned to other avenues. As early as January 1797, when he was only halfway through the year's lectures, he had been looking for opportunities of repeating his teaching away from Glasgow during the six months of freedom that he would have between May and October. In characteristically entrepreneurial spirit, he prepared a printed one-page proposal for two courses, one on natural philosophy, the other on chemistry, for distribution to likely takers. One distinguished recipient was James Watt. In a covering letter, Garnett asked Watt whether the courses might succeed in Birmingham.[49] The proposed lectures drew heavily on what had become his standard offering. For a course fee of a guinea, he would give fifteen weekly lectures on natural philosophy; on chemistry, there would be a total of thirty lectures, given twice weekly for two guineas, both courses spread over four months, beginning on 1 June. In addition, he proposed (for three guineas) a 'complete & scientific' course of daily lectures on the applied aspects of natural philosophy and chemistry, on the model of his morning lectures in Glasgow. Were attendances to match his hopes (100, as he thought, for the first course, 50 for the second and 30 for the third, corresponding roughly to the profile of his audiences at the Andersonian), the income would comfortably exceed his professorial salary.

Watt's response was kindly but realistic. He took the trouble to refer the enquiry to his personal physician, John Carmichael, a near contemporary of Garnett's in the Edinburgh medical school who may have known Garnett as a student. Carmichael was less than enthusiastic. He saw the proposal as over-ambitious and advised Watt that while the first two courses might attract enough subscribers, there would be few takers for the third: 'Four nights in the week which his three courses would require I am affraid would be considered by those who are ignorant of the importance of chemistry as too great a sacrifice of time.'[50] Watt conveyed Carmichael's advice in a four-page letter to Garnett. In it, he leavened a gloomy comment on the depressed state of local trade and its consequences for interest in lectures on 'matters of utility' with the suggestion that an exploratory advertisement in the press might help to gauge possible demand.[51] No such action seems to have been taken, and the proposal for the lectures foundered.

Garnett, though, was undaunted and as ready as ever to offer individual lectures wherever he could find an audience. The seventy-two pages of his *Lecture on the Preservation of Health* began as just such a lecture. In its published form, it offered a carefully pitched mixture of common sense about diet, exercise and fresh air with a dose of undimmed Brunonianism drawn explicitly, in certain passages word for word, from the defence of Brown's principles he had presented before the Royal Medical Society almost a decade before.[52] The lecture became something of a party piece that Garnett was proud to have delivered in 'some of the most populous towns of England'. One of the towns was Liverpool, and Garnett had the lecture printed there in 1797, before reissuing it as a repaginated but otherwise unchanged second edition, in London three years later.[53]

The second session, 1797–8, was by no means a failure. But attendances did fall, by almost half, to about 500, despite determined advertising that made much of accessibility of the lectures and Garnett's use of his own apparatus as well as Anderson's.[54] The reduced numbers had their consequences. Over the winter, there was talk of a possible deficit and a consequent renegotiation of the professor's salary for the following year. And disquiet among trustees made its mark in the growing irregularity of their attendance at meetings.[55] Garnett can only have been alarmed by the sudden change in the Institution's prospects; a one-off 'philosophical' lecture by him on astronomy conveyed his resourcefulness in pursuit of the market for less utilitarian subjects, though in a context that smacked of desperation.[56]

Through it all, Garnett's loyalty to the Andersonian was never in doubt. But it was a mark of his limited bargaining power that he undertook to give the following year's lectures without any assurance as to his prospects thereafter; in this way, discussion of his remuneration could be postponed until the current lectures were finished and the accounts for the year were finalized. The compromise was one that the trustees could scarcely refuse, and in March 1798 they accepted Garnett's 'liberal' offer, which embraced the possibility of his receiving no contractual salary at all and becoming in effect an Andersonian-based independent lecturer with a right to a share of whatever fees accrued.[57] Highly charged though the exchanges were, they conveyed the wealth of good will that existed on both sides. The settlement for 1798–9 was not the end of the story, however. With dark clouds threatening the very future of the institution, Garnett's thoughts turned more urgently than ever to ways of increasing his income, now with a view to resuming medical practice as a complement to his professorial duties. Election to the Faculty of Physicians and Surgeons of Glasgow in 1798 was a step in this direction as well as a personal honour.[58] But it was not enough. Again, as so often in his life, money worries gnawed at his confidence, and once the year's teaching was over, it turned a much-needed interlude in his parents' house in Barbon, with his wife and daughter, into a period of excessive activity.

The Highland tour

Among the summer tasks that Garnett set himself was the preparation of a new course, on the philosophy of natural history. The work united his idea for an attractive addition to his offerings at the Andersonian with a longstanding personal interest, especially in mineralogy and botany. As such, it offered a diversion from his recent anxieties in Glasgow. But it came with its quota of stress and was soon to give way to a venture at once far more disruptive of his summer and burdensome in its consequences. This was the tour of the Highlands and Western Isles of Scotland on which he embarked, on 9 July 1798, with the young portrait painter and landscape artist Walter Henry Watts. To judge by an obituary of him published more than forty years later, Watts would have made a lively and cultivated companion, with a personality and range of literary and artistic interests that cemented an enduring friendship with Garnett.[59] A few years after the tour, he was to turn to journalism, as a long-serving parliamentary reporter for the (Tory) *Morning Post* and then the (Whig) *Morning Chronicle*.

But in 1798, still in his early twenties, he was struggling to make his name as an artist, mainly in the north-west of England, and only too glad to be engaged as Garnett's illustrator.

In the 600-page account of his travels, published two years after the event as *Observations on a Tour through the Highlands of Scotland*, Garnett mentioned the motives that had led him to undertake the tour. One was concern about his health: the hard work and stressful circumstances of his second session at the Andersonian had left him vulnerable to 'some complaints which frequently attend a sedentary life', probably the low spirits that plagued him throughout his career.[60] The other was his, and Watts's, long-standing ambition to see 'the sublime scenery of the North'. In this ambition, Garnett and Watts were following formidable precursors who, over a quarter of a century, had created the by-now abundant corpus of descriptions of the wilder parts of Britain, in particular Scotland, Wales and the Lake District, and fed the unprecedented boom in British travel writing.[61]

Pre-eminent in the genre was the Oxford-educated Welsh naturalist, antiquary and landowner Thomas Pennant, whose descriptions of Highland tours he had undertaken in 1769 and 1772 were still widely read in the 1790s.[62] Significantly, Pennant's 'journal' (probably the volumes describing both tours) was the one work that we know Garnett took with him. The praise he heaped on this 'monument of the talents and industry of its author' is evidence that he admired it, to the point of punctuating his own account with observations and insights drawn from Pennant, most of them acknowledged, though including a number that went unattributed.[63] In both conception and execution, in fact, Garnett saw his tour as building on Pennant's. Even his itinerary was a reduced amalgam of the two followed by Pennant. Embracing the Western Isles and extending northwards to Fort William, Fort Augustus and Inverness before returning to Glasgow via Perth, it broadly corresponded to what had come to be known as the 'long tour'. As such, it was not to be confused with the better-trodden 'short' version, which would barely have extended beyond Inverary, Loch Lomond, Dunkeld and Stirling.

Despite the size of Garnett's account (longer than any Scottish travelogue so far published), his tour fell short of Pennant's, at least in duration (less than six weeks, as opposed to Pennant's, of three and five months) and in rigours that paled in comparison with the ones Pennant had faced in the pioneering days of Highland tourism. By the time Garnett set out, the routes to be followed, locations to be visited and views to be enjoyed were well known, making repetition of familiar material a constant snare. Readers' expectations of travel literature, however, had evolved significantly in the quarter of a century since Pennant, and Garnett slipped easily into the new style of narration.

This was nowhere more obvious than in his appreciative evocations of mountain grandeur, which lent an aesthetic dimension largely absent in Pennant. Especially since the 1780s, emotional responses to scenery had become such staples of Scottish tourist literature that it is hard to know how spontaneous Garnett's sentiments were or how much they owed to a conscious bid to appear as a man of discernment in the now fashionable mode. In his choice of guiding aesthetic principles, he certainly played safe. They were those that the artist, cleric and educationist William Gilpin had elaborated in his writings from the mid-century. In the 1790s, Gilpin was still very much in vogue, thanks most recently to his influential *Three Essays* on the theory of the picturesque in landscape and art, the first two editions of which had appeared early in the decade.[64] In a terminology refined in successive volumes of *Observations* on his travels in widely dispersed parts of Britain, Gilpin had presented the 'picturesque' as intermediate between Edmund Burke's contrasting aesthetic domains of the beautiful (associated with smoothness and delicacy of form and colour) and the sublime (inspiring feelings of awe, even fear).[65] Garnett adopted Gilpin's categories to the letter, and at appropriate points throughout the *Tour*, feelings cast in Gilpinesque language, no doubt filtered through discussions with Watts, lent a subjective cast to his travelogue and commentary.

Garnett's respect for Gilpin was qualified by only the mildest reservations about an authority 'whose taste for the picturesque can seldom be called in question'.[66] A few miles into the tour, on the north bank of the Clyde, he ventured the cautious observation that the ruined fort of Dunglass and its background of mountains fell short of the 'good picture' that Gilpin thought it to be.[67] Deferential endorsements, though, were the norm, often conveyed in language barely modified from Gilpin's. If Dumbarton Castle and its dominant setting formed 'a very picturesque object', they did so because the scene had been given 'consequence' by the combination of the buildings ('though not of themselves beautiful') and the craggy sides of the hill on which they stood.[68] The criteria were, almost word for word, those by which Gilpin made his identical assessment. Similarly, when Garnett judged the widely admired York Cascade in the late Duke of Athol's pleasure grounds at Blair Athol to be wanting in 'sublimity and simplicity', he invoked precisely the deficiencies in an 'undoubtedly beautiful' scene that had disappointed Gilpin (see Figure 4.1).[69] For Garnett as for Gilpin, and in virtually identical language, the cascade (like others along the Tilt) was made to 'appear smaller' through being viewed as a feeder to the 'greater stream'.

Figure 4.1 The York Cascade, falling into the River Tilt on the Duke of Athol's pleasure grounds at Blair Athol, Perthshire. The wild, broken falls of the Cascade were widely praised by admirers of sublime scenery. But both William Gilpin and Garnett felt that the proximity of the 'greater stream' of the Tilt (below the scene depicted) detracted from the sublimity of the view and a 'simplicity' that was lost through the falls' appearing 'frittered' rather than as a single turbulent gush. Aquatint plate from Garnett, *Observations on a Tour through the Highlands and the Western Isles of Scotland*, 2 vols. (London, 1800), vol. 2, facing p. 47. The plate was one of 52 in the book, all drawn by Walter Henry Watts and engraved by William Green. Private collection.

Although Garnett's expressions of feeling introduced elements that were absent from the more sober Pennant, he was at one with Pennant in a central aspect of his mission: to inform and educate. Firmly in the Pennant mould was the prominence he gave to science, though with differences that reflected his own profile of interests. Whereas Pennant, a fellow of the Royal Society, correspondent of Linnaeus and author of a four-volume *British Zoology*, focused primarily on fauna, Garnett's emphasis was on flora, geology and mineral and other natural resources. Scientific material could be off-putting, though, and as an author anxious to please and be read, Garnett recognized that a balance between seriousness and superficiality had to be struck.[70] To that end and so as not to 'terrify or impede the progress of the light reader', he advised any who found the science offputting simply to omit the *Tour*'s more 'philosophical' passages.[71] Nevertheless, such passages were frequent, and they could be lengthy and intrusive. Accounts of an examination of the springs at the Lowland spa of Moffat, recounted from information he had gathered during a stay there in the summer of 1797, and at Pitkeathly, near Perth, were the occasion for extended reflexions on the medical efficacy of sulphureous and chalybeate waters reminiscent of Garnett's Harrogate days.[72] Still heavier-going for the 'light' reader was a lecture-length footnote on changes in the British climate and wind patterns that drew on his earlier meteorological interests and the ideas on winds he had exchanged with Erasmus Darwin.[73]

Commenting on these passages, S. G. E. Lythe has written that Garnett travelled 'with the eye and mind of a professional scientist'.[74] There is truth in the statement. But a scientific 'eye' did not preclude the mingling of scientific and non-scientific genres. Independently of the science, there were not only sentiments and evaluations of scenery to be articulated but also adventures to be recounted, none more vividly than in the twenty-six pages Garnett devoted to his visit to the remote island of Staffa.[75] There, genres coalesced in a tale of a precarious landing on Staffa's only beach, the awe inspired by the cathedral-like grandeur of Fingal's cave, and the scientific challenge of the array of basalt columns whose origins were still debated a quarter of a century after Joseph Banks had been the first outsider to see them, during his expedition to Iceland in 1772.

Banks' account, published in Pennant's second *Tour in Scotland* (1774), had offered no explanation.[76] But where Banks had feared to tread, Garnett did not hold back. Referring to his observations during the few hours he spent on the island, he dismissed not only the fanciful Celtic legend that ascribed the columns to the work of giants building the palace of Ossian's father, Fingal, but also the more serious 'Neptunist' discussion by the Church of Ireland bishop and traveller Richard Pococke, who saw the similar and obviously related columns of the Giant's Causeway in Ireland as formed by sedimentation from a primeval ocean.[77] Garnett came down, instead, in favour of volcanic action in a process analogous to crystallization (though unlike any known process of crystal formation) in the 'bowels of the earth'.[78] In this, as in so much of his science, he drew on his wide reading, including case studies of the basaltic columns in the Auvergne. With an openness undimmed by the current war, he was happy to display his immersion in French sources by associating his acknowledgement to the Irish Vulcanist and Protestant minister, William Hamilton, with recognition of the pioneering work of Faujas de Saint Fond, who had been among the early visitors to Staffa in 1784, and Nicolas Desmarest, whom he credited (rightly) with identifying basalt as a volcanic rock.[79]

Prominent though his aesthetic and scientific digressions were, no theme in the *Tour* mattered more to Garnett than his account of the suffering caused by backwardness and underinvestment in the Highlands. It was a suffering to which Pennant too had been sensitive, and other prominent authorities had taken up the theme. Garnett's sympathies lay firmly with the advocates of agricultural improvement and social welfare, in the manner of John Knox's *View of the British Empire, More Especially Scotland* (1784). A philanthropist and man of independent means (after making a considerable fortune as a bookseller in London), Knox wrote as an energetic pioneer of tourism in Scotland, the country of his birth. Above all, though, his book was a call to action. Knox's fact-gathering tours, including sixteen between 1764 and 1776, conveyed the importance he attached to relieving the 'human misery' of the Highlanders, specifically through the establishment of fisheries to provide employment around the Scottish coast.[80] Garnett cited him frequently, to the point of admitting that, in places, he had cast his own description of the hard lives he had witnessed 'nearly in Mr. Knox's own words'.[81]

Even Knox's carefully documented study, though, paled in volume and thoroughness beside Sir John Sinclair's far richer compendium: the *Statistical Account of Scotland*, published between 1791 and 1799 in twenty-one volumes, most of which were available to Garnett by the time of his tour. With the authority of an Elder in the Church of Scotland, Sinclair assembled parish-by-parish information from more than 900 responses to lengthy questionnaires that he addressed to ministers of the Kirk across the country. Despite their variable quality, the replies provided an unprecedentedly solid foundation for knowledge of the natural and human resources of the Highlands and Hebridean islands, and they did much to fashion perspectives on Scotland until the completion of their better-structured sequel, the *New Statistical Account*, in its definitive fifteen volumes in 1845. Sinclair's *Statistical Account* was an inexhaustible source, and Garnett quarried it liberally. His normal practice was to combine information from 'the best local history that ever has appeared in any country' with testimony of his own.[82] His ten pages on Stirling were typical in retaining a personal quality while resting heavily on the statistical data and summary of the town's history that Sinclair had received from an unusually conscientious and scholarly minister.[83] Other, less disciplined borrowings reflected a liking for curiosities and tales calculated to entertain rather than instruct. The story of the people of a village near Oban who a hundred years earlier had apprehended a group of miscreants and shut them up to die in a local cave was one of the *Statistical Account*'s choicer anecdotes that caught Garnett's imagination, and he recounted it in full, almost in the minister's own words.[84]

What really moved him, however, was the congruence between his own observations of hardship and the evidence he found in Knox, Sinclair and a dismaying account of Argyll agriculture published in the year of his tour by Dr John Smith, a minister of Campbelltown on the Kintyre Peninsula.[85] The deprivation Garnett described was profound, and worse was to come. What he was witnessing, in fact, were the first painful stages of the 'Highland Clearances' that were to continue, in the form of evictions and the erosion of traditional clan-based society, into the mid-nineteenth century. In this, he saw tenants and landowners alike as victims. For tenants, arable farming on marginal land, eked out alongside small-scale fishing and cattle-rearing, yielded livelihoods of barely subsistence level, with little to spare for the payment of rents, while landowners were tempted to seek refuge from precarious incomes by turning to large-scale sheep-farming and easy profits garnered from fewer hands. The consequences, as Garnett observed, were plain to see in levels of despair that fostered the excessive consumption of spirits, high infant mortality, an incipient tide of emigration to North America and the long-term absence of men recruited to Highland regiments or forced to travel south in search of employment.[86]

It was with the spectre of chronic depopulation looming large that Garnett and other champions of improvement made their case. Their goal was an economy for the Highlands and, more particularly, the Hebridean islands that would turn the dismal tide without a wholesale transformation in land use. Possible remedies did not exclude sheep-farming altogether. The important thing, in Sinclair's words, was to avoid the replacement of cattle with 'flocks of wild, coarse wooled, and savage animals' left to roam virtually untended on vast estates.[87] The remedy lay, as Garnett also insisted, in the production of wool of sufficiently high quality and value to make a well-managed, moderately sized flock of perhaps 300 sheep and hence a modest family-holding economically viable. It was in that way, the way of mixed agriculture supported by leases that gave tenants security of tenure and an incentive to improve their land, that the decline of the traditional small Highland farm could best be arrested.[88]

Although commentaries on the eighteenth century's 'Highland problem' had a history going back to the aftermath of the failed Jacobite rising of 1745, Garnett's perspective was rooted firmly in the later 1790s. With the possibility of a Stuart restoration a distant though not extinguished memory, he wrote assertively of the benefits of the union and dismissively of the 'unfortunate and infatuated adventurer' who had led the rebellion and whose defeat at Culloden now fed nothing more than a pathetically dwindling nostalgia.[89] For Scotland, as Garnett insisted, the best might yet be, both for the Highlands and for the industries and port of Glasgow, finally recovering from the calamitous loss of trade in the American war.[90] It was a committed but nuanced stance, one that addressed not only the interests of agriculture, manufacturing and commerce but also, and no less importantly, the harm done to a sense of Scottish identity by the loss of the Edinburgh parliament in 1707.

Garnett's perception of the importance of identity (though he did not use the word) distanced him from Samuel Johnson's scathing dismissal of the Scots as an alien people supinely dependent on the benefits accorded them by their English neighbours. The challenge, for Garnett as for other champions of the union, was to find a way of marshalling Scottish distinctiveness not as a force for separation but in support of a Britain, specifically a Protestant Hanoverian Britain, in which multiple national identities could coexist. In Garnett's strategy, the figure of Ossian, the purported author of a cycle of Gaelic poetry dating from the third century, had an essential role. The Ossianic legend had been a focus for debate since the 'discovery', translation, and publication of the poems by the Scottish poet James Macpherson in the 1760s. From the start, suspicions that the poetry was the work of Macpherson himself, perhaps based on fragments of folk literature, had circulated, with Johnson among the arch-sceptics.[91] Garnett, though, offered more than an endorsement of the authenticity of the poems. He saw them as a way of feeding Scottish and more particularly Highland pride by presenting them as evidence of a deep literary past that had survived for centuries at the heart of a vibrant Gaelic culture and was still ingrained in the consciousness of Highlanders: 'In almost every glen are to be found persons who can repeat from tradition several of these, and other Celtic tales of the same date.'[92] It was a version of history blatantly suffused with politics. As Garnett knew, a tradition whose roots could be shown to long predate the Stuart succession had little prospect of serving any future resurrection of the Jacobite cause.

The tour came to an end in mid-August, when Garnett arrived back in Glasgow with Watts. The time away had been good for him. His spirits were high, and he had gained social and intellectual capital from an association with the world of gentlemanly travel in a Scotland far removed from the one he had come to know through his professorship at the Andersonian. From Glasgow, he was glad to relax with Catherine on excursions to the nearby falls of Clyde and the recently founded cotton mills and model housing at New Lanark. The 'very romantic' setting of New Lanark was exhilarating enough. But even more so was the prospect of healthy employment that the new development offered for some of the displaced Highland families. It was in precisely the improving spirit dear to Garnett that the Glasgow entrepreneur and leading figure in the Andersonian circle, David Dale, had launched the New Lanark venture. And Garnett now saw every reason to think that Dale's 'very worthy friend' Robert Owen, who had recently bought the mills and was soon to become Dale's son-in-law, would 'perfect the work'.[93] With Catherine sharing his hopes, the visit left him 'more gratified' than at any time in his life.[94]

One thing the tour had not done, however, was to relieve the precariousness of his professorial appointment. Should he again be thinking of alternatives in itinerant lecturing or medicine? Soon, though, unanticipated good news from the Andersonian edged the balance in favour of making the most of what he had. On 26 September, in readiness for the 1798–9 session, a group of twelve trustees made a gesture of confidence in the Institution and, by implication, in Garnett himself by completing the purchase, for £1,520, of the Flesh Market, a handsome building newly constructed as a speculative venture on the west side of John Street.[95] There, with the aid of a share issue of £2,000 in 100 shares of £20 each, they soon fitted out what Garnett described as 'one of the most elegant and commodious lecture rooms in Britain'.[96]

What we know of the room comes solely from the description that appeared as one of the many digressions in the *Tour*. Yet there is enough in the description to suggest that the design may have left a material legacy in the famous amphitheatre whose construction Garnett was to witness at the Royal Institution three years later. The disposition of the tiered seating (for up to 500), arranged in a semi-circle centred on the lecturer and with a diameter of forty-five feet, was similar to that adopted at the RI. There were parallels, too, in the lighting by windows that could be darkened in an overhead dome and on the sides, and a generous provision for other activities. This included space for a library of several thousand volumes ('among which are the most celebrated French authors'), a chemical laboratory, workshop and fine mineral collection and museum, as well as an exceptional cabinet of scientific apparatus. The cabinet, 'unquestionably the most complete and extensive in Britain', was the object of special pride, with the instruments bequeathed by Anderson's bequest now augmented through funding from the trustees as well as Garnett's continued readiness to place his personal collection at his employers' disposal.

The investment in the new premises rested on a tide of commercial confidence and civic pride that in less than a decade had seen Glasgow endowed with other notable public buildings, including not only the Trades Hall and Grammar School but also a new Royal Infirmary and Assembly and Concert Rooms, all in the best Adam style. In Garnett's words, Glasgow was 'the most improving place in Britain'; no other city in the British Empire was growing so rapidly in 'population and opulence'.[97] At odds with the investment, however, was the unreliability of the Andersonian's income stream for running costs. That problem remained unresolved, and it only heightened Garnett's sensitivity to his financial anxieties. His response, characteristically, was to prepare for an additional course of lectures that he had been invited to give in Newcastle once the coming year's teaching was over.[98] The invitation had come from the recently established Newcastle Literary and Philosophical Society, in the person of the Unitarian minister and indefatigable joint secretary of the society, the Revd William Turner. Fashioning the programme for Newcastle was an easy matter. Garnett simply resurrected the one he had proposed to James Watt for delivery in Birmingham two years earlier: fifteen or more lectures on natural philosophy (with a course-fee of one guinea, admitting a gentleman or a lady accompanied by a gentleman) and at least thirty on chemistry (two guineas) followed 'if desired' by a course on botany, all to be given between July and September 1799. By now, the individual lectures and demonstrations were well honed too. Even so, a summer spent giving at least three lectures a week remained a far from trivial undertaking. Yet the prospect of a significant supplement to his income carried the day against the inevitability of domestic upheaval, whether a three-month relocation to Newcastle with his wife and daughter or a lengthy separation from them.

Tragically and with brutal suddenness, these and all other plans were curtailed in Glasgow on Christmas Day 1798, when Garnett's wife died from uncontrollable bleeding barely an hour after giving birth to a second daughter, Catherine Grace. It was a blow from which he never fully recovered. Within days, letters to members of his close family conveyed his grief. To his cousin Richard Ortt in Bury, he described himself as 'cast ashore, friendless, and deprived of every comfort': his infant daughters were his sole consolation, and henceforth he would live 'only for the sweet babes'.[99] To his late wife's brother, William Cleveland, he wrote in the same distraught tone:

> Oh, My dear Brother, how can I tell you the sad story of my woe. The companion of my studies, the friend of my bosom is no more, and I am wretched beyond conception. The cold earth has closed on that form which was so lately animated by every virtue, & whose only wish was to promote my happiness. Oh! what a blank is life now to me![100]

He had the consolation of Mary Worboys to look after his 'little orphans', but little else.

The depression that had unsettled him during the winter months in Harrogate now struck more debilitatingly than ever. The most ordinary reverses of life played on his natural sensitivity and provoked periods of extreme distress. A modest increase in attendances at his lectures in 1798–9, to 525, and the pride he took in the new premises in John Street were not enough to console him. But through the spring of 1799, he struggled on, encouraged by an allocation of £100 towards his salary for 1799–1800 to supplement a profits-based agreement of the kind he had accepted for the previous year.[101] As he knew only too well, audiences were key to the very survival of the institution. And it was with enrolments in mind that he resurrected his proposal for the popular course on the philosophy of natural history on which he had been working before his wife's death.

Garnett's case for the new course rested on the commercial advantage of substituting it for the Friday evening lectures on chemistry, which remained persistently less popular than those on natural philosophy. Presenting his proposal to the managers in June 1799, he insisted on the 'novelty' of an offering that would be 'as entertaining and interesting as any of the popular courses that have been given in the Institution'.[102] But there was more to the course than entertainment alone. The accompanying outline of the lectures also caught the eye for the visionary worldview they promised. They would begin with a discussion of the fixed stars, including the 'probability' that some of them would have worlds in orbit around them. They would then focus on our own planet: how it was formed, the causes of meteorological phenomena and the nature of life on earth, including skin colour and other varieties of human life and the 'progress of man in society from rudeness to refinement'. It was heady stuff, too heady and probably too tarred with echoes of Erasmus Darwin's evolutionary ideas and the brush of French cosmological speculation for the Revd James Stewart. With the authority of an Andersonian trustee and minister of the Presbyterian Relief Congregation of the Anderston area of Glasgow, Stewart aired his concerns during more than two months of reflexion by managers and trustees, culminating in approval for what promised to be an emasculated version of Garnett's original conception: delivery of the lectures was to be rigorously monitored and the word 'philosophy' was to be removed from the title.[103]

Other anxieties about the appropriateness of the lectures may have gone further than Stewart's. A contemporary account of Garnett at the Andersonian refers enigmatically to aspersions that had been cast on his 'political principles'.[104] Nothing more is known, though in the charged atmosphere of the 1790s, displays of cosmological unorthodoxy of the kind that he proposed for his course would have been quite enough to ignite suspicion. To someone as sensitive to the dangers of political subversiveness as Garnett was now and throughout his life, such suspicion would have been unjust and hurtful. In fact, by the time the course was finally approved, on 28 August, the mere hint of suspicion would have been enough to distress him. With the lectures in Newcastle long since cancelled, his hopes of resuming medical practice getting nowhere and his loyalty to the Andersonian now sorely tried, he was close to breaking point.

In the circumstances, any realistic possibility of making a new start away from the scene of his grief in Glasgow was certain to attract him. And the possibility presented itself, apparently unsolicited, in mid-September, when he received an invitation from Benjamin Thompson, Count Rumford in London to become the first professor at the Royal Institution. He did not hesitate for long. On 15 October he submitted his resignation to the managers of the Andersonian and was soon planning his move to the capital and yet another change of life, this time in the socially very different world of Mayfair.

Notes

1 From a conversation (19 August 1773) quoted in Boswell, *Journal of a Tour to the Hebrides*, 55–6.

2 Both Currie (5 guineas) and Roscoe (3 guineas) were among the more generous subscribers to Garnett's posthumous publication, *Zoonomia*; see ch. 5, 135.

3 Kelly, *George Birkbeck*, 59–60.

4 Catherine to Sarah Cleveland, 5 October 1795, in Hardy, ed., *Benenden Letters*, 243–6.

5   Announcement in the weekly *Manchester Mercury*, 26 January 1796.
6   'Life of Garnett', xii.
7   A figure that includes the adjacent town of Salford. See Aston, *Manchester Guide*, 45–9.
8   Garnett, 'Meteorological observations' (1793 and 1796).
9   See ch. 3, 68–9 on the opening they gave him to Darwin, for example.
10 Watt to Thomas Walker of Manchester, 18 May 1796, in Musson and Robinson, *Science and Technology in the Industrial Revolution*, 146–7.
11 'Life of Garnett', xiii.
12 Garnett, 'Observations on rain gages'.
13 Aston, *Manchester Guide*, 271.
14 See, for example, the 1790 edition of Walker, *Syllabus of a Course of Lectures*, where Walker advertises himself as lecturer to the Duke of Gloucester and offers to read his course privately in the homes of the nobility.
15 Coley, 'John Warltire' and Harrison, 'Blind Henry Moyes'.
16 Walker's radical associations are explored in Ruston, 'Shelley's links to the West Midlands Enlightenment'.
17 On Anderson and the plan for his institution, see Butt, *John Anderson's Legacy*, esp. 1–45 and the more detailed Muir, *John Anderson*.
18 Sher, 'Commerce, religion and the Enlightenment', 342–51.
19 For a typical expression, see 'Letter to J____ M____, Esq. on the defects of a university education', in Thom, *Works*, 263–301; dated October 1761.
20 For the Will and Codicil, see Anderson, *Extracts from the Latter Will and Codicil*; also in Muir, *Anderson*, 129–62.
21 Will, articles 2 and 8, in Muir, *John Anderson*, 131 and 143–4.
22 And. MM, vol. 1, f. 77 (21 July 1796).
23 Muir, *John Anderson*, 93–4.
24 And. MM, vol. 1, ff. 53–6 (23 March 1796).
25 For a contemporary account of the buildings, see Denholm, *History of the City of Glasgow*, 123–4.
26 Muir, *John Anderson*, 95.
27 And. MM, vol. 1, f. 73 (21 June 1796).
28 Ibid., vol. 1, ff. 76–7 (21 July 1796).
29 *View of the Constitution and History of Anderson's Institution*, separately paginated, bound in *Report by the Mangers to the Trustees* (1832?), 4. Copy in University of Strathclyde Archives and Special Collections (OB/3/1); scan kindly supplied by Dr Anne Cameron.
30 And. MM, vol. 1, ff. 85–7 (21 September 1796).
31 Ibid., vol. 1, f. 83 (1 September 1796). On Headrick, see Burns, 'Twilight of the Enlightenment'.

32   Conditions agreed to by the managers on 12 September before their endorsement by the trustees on 21 September; And. MM, vol. 1, ff. 83 and 86 (12 and 21 September 1796). Garnett's letter of 6 September, referred to in the minutes, is now lost.
33   Anon., 'Dr Garnet [sic], M. D.', 409–10.
34   And. MM, vol. 1, f. 94 (2 November 1796).
35   For the advertisement, prepared by Garnett and approved by the managers, see And. MM, vol. 1, ff. 90–3 (24 October 1796); reproduced in Muir, *John Anderson*, 98–9.
36   On the Trades Hall, see Denholm, *History of the City of Glasgow*, 1st edn. (1798), 119–21; 3rd edn. (1804), 201–3.
37   And. MM, vol. 1, f. 92 and Muir, *John Anderson*, 99.
38   Will, article 9, in Muir, *John Anderson*, 146–7.
39   And. MM, vol. 1, f. 116 (28 April 1797). See also the account in Garnett, *Tour through the Highlands* (1800), vol. 2, 193–205. Cited hereafter as Garnett, *Tour*.
40   And. MM, vol. 1, f. 116 (28 April 1797).
41   Garnett, *Tour*, vol. 2, 202–5. On Garnett as a champion of women's education at the Andersonian and subsequently at the Royal Institution, see Smith, 'Retaking the register', 317–19.
42   Financial summary for 1796–7, in And. MM, vol. 1, 135 (19 June 1797).
43   And. MM, vol. 1, ff. 106–7 (20 March 1797).
44   Ibid., vol. 1, 109–11 (22 March 1797).
45   Garnett, *Outlines of a Course of Lectures on Natural & Experimental Philosophy* (1796) and *Outlines of a Course of Lectures on Chemistry* (1797).
46   Garnett, *Course of Lectures on Chemistry*, esp. lectures 5, 10, 24–8, and 55–9.
47   And. MM, vol. 1, 113–14 (20 April 1797).
48   The passage from early enthusiasm for the proposal to its final abandonment can be traced in discussions in And. MM, vol. 1, 114 (20 April 1797), 115 (28 April 1797), 149 (5 October 1797), 151–2 (30 October 1797) and 153 (7 December 1797).
49   Garnett to Watt, 24 January 1797, James Watt papers, Library of Birmingham, MS 3219/4/29/42. I am grateful to Frank James for drawing this correspondence to my attention.
50   Carmichael to Watt, 9 February 1797, ibid., MS 3219/4/29/33.
51   Watt to Garnett, 9 February 1797, ibid., Copy press letter book. 1797–1803, letter 3.
52   Cf. Garnett, *Lecture on the Preservation of Health* (1797), 6–32 with the presentation of Brown's system in his RMS dissertation 'In what does life consist?', RMS diss., vol. 21 (1787–8), dissertation no. XI. In the 'Preservation of health' lecture, Garnett generously acknowledged his debt to 'the much injured and unfortunate author of the *Elementa medicinae*', rather than to Brown by name; see Preface, iv.

53 Garnett, *Preservation of Health*, ii; 2nd edn (London, 1800), ii.
54 And. MM, vol. 1, ff. 147–50 (5 October 1797), on advertising for the new year's courses.
55 And. MM, vol. 1, ff. 156–9 (21 December 1797), where twenty-seven of the eighty-one trustees are recorded as disqualifying themselves by their absence from six meetings.
56 Advertisement in *Glasgow Courier*, 16 November 1797.
57 And. MM, vol. 1, ff. 167–77, recording meetings of managers and trustees between 15 and 21 March 1798.
58 Duncan, *Faculty of Physicians and Surgeons*, 267.
59 Dodd, *Annual Biography ... MDCCCXLII* (1843), 457–8.
60 Garnett, *Tour*, vol. 1, 1–2.
61 In a rich secondary literature on the genre, I am especially indebted to Leask, *Stepping Westward*.
62 Pennant, *Tour in Scotland MDCCLXIX* (1771) and *Tour in Scotland MDCCLXXII* (1774–6); both republished in later editions, most recently in 1790. For modern perspectives on Pennant, see Leask, *Stepping Westward*, esp. ch. 3 and Constantine and Leask, eds., *Enlightenment Travel and British Identities*, a collection of essays arising from the 'Curious travellers' project of the University of Wales Centre for Advanced Welsh and Celtic Studies and the University of Glasgow between 2014 and 2018. The website *curioustravellers.ac.uk* is a valuable resource on Pennant's and other domestic tourism in the mountainous regions of Wales and Scotland. I am grateful for exchanges with Dr Constantine and Professor Leask, the joint leaders of the project.
63 Garnett, *Tour*, vol. 1, v. S. G. E. Lythe notes the irregular pattern of attribution of borrowed material in his *Garnett*, esp. 32.
64 Gilpin, *Three Essays* (1792), esp. 'Essay I. On picturesque beauty', 1–33. On Gilpin in Scotland, see Leask, *Stepping Westward*, 171–9.
65 On landscape and picturesque taste, see Andrews, *Search for the Picturesque*, esp. 39–66 and (on Highland tourism) 196–240.
66 Garnett, *Tour*, vol. 2, 47.
67 Ibid., vol. 1, 10. Cf. Gilpin, *Observations Made in the Year 1776*, vol. 2, 55.
68 Garnett, *Tour*, vol. 1, 11. Cf. Gilpin, *Observations*, vol. 2, 46.
69 Garnett, *Tour*, vol. 2, 47. Cf. Gilpin, *Observations*, vol. 1, 140–1.
70 Garnett, *Tour*, vol. 1, 174–8 and vol. 2, 241–57.
71 Ibid., vol. 1, vii.
72 Ibid., vol. 2, 129–32 and 240–57. Lightly edited versions of the account of the Moffat waters appeared in *Med. Phys. J.*, 2 (1799), 354–60 and as *Observations on Moffat* (1800).
73 Garnett, *Tour*, vol. 1, 174–8. And see ch. 3, 68–9.
74 Lythe, *Garnett*, 31.

75 Garnett, *Tour*, vol. 1, 217–43.
76 'Account of Staffa, communicated by Joseph Banks, Esq.', in Pennant, *Tour in Scotland MDCCLXXII*, part I, 299–309.
77 See Pococke, *Irish Tours*, 197–205 for Pococke's accounts of the Giant's Causeway, from *Phil. Trans.*, 45 (1748), 124–7 and 48 (1753), 226–37.
78 Garnett, *Tour*, vol. 1, 235.
79 For Hamilton's Vulcanism, see his *Letters concerning the Northern Coast of the County of Antrim*, esp. 137–73.
80 Knox, *View of the British Empire*, i–ii.
81 Garnett, *Tour*, vol. 1, 184.
82 Ibid., vol. 1, vi.
83 Ibid., vol. 2, 149–58.
84 Ibid., vol. 1, 276–7. The original passage was in the report of the Revd Patrick McDonald, minister of the united parishes of Kilmore and Kilbride, in Sinclair, *Statistical Account*, vol. 11 (1794), 121–37 (126–7n.)
85 Smith, *Agriculture of the County of Argyll*, esp. 24–38 and 51–6.
86 Garnett, *Tour*, *passim*, but see especially vol. 1, 159–91 and 296–301.
87 Sinclair, *Address to the Society for the Improvement of British Wool*, 11. Sinclair was addressing the newly founded Society for the Improvement of British Wool in 1791.
88 Garnett, *Tour*, vol. 1, 271–2 and 296–301.
89 Ibid., vol. 2, 31.
90 Ibid., vol. 2, 187–91.
91 Cf. Johnson's rejection of Ossian's poems as a fabrication of Macpherson's that had 'never existed in any other form than that which we have seen'; Johnson, *Journey to the Western Islands*, 273.
92 Garnett, *Tour*, vol. 1, 285.
93 Ibid., vol. 2, 236–7.
94 Ibid., vol. 2, 231–7 (236).
95 Butt, *Anderson's Legacy*, 29–31.
96 Described in Garnett, *Tour*, vol. 2, 193–205, and more briefly in Denholm, *History of the City of Glasgow*, 3rd edn. (1804), 328–33.
97 Garnett, *Tour*, vol. 2, 185.
98 Watson, *History of the Literary and Philosophical Society of Newcastle-upon-Tyne*, 206–7.
99 Garnett to Ortt, 1 January 1799, in 'Life of Garnett', xiv–xv.
100 Garnett to William Cleveland, 2 January 1799, Strathclyde MSS, GB 249 OM/64/2/1. Also in Hardy, *Benenden Letters*, 263–4.
101 And. MM, 7 and 21 March 1799, ff. 216 and 222.
102 Ibid., 21 June 1799, ff. 226–8.

103 Ibid., 28 August 1799, ff. 239–40.
104 Anon., 'Dr. Garnet, M.D.', in the Dublin edition of *Public Characters of 1799–1800*, 317–18 and the earlier of the two London printings of 1799, 421–2. The mention of political attacks on Garnett is omitted from the later London edition.

5

London

Trials and tragedy in Mayfair

The initiative that took Garnett to London had been maturing in the same winter months of 1798–9 in which his life had passed from the happiness of anticipation of the birth of his second child to shock and grief following Catherine's death. The first he knew of the initiative was through a letter he received from Rumford in May 1799. The purpose of the letter was to ask for his views on the rapidly developing plans for what had been constituted two months earlier as 'the Institution' and was soon to be formally designated the Royal Institution of Great Britain.[1] The RI's core aim of promoting science in its application to manufacturing and agriculture had much in common with the Andersonian's, and news of the venture in Glasgow made Garnett an object of particular interest, initially as a source of advice and four months later, in September, as the institution's choice as its professor. A move from the booming port and capital of Scottish industry to the world of refined metropolitan culture was not one to which, in normal circumstances, he would necessarily have aspired. He had fitted well in Glasgow and, until the death of his wife, shown no inclination to leave, to the point of planning to renovate an 'old but substantial house' near Moffat as a family retreat.[2] But a combination of his personal tragedy and the Andersonian's precarious finances effectively made the decision for him, and he was soon set on a path that would test his capacity for adaptation to new circumstances more searchingly than ever before.

The Royal Institution: Science and improvement

By the time Garnett arrived in London, on 23 December 1799, the Royal Institution had begun to acquire a distinctive character and profile of support. An aspect of the RI's founding mission that would have appealed to him was its philanthropic concern with the challenges of industrialization, especially the privations and social conflicts that had escalated across Britain in the war-torn years of the 1790s. Crucial in this were the wealth and generosity of Thomas Bernard, the Harvard-educated son of the governor of the colonial provinces of New Jersey and then Massachusetts Bay. By now long-established in London as a barrister and energetic promoter of good works, Bernard had taken a leading role in the recently formed Society for Bettering the Condition and Increasing the Comforts of the Poor. Through the Society, commonly known as the 'Bettering Society', he had found ample scope for his charitable objectives but also struck personal alliances that did much to fashion the profile of opportunities and constraints within which Garnett would have to work in his new post.

The most important of Bernard's alliances was the one he had cultivated with Rumford through personal contacts and correspondence since the spring of 1797. Through his own experience of a childhood in colonial America, Rumford had natural common ground with Bernard. Born and brought up in Massachusetts, he had married early into a family of some wealth and influence and seemed set for a life of prosperous stability. But with the coming of the American Revolution, his fortunes had taken a colourful turn: first to military service in the loyalist cause, then on to a knighthood by George III, eleven years as aide-de-camp to the Prince Elector of Bavaria, during which he was made a Count of the Holy Roman Empire, and finally, in September 1798, appointment by the Elector as the Bavarian Minister Plenipotentiary and Envoy Extraordinary to the Court of St James.[3] When he arrived from Bavaria, in mid-September, he believed that he was coming to take up his ambassadorial position. The British government, though, refused to recognize him, on the grounds that he had all along been a subject of the king. And it was with the diplomatic avenue suddenly closed that he threw in his lot with Bernard's philanthropic mission.

Once Rumford was established in London, the meeting of minds between him and Bernard was cemented in both friendship (though this eventually soured) and their shared ideals of public welfare, mainly in Rumford's case through improved kitchens and stoves for heating. Through Bernard, Rumford met a number of leading figures in the Bettering Society who were to have crucial roles in the founding of the RI, among them the slavery reformer William Wilberforce and George, ninth Earl of Winchilsea and Nottingham. Their support, along with Bernard's, was enough to ensure action, and Rumford was soon at work on the detailed proposals and appeal for support for the new institution. His draft appeal was approved at a meeting of the Bettering Society, chaired by Shute Barrington, Bishop of Durham, on 1 February 1799, and a month later a definitive fifty-page version, *Proposals for Forming by Subscription ... a Public Institution*, launched what was now an independent project into the public domain.

The call was for subscriptions at three levels: perpetual proprietors, subscribing a minimum sum of fifty guineas; life subscribers, paying ten guineas; and annual subscribers, paying two guineas per annum. The levels were pitched astutely, and the call, crucially endorsed by the president of the Royal Society, Sir Joseph Banks, was an instant success. On 7 March, at Banks' London home, a first meeting of proprietors, already numbering 58, formally approved the next step of petitioning the king for a royal charter.[4] And within days 500 further copies of the *Proposals*, printed free of charge by the booksellers Cadell and Davies, were ready for distribution to individually targeted recipients.[5] The campaign that followed captured imaginations and opened pockets. By 1 May 1799, the number of proprietors stood at 132, in addition to 70 life subscribers and 72 annual subscribers. The result was a financial base that had already made it possible to negotiate with the family of the late William Mellish, a prominent government administrator and M.P., for the purchase of a property and adjacent garden space at 21 Albemarle Street for £4,500 and to begin fitting out what has been the RI's home ever since.[6] A body of nine managers, required to meet weekly, and a more detached committee of visitors, both groups chosen from among the proprietors, sustained the momentum through a busy summer. The agreement by Winchilsea, well placed at court though better known for his patronage of cricket, to serve as the Institution's president completed an imposing list of aristocratic and other gentlemanly officers. With such backing, the grant of the title 'Royal' became a formality, delivered after a conversation between Winchilsea and the king in June.[7]

As defined in the *Proposals* and, in slightly different words, the *Prospectus of the Royal Institution of Great Britain* (a promotional publication that followed some months later), the aim of the RI was two-fold: to diffuse the knowledge and application of 'useful mechanical inventions and improvements' and to teach 'the application of science to the common purposes of life'.[8] To those complementary ends, manufacturers, enlightened landowners and men of science were to be brought together in a common pursuit of improvement. In seeking the realization of the long-familiar rhetoric about the benefits of a union of science and practice, the programme was aiming high. As presented by Rumford, however, it had the concrete quality of a project well on its way to fulfilment. In the immediately utilitarian spirit of the institution, there would be a permanent exhibition of models and other objects that would 'fix the attention, and determine the choice' of workmen and manufacturers and so advance best practice and innovations of the functional kind that were his personal priorities.[9] Science, for its part, would be served in more conventional ways. There would be a library of books and learned journals, a laboratory equipped for 'chemical and philosophical experiments', and a room for lectures on 'Natural Philosophy and Philosophical Chemistry', supplemented as appropriate by lectures on specific trades and techniques: here, 'men of the first eminence in science' would be appointed to officiate.[10] As was soon to become apparent, the dual structure harboured the seeds of a tension that was to have damaging consequences during and beyond Garnett's time as professor. But, for the moment, the rhetoric of a marriage of scientific and utilitarian interests struck a responsive chord with the metropolitan and land-owning elites from which the RI drew its main promoters.

The chain of events that culminated in the appointment of Garnett is poorly documented. What we do know is that by early May 1799, Rumford and two other managers, the distinguished lawyer and diplomat Sir John Coxe Hippisley and the writer and future Baronet Richard Sullivan, had had discussions with the Revd William Farish, the professor of chemistry at Cambridge. The plan they discussed was for Farish to offer a one-off inaugural course of lectures, to begin in December and run through to the following February.[11] For this, Farish was a safe choice. As an evangelical clergyman with a commitment to philanthropy, a Senior Wrangler and First Smith's Prizeman when he graduated from Cambridge in 1778, and a successful lecturer with interests embracing mechanics, naval architecture and the applications of chemistry, he combined outstanding intellectual achievement and proven charitable interests with an openness, rare among Cambridge professors, to the worlds of industry and agriculture. The headings of the lectures on 'arts and manufactures' that he had given in Cambridge in 1796 show how well he would have fitted in the emerging plans for the RI.[12] Despite Farish's early show of interest, however, the discussions came to nothing. He declined the engagement and stayed in his university post.[13]

It was in the wake of Farish's withdrawal, and with the pace gathering, that Rumford made his initial approach to Garnett later in May and renewed the search for the RI's first and (as was intended at this stage) only professor. There is no record of further exchanges with Garnett during the summer. But by the time the managers authorized Rumford to engage him on 14 September, the terms of the appointment were precisely defined. Garnett's title would be 'Professor & Public Lecturer in experimental Philosophy, Mechanics, & Chymistry', modified soon afterwards to 'Professor of Natural Philosophy and Chemistry'.[14] In addition, he would be expected to act as scientific secretary to the RI and to edit its *Journals*, an occasional (and never very successful) bulletin of reports on administrative matters, lectures and publications originating in the RI, with brief notices of other books and communications, especially at the Royal Society. The annual salary of £300 (with the expressed possibility of an increase to £500, if and when funds allowed) was adequate rather than conspicuously generous. But it was significantly more than he had been paid at the Andersonian and came with the added attraction of lodgings in the Institution. Most importantly, it offered the fresh start that he desperately needed.

When Garnett's letter of resignation came before the Andersonian's managers on 15 October, the good will towards him was evident. They immediately expressed their warm thanks for 'the unremitted attention he has paid to the interest of the Institution' and wished him 'every happiness and success in the enlarged, and venerable sphere he is called to act in'.[15] Two days later, a specially summoned meeting of the trustees endorsed the managers' acceptance of the resignation.[16] It was a measure of the managers' and trustees' satisfaction with what Garnett had achieved that they moved immediately to fill the chair and even acted on his recommendation of George Birkbeck, a younger friend and fellow-northerner, as his successor.[17] In appointing the twenty-three-year-old Birkbeck, they were acquiring another professor in the 'hardy progeny' mould. As a Yorkshireman from Settle (less than twenty miles from Barbon), a pupil of John Dawson (in the early 1790s, when he was living close to Sedbergh) and a recent graduate in medicine from Edinburgh (where he had been prominent in the Royal Medical Society), Birkbeck had much in common with Garnett.[18] Before going to Edinburgh, and probably on Dawson's advice, he had even worked as a pupil of Garnett's in Knaresborough in 1792–3, and it was his time there that had determined his vocation in medicine rather than in the mixed family business of wool-combing and banking. Birkbeck never forgot his debt to Garnett, and Garnett in turn must have been gratified to be leaving such a kindred spirit in the post that the tragic turn in his personal circumstances had led him to vacate.[19]

Once Garnett had made his decision, practical considerations crowded in. Transporting his personal effects to London would have been complicated enough. But the sixteen cases of his scientific instruments, many of them by the leading London maker George Adams, presented a special challenge: insurance cover of £300 for the sea-passage from Leith reflects the quality of what was already a rich collection.[20] For Garnett, though, no priority was higher than the welfare of his daughters. From Glasgow he took them to Barbon and prepared to leave them there, in his parents' home and in the care of Mary Worboys, pending (as he hoped) their joining him in Albemarle Street. It was a consequence of his troubled year that Catherine Grace's baptism took place only now, on 19 November in Kirkby Lonsdale, when she was almost a year old. The baptism must have been a poignant family occasion, given added significance by the imminence of Garnett's departure for an unknown metropolitan destination far from his roots.[21]

Albemarle Street

In London, Garnett found physical preparations for the RI moving ahead, albeit rather fitfully. As early as 5 June, work on 21 Albemarle Street had been sufficiently advanced for the managers to begin meeting there,[22] and through the summer of 1799, the number of proprietors and subscribers had continued to grow. In September, the appointment of a young Scottish architect, Thomas Webster, as an energetic new clerk of works, with the additional duties from September as clerk to the RI, had given new momentum to the refitting and enlargement of the building.[23] But in December improvisation rather than orderly implementation remained the order of the day. For Garnett, this only added to what would in any circumstances have been the formidable task of settling in at an institution still finding its feet. Since he had had no face-to-face discussions with the managers, indeed with anyone from the RI, he knew little of what was expected of him and even less of Rumford, the man with whom he would be working most closely. A particular source of frustration was Rumford's absence; he was not to return to London until the end of January, following nearly five months away, mainly spent travelling in Britain for his health. How, without the guidance and support that he might reasonably have hoped to receive, was Garnett, himself an unknown quantity, to affirm his position? Some in RI circles may have read his publications on the Harrogate spa waters or even taken the waters themselves. Otherwise, he came as an outsider with a professorial reputation fashioned in a country and culture unfamiliar to the great majority of the Institution's promoters. It was a situation fraught with potential difficulty.

Being left to his own devices added a layer of complexity to Garnett's immediate priority of preparing for his lectures. Following an outline that he had addressed to the managers (at Rumford's request) just before his move to London, he planned to tackle the full range of both natural philosophy and chemistry, as he had done at the Andersonian.[24] There was continuity also in his decision to maintain a distinction between two types of audience: one attending 'chiefly for amusement or because it may be fashionable', the other for 'instruction'. His initial proposal was that he should give eight lectures a week spread over eighteen to twenty weeks, which would have been an even greater burden than he had shouldered in Glasgow. Rumford was clearly pleased with the plan, and the tone of a letter he wrote to Garnett (whom he had yet to meet) on 26 January was encouraging:

> I am much delighted to find you have made such rapid progress in your preparations. I hope no expense will be spared in providing suitable apparatus for your Course of Lectures, and that the Experiments will all be made on a large scale and in all respects in a manner worthy of the Royal Institution of Great Britain.[25]

Already, however, Rumford harboured reservations. Two weeks earlier, these had surfaced privately in a letter to Banks in which he expressed his clear preference for Webster, of whom Banks, too, evidently thought well:

> I am very glad indeed that you like Webster. I am much deceived if he does not turn out to be a very useful acquisition. I hope Dr. Garnett will do well, but I must own that I am not as prepossessed in his favour as I am in favour of Webster.[26]

It was, at best, a hollow expression of support for Garnett, and a first encounter at the beginning of February did nothing to calm Rumford's reservations.

Despite the signs of incipient tension, Garnett's lectures got off to a good, if delayed, start on 11 March. By now, he had trimmed the number of weekly lectures to six. But what remained, however, was still a gruelling schedule.[27] The more popular, 'early' lectures would be delivered on Tuesdays (on experimental philosophy) and Thursdays and Saturdays (on chemistry) at 2 pm; these lectures would be illustrated by 'interesting & pleasing Experiments', and they would last only one hour, 'that the Attention may not be fatigued'. For the necessarily smaller public seeking 'instruction', Garnett offered something more demanding: 'a full & scientific course of experimental Philosophy, on the plan generally adopted in Universities' on Mondays, Wednesdays and Fridays at 8 pm. In these lectures, working models would be used, though only as adjuncts to a mathematical underpinning of mechanics, hydrostatics, hydraulics and pneumatics, and a systematic coverage of applications in 'the mechanical and chemical arts'. The full course promised to be a serious, not to say austere affair. But large admiring audiences for both this and the popular courses suggest that Garnett performed at both levels with his old flair.

Flair, though, did not imply showmanship, and there was nothing showy about Garnett's lectures, whichever audience he addressed. One obituarist, who had evidently known him well, remembered a sober style, reinforced by judiciously placed practical demonstrations, that distinguished him from more flamboyant lecturers:

> He did not use the rhetorical action and declamation, which so frequently impose on the world, and which, in matters of science, are perhaps worse than useless. What he said was easily apprehended, and he never allowed an opportunity to escape of illustrating and confirming by experiment what he had advanced in theory.[28]

In the same vein, another unidentified acquaintance described him as 'too modest for a shining orator, even if his subjects had admitted of oratory'; yet 'his style was good, and his illustrations, to those who could not be expected to understand his demonstrations, apt and luminous'.[29]

It seems clear that with Garnett's methodical approach there went a certain dryness. Jane Ewbank, the daughter of a York pharmacist, who probably heard him in his last, difficult months at the RI, found his delivery 'ungraceful', even 'automaton-like'.[30] At the same time, however, she appreciated his habit of pausing and repeating things, so as to be understood and leave time for notetaking. This was in sharp contrast with Henry Moyes, whose lectures (which she attended in York) were 'all grace and animation', but often difficult to follow. Ewbank's Garnett comes across as more of a pedagogue than a performer or entertainer. That, though, was his strength. At the RI, as at the Andersonian, clarity and careful preparation were the foundation for the calm authority that comes across in Thomas Phillips' striking portrait of him in his prime (see Figure 5.1).

Studiedly untheatrical though his manner appears to have been, Garnett's success as a lecturer was crucial to the surge of support for the RI through the first half of 1800. By 1 May, the number of proprietors had more than doubled in a year, to 281, while the numbers of life subscribers (267) and annual subscribers (413) had increased even more dramatically.[31] All this despite material conditions that left much to be desired. The lecture-theatre, in a first-floor room (now one of the main rooms of the library), was a makeshift installation, created by knocking two rooms into one. A draft plan, one of a number apparently sketched by Webster, suggests that Garnett may have lectured from a raised dais in the centre of the room, surrounded on all four sides by rows of seats at floor level and on a small gallery (see Figure 5.2).[32]

Figure 5.1 Portrait of Garnett as professor of natural philosophy at the Royal Institution. Stipple engraving by Simon Phillips, after a painting by Thomas Phillips, now lost. Garnett's commanding pose, with one hand holding a book, the other on the receiver of an air pump, conveys the authority associated with a man of learning, though one who also engaged in the active investigation of nature. The engraving is dated 1 May 1801, only a month before Garnett's unhappiness at the RI forced his resignation. But his confident appearance suggests an earlier date for the original painting, probably during his first year as professor. Courtesy of the Wellcome Collection. Public Domain Mark.

Figure 5.2 One of two surviving designs for the temporary lecture-theatre at the Royal Institution. The lecturer is shown on a dais in the centre of the room (now part of the library on the first floor of the RI), with ladies seated in the lower rows. Although the designs bear no signature, they are thought to be by Thomas Webster, clerk of works, then clerk, to the RI. The design is in the Drawings & Archives Collection of the Royal Institute of British Architects (SD/55/4/6). Courtesy of RIBA Collections.

Whatever the precise arrangement, it was a recipe for claustrophobia rather than comfort. The always vociferous Sir John Coxe Hippisley judged the space wholly inadequate in size, and uninviting in its disposition. It was not just that barely half of the current subscribers could be accommodated. More off-putting, as Hippisley put it in a report to his fellow managers, were seating arrangements of such inconvenience as to call for 'a superabundance of scientific ardour' on the part of those attending. This promised to be a particular impediment for the more than a hundred lady subscribers, to whose presence he, like Garnett, attached a high priority. His description, with its implied criticism of Webster and its evocation of Garnett's success in attracting women to his lectures at the Andersonian, was damning:

> We invite ladies to subscribe; & our Professor informs us, that the Fair Sex constituted a large Proportion (& not the least observant) of his numerous Auditors, which sometimes bordered on 1000 Persons. The Ladies of this

Metropolis are not the earliest attendants at public assemblies; and with us, unless they should be early enough to occupy the two or three lowest Ranges of seats, no Female of Condition or Delicacy can find suitable accommodation.[33]

The conditions, of course, were trying for everyone concerned, including Garnett himself. Other worries accumulated, too. Even as his lectures were winning praise, Garnett was conscious of being disadvantaged in a structure that gave Rumford an ease of access to the managers from which he himself was excluded. Things had been very different at the Andersonian, where the managers had made a point of engaging with him and inviting him to attend at least some of their meetings. A smouldering divergence of opinion among the managers and leading subscribers as to where the balance of the RI's priorities should lie did not help either. While Rumford recognized the importance of the refined audiences whose subscriptions sustained the institution, his primary goal remained the instruction of artisans and labourers. In this, he drew on his alliance with Webster, who had arrived with previous experience of teaching workmen and now wished to implement a proposal for a Royal Institution school for mechanics that he had put to Rumford before Garnett's arrival.[34] The alliance set Rumford at odds, in particular, with Hippisley, whose prominence in the worlds of law and diplomacy drew him more naturally to the interests of the RI's society following.[35] Also in the Hippisley camp was Bernard, now the treasurer of the RI and increasingly uneasy about Rumford's preoccupation with boilers, culinary gadgets and the like. By the summer of 1800, relations between Rumford and his critics had deteriorated badly. In a statement that smacked more of bravado than of calm judgement, Rumford boasted (to his Swiss friend Marc-Auguste Pictet) that he had seen off 'those who attempted to wrest the affairs of the Institution out of my hands, in order to put themselves at the head of this new Establishment'.[36] The truth is that his critics were still fighting their corner. The tensions were far from over.

The divide on such a fundamental matter of policy left Garnett uncomfortably positioned between the factions. His own view had always been, and it remained, that it was possible for the worlds of cultivated discourse and practical teaching to co-exist, at the RI as they had done at the Andersonian. But the success of his lectures to audiences seeking 'amusement' and his perceived lack of interest in the exhibition of models and machinery and the proposed school for artisans left him close, in Rumford's eyes, to Hippisley and Bernard. As the broader issue of the institution's mission played out, the prospect of anything approaching a friendly rapport between Rumford and Garnett receded.

Pressures on Garnett came from every quarter. The constant disruption and consultations to do with the building of the new lecture-theatre as part of a major extension to the north of the original Albemarle Street property took a relentless toll. And making things worse, as the year progressed, was the daily proximity of Rumford, who had moved into accommodation in the RI's house soon after arriving back in London on 31 January. The arrangement exposed Garnett to the full thrust of Rumford's authoritarian manner and aggravated his sense that, amid the ongoing internal strife about priorities, at least a faction among the managers was beginning to lose confidence in him and see him as a member of the anti-Rumford camp. An early warning sign was the managers' decision, on 31 March, to establish a standing committee to examine the syllabuses of lectures and superintend experimental work in chemistry and natural philosophy; the so-called 'Scientific Committee of Council', with men of the eminence of Henry Cavendish, William Farish, Charles Blagden and Nevil Maskelyne among its initial nine members, had no place for Garnett.[37] Along with a resolution of the managers that Rumford should oversee, and in effect take over, the composition, publication and sale of the planned but as yet unlaunched *Journals*, the measure struck pointedly at Garnett's authority, the more so as Rumford's impact on the project was immediate; the first issue of the *Journals* appeared within days.

Two months on, Rumford's critical oversight of Garnett had another menacing consequence, this time in an unpleasant and all too public spat following a lecture on 28 May in which Garnett had mistakenly attributed the recent invention of the electric pile to 'the French philosophers' rather than to Alessandro Volta. News of what appears to have been an innocent misstatement during Garnett's demonstration of the pile (the first public demonstration in Britain) had immediately reached Joseph Banks, probably through his friend Charles Blagden. The lecture had not been a success. As described in Blagden's diary, it had been a bungling affair, not surprisingly perhaps, given the novelty of the apparatus, which Garnett had borrowed from the pharmacist and meteorologist Luke Howard.[38] What mattered, however, was not the quality of the lecture but its timing. Since Volta had announced his experiments in a personal letter of 20 March 1800 to Banks that had not yet been presented before the Royal Society, still less published in the *Philosophical Transactions*, Banks felt a proprietary interest in the information and was irked by the leak.[39]

Banks' sense of privileged ownership has to be seen as distinctly contrived. In the spring of 1800, William Nicholson and Anthony Carlisle were already engaged in intense, though unannounced research on the properties of the pile, notably its capacity to decompose water into its constituent elements.

Nevertheless, Banks' irritation was enough for Rumford to take his side and, within a day of the lecture, to issue a peremptory written rebuke to Garnett.[40] On the following day, 30 May, the affair took a graver turn when the *Morning Chronicle* carried the first published account of the pile in English, how to build it and what it could do.[41] The danger for Garnett's relations with Rumford was that the account was plainly based on his lecture of two days before. With reports multiplying in an eager press, both in Britain and abroad, the loss of control of the news provided Rumford with a golden opportunity of at once pleasing Banks and further disciplining Garnett. What followed was an exercise in calculated humiliation. In his next lecture, Rumford wrote to Banks, Garnett would be required to read a lengthy prepared statement acknowledging his mistake and confirming unequivocally that the discovery belonged to Volta alone.[42]

The ending of the RI year promised Garnett at least temporary relief from the tide of harassment. On 9 June, as soon as his lectures ended, he left to join his daughters and Mary Worboys in Barbon, after assuring the managers that he would make himself available for consultation at any time in the long period before his courses were to resume.[43] He must have had high hopes of the benefits of his time away. Through what had been a lonely first winter in London, separation from Louisa and Catherine had taken a heavy toll. And the managers', and Rumford's, uncompromising opposition to his expectation that they would come to live with him had deepened the wound, despite the unrealistic prospect of anything approaching a comfortable family life in the two rooms allotted to him as living space on the second floor.

Pleased though he was to see his daughters again, revisiting his old haunts in Westmorland had the effect of lowering, rather than raising, his spirits. In a state of such vulnerability, he must have been especially hurt by the unsigned review of his *Tour through the Highlands* that appeared in the May and August issues of the *Critical Review*, a Tory monthly with a reputation for acerbic reviewing. The reviewer focused unsparingly, and with some justice, on the work's digressions, loose composition and lack of originality, all of them signs of the haste and distracting circumstances in which it had been written. A smattering of perfunctory praise did something to soften the disparagement: most of Watts' illustrations were judged to be 'clear, beautiful, and appropriate', and Garnett's descriptions were 'clear and intelligible, without the obscurity, we had almost said the cant, of the picturesque artist'.[44] Garnett, though, could not expect a periodical that prided itself on its loyalty to the classical tradition to treat him gently. His belief in the authenticity of Ossian's Celtic poems marked him as a breaker of the established literary mould. And he could hardly have been surprised to see the case he made in the *Tour* for learning modern rather than ancient languages dismissed as 'a trite declamation' typical of 'the cant of modern reformers'.[45] Responding to Garnett's argument against 'tormenting the young mind ... with studying Latin and Greek for seven years', the reviewer fell back on the traditional conservative defence of a well-tried preparation that had done so much to fashion the nation's 'men of knowledge and science'. Such comments mapped the dividing lines unerringly and measured the mountain of entrenched opinion against which Garnett's reforming instincts had to struggle, perhaps as much in his own head as in his published statements.

The summer months of 1800 were made all the more painful for Garnett by events back at the RI. He had barely left London when his able, if rather erratic, laboratory assistant John Sadler, the son of the pioneer balloonist James Sadler, was discharged along with the porter, housekeeper and one of the two housemaids.[46] The managers followed Rumford in justifying the dismissals as a necessary economy at a time when building work was in any case likely to disrupt the RI's normal functions. Garnett, though, saw the move against Sadler as a hostile act that would only add to his already heavy workload. An opportunistic intervention by Webster, suggesting that he might fill the gap left by Sadler's departure, only heightened his apprehension. Garnett rightly saw the hand of Rumford behind the approach, and his reply to Webster's letter to him in Barbon was deliberately guarded, though polite enough.[47] Was Webster, despite his 'industry and abilities', prepared for the hard work and 'many dirty jobs' that the post of 'operator' involved, especially in preparing the chemical lectures? At the very least, by way of preparation, he would have to follow 'an autumnal course of lectures', which itself raised the spectre of a lengthy delay before he was fully trained. Webster's reply conveyed a readiness to adjust to whatever might best serve Garnett's and the RI's interests.[48] But it seems unlikely that the matter went any further.

It was no easy matter to deal with such problems from two hundred miles away. By the time Garnett returned to London after the summer, his confidence was at a low ebb. And things took a further turn in November, when Rumford came back to the RI, after a four-month absence, mainly in Harrogate (for the waters) and Edinburgh, to discover that Garnett had arranged for the syllabuses of the courses he was to deliver in the forthcoming session to be printed without consulting him or any of the other officers or managers. The syllabuses, based on the ones Garnett had put out for his lecture-series at the Andersonian, were innocuous enough.[49] Nevertheless, Rumford's feelings ran high, the more so as he had no choice but to accept that it was too late for them to be withdrawn.

His remedy, predictably, was a mechanism for even more rigorous control, now through a three-man committee, of Banks, Cavendish and himself, that would take over the task of vetting future course outlines from the already-coercive Scientific Committee of Council.[50]

The measure put Garnett firmly in his place and set the tone for another tense winter. By early January 1801, Rumford was searching for an assistant for the chemical lectures, with a determination and ulterior motives of which Garnett would have been all too aware. Responding to Rumford's request for advice, Thomas Charles Hope, Black's successor as professor of chemistry at Edinburgh, recommended Humphry Davy, superintendent of the laboratory of Thomas Beddoes' Medical Pneumatic Institution in Bristol, where Hope had met him.[51] The same recommendation came from two other admirers of Davy: the young chemist and calico-printer James Thomson and Thomas Richard Underwood, geologist, RI proprietor and friend of Samuel Taylor Coleridge. The trio of Hope, Thomson and Underwood formed a persuasive lobby, and the scene was soon set for a hastily arranged meeting in London between Rumford and Davy. It was a decisive encounter. Though initially discomfited by Davy's manner and his association with a figure as radically inclined in politics as Beddoes, Rumford was quickly bowled over by him.

Davy was still only twenty-two and a relative newcomer to chemistry (which he had been studying for less than two years). Yet he had the aura of a rising star. He had already published a substantial essay in which he broached the idea that light could be considered as a chemical substance capable of combining with others.[52] He had also shown his mettle as a hands-on chemist in research on the chemical properties of nitrous oxide and other gases and the physiological effects of inhaling them.[53] It was partly through this work, allied to Beddoes' broader advocacy of pneumatic medicine, that laughing gas (as nitrous oxide had quickly come to be called) had attracted attention, even notoriety, for the sensations and behaviour it induced. James Thomson, Coleridge and Robert Southey were among the younger bloods who had experienced the pleasure of breathing it.[54] But when men of the stature and sobriety of James Watt, James Keir and others in and close to the Lunar Society circle showed an interest in the gas's medicinal properties as well, the connotations of louche conduct associated with its recreational use lost their force. That, at least, was so in Rumford's eyes. By mid-February, with the managers' approval, he had offered Davy ('a nice able man', as he described him soon afterwards in a letter to his daughter[55]) the combined post of assistant lecturer in chemistry, director of the chemical laboratory and assistant editor of the *Journals*.[56]

Discomfort and departure

Davy's appointment, albeit at a salary of only 100 guineas, compounded the assault on Garnett's position that had been in train for a year. The effect on him was immediately apparent in a bout of illness, probably again linked to depression. When he began the year's lectures, in February 1801, those attending found his manner 'languid and hesitating'.[57] The prospect of Davy's imminent arrival and residence in the RI was bad enough. But Rumford's decision to house him in one of the two rooms that Garnett had already furnished for himself and at his own expense raised provocation to a new level. And an offer to reimburse Garnett for his expenditure on chairs and a carpet for the room, now to be reallocated to the managers' room, only added insult.[58] Dismayed at the trimming of his quarters, Garnett discussed with Rumford the possibility of moving out of the building altogether and put the idea to the managers, via Rumford, with a request for an addition of £100 to his salary as compensation.[59] The managers declined to engage with the proposal and simply ignored Garnett's deferentially worded suggestion that they might in any case consider such an increase, in the light of their initial agreement of a possible future rise to £500. The excuse that nothing could be done until the accounts were made up and the RI's financial position was clearer left Garnett helpless. It was to take almost three months and a further approach from him before they responded.

In those three months, Garnett's already precarious situation continued to deteriorate. On the morning of 2 March 1801, with his confidence undermined and health problems bearing down on him, he reported to Rumford that he would be unable to lecture that evening.[60] As a temporary expedient, Rumford arranged for the Scottish chemist and physician Alexander Crichton, currently practising and lecturing at Westminster Hospital, to stand in for him, with similar ad hoc arrangements to follow so long as he remained unwell. Crichton accepted the invitation, and we must assume that he gave the lecture.[61] For Garnett, the episode was an embarrassment that made it all too easy for Rumford to present his withdrawal as a sign of weakness. Once Davy arrived in Albemarle Street, on 11 March, he too pitched in. Immediately, no doubt with Rumford's approval, he moved to affirm his ascendancy by launching a course of five evening lectures on galvanism, one of Garnett's favoured subjects. Both Rumford and Joseph Banks attended the first lecture, on 25 April, and found it enthralling; the rest of the audience, too, responded enthusiastically. Davy, emerging as a consummate performer, was exhilarated by the 'general applause' that greeted the lecture and presumably those that followed.[62]

By now, events were escalating fast. On 25 May, a month after Davy's dazzling first lecture, the managers gathered for a specially convened meeting that was to seal Garnett's fate. At the meeting, they finally agreed on their reply to his proposal of three months earlier (and to a follow-up letter from him on 11 May) about moving out of Albemarle Street, with financial compensation. They were in no mood for compromise, and they rejected the proposal.[63] No less menacingly, at the same meeting they approved a lengthy upbeat report from Rumford outlining the present state and 'probable future Prosperity and Utility' of the RI; the report, needless to say, made no mention of Garnett.[64] It would be hard to imagine a more calculated affront, and Davy's promotion from assistant lecturer to the rank of lecturer in chemistry a week later, albeit with an unchanged salary, soon removed any lingering illusions that Garnett may have had.[65] The show of favour to Davy, clearly already seen as Garnett's successor, was the last straw. On 3 June, two days after Davy's promotion, Garnett wrote to the managers offering his resignation.[66] When the managers met again, on 15 June, they moved quickly to accept the offer and settle with Garnett by paying the arrears of his salary, £200.[67]

Suddenly the field was clear for Rumford to recruit Davy to his personal priority of relaunching a lecture-programme that he felt had drifted away from the RI's core utilitarian mission. With Garnett gone (back, within days, to his daughters in Barbon), Rumford's hand was unmistakable in the managers' instruction that Davy should prepare short courses of lectures on the chemistry of tanning and dyeing and the arts of staining and colour printing on fabrics.[68] As soon became apparent, however, Davy's energies were not so easily channelled. The proposed courses never materialized, and while he compromised to the extent of incorporating a substantial section on 'the chemistry of the arts' in his new syllabus for 1802, his gifts as a society lecturer won out.[69] In a much-admired introductory lecture to his course in January 1802, he gave another dutiful nod to Rumford's demands in arguing for the relevance of chemistry to 'the processes and operations of common life'.[70] But in the same lecture, obedience yielded to passion in his evocation of a higher 'love of the beautiful and the sublime' that human beings expressed in pursuing the study of nature.[71] It was a vision with readier echoes in the nascent romanticism of Mary Shelley's *Frankenstein* than in the factory or workplace.[72]

Such flights were not what Rumford had expected of Davy. Yet, as he knew, the audiences that Davy attracted, numbering by his own count between 400 and 500, or more, drew prestige and income to the institution.[73] Increases in salary and, in May 1802, promotion to the rank of professor followed.[74] Rumford's departure for the Continent in the same month further strengthened Davy's position, as did the final abandonment of Rumford's and Webster's plans for the instruction of mechanics in the following year. Freed of these and most other constraints within the institution, Davy prospered, now with the cultivated persona of a man of genius (in Jan Golinski's characterization) rather than the purveyor of useful knowledge.[75] It was a freedom, above all from the overbearing Rumford (who never returned to England), that Garnett would have envied. But it all came too late.

The abruptness of the break with Garnett was reinforced, only three weeks after his departure, by the appointment of Thomas Young as professor of natural philosophy, editor of the *Journals* and superintendent of the RI's house.[76] Though still only twenty-eight, Young was a notable catch, and he knew it, as he showed in his brusque response to Rumford's offer of a salary of £225 rather than the £300 that was eventually agreed.[77] Like Davy, he was judged a success, albeit in a quite different way. His lecturing skills never matched Davy's; his 'too severe and didactic a style' made for a delivery that many in his inevitably dwindling audiences found pedestrian, and he made little effort to adjust.[78] But his status as an established metropolitan physician and Fellow of the Royal Society allowed him to move with ease in the medical and scientific circles of London and, in doing so, to play his part in raising the profile of the RI. In the event, he only stayed for two years, before resigning to allow more freedom for his medical and dazzlingly varied other interests, among them, a decade later, Egyptian hieroglyphs.[79] Nevertheless, it was in his short time as professor that he fashioned his wave theory of light and laid the foundations of his *Course of Lectures on Natural Philosophy and the Mechanical Arts*, a ground-breaking compendium of his own discoveries and the physics and 'mechanical arts' of his day, duly and eloquently acknowledged as the product of his time at the RI.[80]

The experience of Davy and Young as professors was a world away from that of the overworked Garnett, struggling to cope with both chemistry and natural philosophy and do so during the RI's troubled first two sessions. It was a matter for comment that Young gave as many as ninety-one lectures in his two years as professor.[81] That burden, however, pales by comparison with Garnett's load, both in the number and in the range of the lectures he was called upon to offer. As Garnett knew all too well, he deserved better. Yet, with time, memories of the debt the RI owed to him inevitably faded, and Davy, in particular, was happy to hasten the process. With a cavalier disregard for proprietary rights, he arranged for the 1801 edition of Garnett's *Outlines of a Course of Lectures on Chemistry* (the one to which Rumford had taken such objection) to be reissued as a companion volume to accompany his own first series of lectures. Only the title page, which had borne Garnett's name and which Davy replaced with one that gave no author, was changed. Over a year later, despite the new syllabus he put out in January 1802, Davy was still shamelessly distributing copies of Garnett's version of the *Outlines* as if they were his own work.[82]

Garnett's departure from the RI left him with yet another new future to fashion, once again in stressful circumstances. Dejected and bitter though he must have been, he responded positively by reviving his thoughts of returning to medical practice, allied to another reversion to an earlier existence, as an independent lecturer. It was with both activities in view that he purchased a lease on a property at 51 Great Marlborough Street, a fashionable address on the northern edge of Mayfair, and built a lecture-theatre at the house. How he financed the venture remains a mystery, though Cleveland money may well have helped. Even at a time of undimmed demand for both public lectures and medical care, vision and determination were essential if the new departure was to be a success, and Garnett displayed both. In a prime position on the front page of the *Times*, in October, he announced an introductory lecture, to be followed by what he appears to have conceived as a trial offering of two courses, each of fifteen lectures.[83] One, on experimental philosophy, would begin on Friday 6 November and continue on Monday and Friday evenings at 8 pm; the other, on chemistry, would be held on Tuesdays and Thursdays at 1 pm. There were to be the usual inducements of attractive demonstrations and up-to-date coverage, all at a guinea for each course, half a guinea for ladies. The combined charge of two guineas for both courses undercut the fee for annual subscribers to the RI, now increased to three guineas. But it left Garnett courting much the same clientele and doing so with the handicaps of a newcomer in a fiercely competitive field.

If he was to succeed, Garnett had to offer more than was available at the RI. Looking ahead, he envisaged an even richer programme to come. Before the end of January, as he promised, there would be lectures on the theory and practice of medicine, followed by a 'full' course on chemistry, including its applications to medicine and pharmacy. Through the winter of 1801–2, he delivered as much of this as his energies and time allowed. The eight courses that he is known to have given spanned the whole range of his interests: experimental philosophy and chemistry (two courses on each), mineralogy, botany (two courses, one delivered in Brompton, the other in his own lecture-theatre) and the vast subject that he called 'the animal economy'.[84] It was this last course, given at his home and repeated for medical students and others at Tom's Coffee House (one of at least three of that name known to exist in London at the time) that his executors published, two years after his death, as *Popular Lectures on Zoonomia*.[85] The pace was relentless, and now as so often in his life Garnett did nothing to protect himself. He even tried to continue as editor of *Annals of Philosophy, Natural History, Chemistry, Literature, Agriculture, and the Mechanical and Fine Arts*, an annual digest of reviews, reports and other scientific news that he had launched early in his time at the RI.[86] Although the work had never carried the institution's formal imprint, it had drawn on information and contacts to which his position as professor had given him unique access. Its first volume, of almost 500 pages covering the year 1800, was a monument to the high point of his tenure of the RI chair. Unnamed 'other gentlemen' were acknowledged to have played their part, but Garnett's personal diligence and familiarity with foreign as well as domestic publications, despite the disruption of the Revolutionary Wars, shone through. This was especially so in a strong coverage of chemistry and natural philosophy, including a lengthy opening article on the history and present state of galvanism, signed 'G', that was unmistakably his doing.[87]

As a private initiative managed by a single person, the *Annals* was a huge undertaking and, sustaining it without an institutional affiliation or the support of a patron or publisher, became an impossible task. The delayed and significantly reduced second volume, for 1801, on which he began work after leaving the RI, already bore the scars of his unfolding personal tragedy. In desperate need of relief, he ceded responsibility for even the sections on chemistry and natural philosophy to the brothers Arthur and Charles Rochemont Aikin, both emerging as public lecturers and prominent figures in scientific and medical circles in London.[88] All, though, in vain. After a slender third and last volume, covering 1802 but not published until 1804, a significant landmark in the history of information management and retrieval foundered, leaving Garnett's efforts unacknowledged and his venture virtually forgotten. In 1813, the new monthly *Annals of Philosophy* assumed the title and something of the style of the earlier initiative, under the editorship of the Scottish chemist Thomas Thomson. But a preface recording the new journal's debt to its precursors and rivals made no mention of the annual volumes that had been published a decade before.[89]

The faltering of the *Annals* was just one sign that during Garnett's winter of freedom, following his bruising experiences at the RI, exhaustion and anxiety again got the better of him. His lecture courses on botany were among the casualties; both were prematurely terminated by ill health. But the only refuge he knew was the familiar one of yet more work, now embracing the relaunching of his medical career as well.[90] On 22 December 1801, he fulfilled an indispensable condition for high-level practice in the capital by securing admission as a licentiate of the Royal College of Physicians.[91] Chance, though, was to intervene once again, in the form of an advertisement for a post as physician to the St Marylebone Dispensary in Margaret Street. On 6 April 1802, attracted by the prospect of a regular position, Garnett announced his candidature in *The Times*.[92] And a month later he was appointed.[93]

It was to be a fatal move into a setting fraught with risk. Long hours of contact with the sick in unsavoury conditions left dispensary physicians dangerously exposed. His immediate predecessor at the dispensary, Robert John Thornton, had been fortunate to survive for four years, and Richard Temple, a Leyden M.D. who was appointed to a second position as physician at the same time as Garnett, was to be even luckier, living on in the post for almost a quarter of a century. Garnett's weakened state, though, left him especially vulnerable. He had barely started at the dispensary when he contracted typhus fever. After an illness variously reported as lasting between a few days and two or three weeks, he died at his home in Great Marlborough Street on 28 June.

Notes

1. In a rich literature on the early history of the Royal Institution, Jones, *Royal Institution*, esp. 114–79 remains a standard source, while Berman, *Social Change and Scientific Organization* offers interesting alternative perspectives. But see also Vernon, 'Foundation and early years of the Royal Institution'; Martin, 'Origins of the Royal Institution' and 'Early years at the Royal Institution'; and Caroe, *Royal Institution*, as well as the biographies of Rumford cited in note 3. Indispensable on the design and development of the Albemarle Street site is James and Peers, 'Constructing space for science'.
2. The plan, dating from the summer of 1797, is referred to by the unidentified editor of Garnett, *Observations on Moffat* (1820), iii.
3. On Rumford's life, see Ellis, *Memoir of Sir Benjamin Thompson* and Brown, *Benjamin Thompson*.
4. Rumford, *Proposals*, signed by Rumford from his home in Brompton-Row and dated 4 March 1799. See especially pp. 43–50 on the meetings leading to the founding of the Institution.
5. RI MM, vol. 1, f. 30 (9 March 1799).
6. James and Peers, 'Constructing space for science', 142–3. Subsequent adjustments brought the cost to £4,850. The sale of the house took place following the murder of the current occupier, Mellish's son John, by a highwayman on Hounslow Heath in 1798.

7   RI MM, vol. 1, f. 45 (29 June 1799).
8   See the title page of Rumford, *Proposals* and the prefatory pages of the two editions of the *Prospectus*, dated January and May 1800.
9   *Prospectus*, 18–19 (January 1800) and 8–9 (May 1800).
10 Ibid., 22 (January 1800) and 10 (May 1800).
11 RI MM, vol. 1, ff. 27–8 and 31 (27 April and 4 May 1799).
12 Farish, *Course of Lectures*.
13 On 4 May 1799, the managers' minutes recorded that 'Mr Fayrish [sic] seemed not disinclined to offer his services towards the end of the year'; see RI MM, vol. 1, f. 31. But there was no further mention of Farish's engagement.
14 RI MM, vol. 1, f. 57 (14 September 1799).
15 And. MM, 15 October 1799.
16 Ibid., 17 October 1799.
17 An advertisement for a 'Professor of Natural Philosophy and Lecturer in Chemistry' appeared in the *Caledonian Mercury*, 21 October 1799.
18 Kelly, *George Birkbeck*, 1–36.
19 Birkbeck dedicated his M.D. thesis, *De sanguine* (1799) to Garnett and to John Allen, a recent medical graduate (1791) and lifelong champion of political reform who had stayed on in Edinburgh, lecturing extramurally, for much of the 1790s.
20 Receipt for transport, 8 November 1799, Strathclyde MSS, GB 249 OM/64/11/6.
21 On the baptism, see Whelprigg Papers, WD WHELP/4/T 41.
22 RI MM, vol. 1, f. 42 (5 June 1799).
23 Ibid., vol. 1, f. 57 (14 September 1799).
24 Garnett to the managers of the Royal Institution, 21 December 1799, copied in RI MM, vol. I, ff. 77–81 (23 December 1799); also in Jones, *Royal Institution*, 167–70. See too RI MM, vol. 1, f. 83 (6 January 1800).
25 Rumford to Garnett, 26 January 1800, Dartmouth College, Rainer Special Collections Library, Rumford MS 800126.
26 Rumford to Banks, 15 January 1800, letter now at Boston University, quoted in Jones, *Royal Institution*, 151.
27 Resolution of the managers, 31 March 1800; reported in *J. Roy. Inst.*, 1 (1802), 7–8. See also report in *Gent. Mag.*, 70 (April 1800), 302.
28 W., 'Some account of the late Dr. Garnett', 49.
29 Unsigned preface in Garnett, *Observations on Moffat* (1820), v–vi.
30 'Journal of Miss Ewbank of York, 1803–5', annotated transcription of the original diary in the National Library of Scotland (NLS MS 9481), 42; online at https://www.york.ac.uk/media/eighteenth-century/Diary-of-Jane-Ewbank.pdf. I am grateful to John Christie for drawing this mention of Garnett to my attention and to Jane Rendall for allowing me to quote from the transcription.
31 *Prospectus*, 63–81 (May 1800). Cf. the corresponding figures of 147, 126 and 114 in *Prospectus* (January 1800), 57–70.

32 James and Peers, 'Constructing space for science', 143–4.
33 RI MM, vol. 1, f. 93 (27 January 1800).
34 See Webster's letter to Rumford, reproduced in RI MM, vol. 1, ff. 58–65 (14 September 1799); copy in Webster's hand appended to 'Autobiography of Thomas Webster', ff. 65–9 (RI MS HBJ). In accordance with Webster's plan, and with Rumford's support, mechanics were briefly instructed through machines and other appliances installed on the ground floor, with access separate from the entrance for those attending the public lectures. Subsequent abandonment of the scheme provoked Webster's extreme disappointment, aggravated by his indignation that Birkbeck went on to receive credit for an initiative in the education of working men that he (Webster) insisted he had pioneered. See 'Autobiography of Thomas Webster', ff. 10–17.
35 The diverging perceptions of the RI's functions are well treated in Brown, *Benjamin Thompson*, 225–42 and, with special reference to the interest of some of the RI's key founders in agricultural improvement, Berman, *Social Change and Scientific Organization*, chapters 1–3. Brown draws to particularly good effect on correspondence between Rumford and the Swiss physicist Marc-Auguste Pictet.
36 Rumford to Pictet (copy), 5 July 1800, American Academy of Arts and Sciences, quoted in Brown, *Rumford*, 230.
37 RI MM, vol. 2, ff. 39–43 (31 March 1800) and *J. Roy. Inst.*, 1 (1802), 9–10. Also in *Prospectus*, 85–6, where Maskelyne's name is omitted. Maskelyne had asked to be relieved of service on the committee on 5 May 1800; see RI MM, vol. 2, f. 76.
38 Diary of Sir Charles Blagden, entry for 28 May 1800; Royal Society Archives, CB/3/3. I am indebted to Iain Watts for his insights on this episode; see Watts, 'Current events', chapter 1.
39 See Volta's letter, 'On the electricity excited by the mere contact of conducting substances of different kinds', eventually read before the Royal Society on 26 June 1800.
40 Rumford to Banks, 29 May 1800, Dartmouth College, Rainer Special Collections Library, MS Rumford 800329 (192); reproduced in Jones, *Royal Institution*, 156.
41 *Morning Chronicle*, 30 May 1800.
42 Rumford to Banks, 30 May 1800, Dartmouth College, Rainer Special Collections Library, MS Rumford 800329 (193); also in Banks, *Scientific Correspondence*, vol. 5, 43–4 and Jones, *Royal Institution*, 156–7. In the letter, Rumford submitted a proposed form of apology, following the regrets he had expressed to Banks on the previous day; see note 40.
43 RI MM, vol. 2, f. 101 (9 June 1800).
44 *Crit. Rev.*, 2nd ser. 29 (May and August 1800), 1–12 (2) and 416–28 (427).
45 *Crit. Rev.*, 2nd ser. 29 (August 1800), 416–18 and Garnett, *Tour*, vol. 2, 5–7.
46 RI MM, vol. 2, f. 104 (12 June 1800). See also Rumford to Banks, 12 June 1800, in Banks, *Scientific Correspondence*, vol. 5, 46.

47　Garnett to Webster, 27 Sept. [1800], tipped into 'Autobiography of Thomas Webster' (RI MS HBJ).
48　With the letter cited in note 47 are Webster's draft of a reply to Garnett and a draft letter to Rumford enquiring whether he could be released to attend George Pearson's chemical lectures, daily and for three months in the autumn; ibid.
49　Garnett reissued his *Outlines of a Course of Lectures on Natural & Experimental Philosophy* of 1796 without modification. But he made minor changes to the *Outlines of a Course of Lectures on Chemistry* as published in 1797, notably in the addition of brief bibliographies for each lecture. Both of the new *Outlines* bore the date 2 February 1801.
50　RI MM, vol. 2, ff. 126–7 and 134 (2 and 16 February 1801).
51　On Davy's appointment and early rise in the RI, see Paris, *Life of Davy*, vol. 1, 114–49, a critical perspective to which Davy's brother John responded vehemently in his *Memoirs of the Life of Davy*, vol. 1, 134–252. For modern studies of Davy's rise, see Knight, *Humphry Davy*, esp. 42–56; Golinski, *Experimental Self*, esp. 47–64; and, on the complex history of Davy biography, James, 'Constructing Humphry Davy's biographical image'.
52　Davy, 'Experimental essays on heat, light, and on the combinations of light'.
53　Davy, *Researches, Chemical and Philosophical*.
54　Jay, *Atmosphere of Heaven*, 169–99.
55　Rumford to Sarah Thompson, 2 March 1801, in Jones, *Royal Institution*, 70; also in Ellis, *Memoir of Sir Benjamin Thompson*, 535–6.
56　RI MM, vol. 2, f. 134 (16 February 1801).
57　'Life of Garnett', xviii.
58　RI MM, vol. 2, ff. 150–1 (16 March 1801).
59　Garnett to Rumford, 22 February 1801, letter transcribed in RI MM, vol. 2, ff. 136–8 (23 February 1801). On the managers' rejection of a second approach from Garnett, dated 11 May 1801, see below, 123.
60　RI MM, vol. 2, ff. 142–3 (2 March 1801).
61　On later evidence of Crichton's respect for Garnett, and possible friendship with him, see ch. 6, 136.
62　As reported in *Phil. Mag.*, 9 (1801), 281–2. See also the extended digest of Davy's course, 'Outlines of a view of galvanism', *J. Roy. Inst.*, 1 (1802), 49–66.
63　RI MM, vol. 2, f. 180 (25 May 1801).
64　Ibid., 183. For the report, see *J. Roy. Inst.*, 1 (1802), 17–28.
65　RI MM, vol. 2, f. 185 (1 June 1801).
66　Garnett's letter, referred to in RI MM, vol. 2, 189–90 (15 June 1801), is missing from the minutes.
67　RI MM, vol. 2, ff. 189–90. On the final payment to Garnett, see Rumford to Banks, 19 June 1800, in Banks, *Correspondence*, vol. 5, 51–2.
68　RI MM, vol. 2, ff. 197–8 (29 June 1801).

69 Davy, *Syllabus of a Course of Lectures on Chemistry*, 69–91; also in Davy, *Works*, vol. 2, 327–436 (410–36).
70 Davy, *Discourse*, 11; also in Davy, *Works*, vol. 2, 307–26 (315).
71 Davy, *Discourse*, 24; also in Davy, *Works*, vol. 2, 325.
72 See the chapter on 'Humphry Davy and the sublime' in Ruston, *Creating Romanticism*, 132–74.
73 Davy to Giddy, 12 June 1802, letter 51, in Davy, *Collected Letters*, ed. Fulford and Ruston, vol. 1, 109.
74 The increases, to £200 and then £300, followed in February 1802 and March 1803; see RI MM, vol. 2, f. 241 (15 February 1802) and vol. 3, f. 106 (7 March 1803). The managers granted the title of 'Professor of Chemistry' on 31 May 1802; see RI MM, vol. 3, f. 43.
75 On Davy's persona as a man of genius, I draw on Golinski, *Experimental Self*, 47–73.
76 RI MM, vol. 2, f. 203 (6 July 1801).
77 Young to Rumford, 9 July 1801, in Jones, *Royal Institution*, 417–18.
78 Paris, *Life of Davy*, vol. 1, 140. Cf. the similar judgement in Peacock, *Life of Thomas Young*, 135–6.
79 For an evocation of Young's brilliance as a polymath, though not as a lecturer, see Robinson, *The Last Man Who Knew Everything*.
80 Young, *Course of Lectures* (1807), vol. 1, v.
81 Peacock, *Life of Thomas Young*, 135.
82 See, for example, the copy in the American Philosophical Society, Philadelphia, which bears a handwritten dedication, characteristically to an aristocratic recipient: 'The most noble the Prince of Mecklenburgh Strelitz August 16 1802 by Humphry Davy Esquire'; APS, 540.4 G190.
83 'Dr. Garnett's lectures, at his house, No. 51 Great Marlborough-Street', *The Times*, 21 October 1801.
84 'Life of Garnett', xx, and Garnett's introductory comments, in Garnett, *Zoonomia*, 1.
85 The likeliest venue was Tom's Coffee House in Russell Street, Covent Garden, close to Great Marlborough Street, though see Lillywhite, *London Coffee Houses*, 580–96 on other possible locations.
86 Topham, 'Anthologizing the book of nature', 142–5.
87 G., 'Discovery, progress, and present state of galvanism', *Annals of Philosophy ... for the Year 1800*, 1 (1800), 3–25.
88 'Preface', in *Annals of Philosophy ... for the Year 1801*, 2 (1802), v–vii.
89 *Ann. Phil.*, 1 (1813), 1–4.
90 'Life of Garnett', p. xxi.
91 *Munk's Roll*, vol. 3, 3–4.
92 *The Times*, 7 April 1802, p. 1.
93 Ibid., 7 May 1802, p. 3, and *Munk's Roll*, vol. 2, 421.

6

Reputation and legacy

Garnett's death and interment in the recently inaugurated burial ground of the parish of St James, Westminster, today a large and partially built-up public space on Hampstead Road, behind Euston Station, did not go unnoticed. The inscription on the stone slab of his tombstone, rediscovered in 2020 during preparatory work for the HS2 rail line, was simple (though inaccurate in its dates): 'Thomas Garnett, M.D./Obiit Tertio Julius/MDCCCIII/Aetatis suae XXXV'.[1] Announcements appeared in the press within days.[2] And the *Gentleman's Magazine, European Magazine* and *Monthly Magazine* soon carried extended notices, followed by the *Annual Register*. Without exception, the notices conveyed respect for Garnett's attainments as a physician and man of science, usually twinned with admiration for what 'W.' (possibly Watts) in the *Monthly Magazine* described as his 'amiableness of disposition' and 'the unassuming modesty of his deportment'.[3] They were the obituaries of a public figure of distinction whose departure from the RI and new start in Great Marlborough Street had betokened not failure but the promise of more to come.

His Will, written in February 1802 and proved nine months after his death, in March 1803, provided in meticulous detail for his daughters and appointed three executors: Mary Worboys, James Cadwallader Parker (a major benefactor of the church and workhouse of St Martin in the Fields and variously described in other documents as a plumber, painter, glazier or wine-merchant) and Thomas Parker (a 'gentleman' resident in London, though with property and land at Kidwelly in Carmarthenshire). In addition to administering Garnett's estate, the executors were to act as guardians until Louisa and Catherine reached maturity and were able to inherit the equal shares due to them.[4] The Will conveyed not only Garnett's concern for his daughters but also how present Barbon remained in his thoughts. It identified Worboys and his sister Margaret as the residual legatees, in the event of his daughters' dying without children before the age of twenty-one. Whatever happened, lifetime provision was to be made for

Worboys. And, most revealingly, it was in Barbon, 'in some cottage near Bank House', that Garnett asked for the two orphans to be brought up. In that request, he was conveying something of his own hopes of an 'autumn of life' in which, as his daughter Catherine later recorded, he might himself return to Westmorland.[5]

The estate to which the Will referred amounted to little more than the scientific apparatus that Garnett had acquired over many years and at considerable expense, most recently for use in his Great Marlborough Street lectures. Even when augmented by financial assistance of up to £300 that he anticipated on his death through his membership of the Faculty of Physicians and Surgeons in Glasgow, there was little to spare, and sale of the collection became a matter of urgency. The opportunity attracted the attention of the Literary and Philosophical Society of Newcastle-upon-Tyne, whose joint secretary, the Revd William Turner, had negotiated the lecture series that Garnett had hoped to give there in the summer of 1799. The instruments could not have become available at a more opportune time on both sides. Shortly before Garnett died, Thomas Bigge, a local landowner with a cautiously modernizing agenda similar to that of many of the RI's early promoters, had led a campaign for the creation by the Society of a permanent lectureship in natural and experimental philosophy and the acquisition of equipment to support the lecturer, who was soon to emerge as Turner himself.[6] With the case for acquisition already made, and Bigge's a powerful voice, the Society moved quickly. Helped by two or three major donations and a public subscription, the deal was done in January 1803.

Of a total investment of nearly £1,000 in apparatus, almost half (£457.11s.9d) went on the purchase of Garnett's cabinet and its installation in an 'apparatus room' for use in lectures and by members.[7] Along with instruments acquired on the death of John Rotheram, professor of natural philosophy at St Andrews, Garnett's collection was a prized item, and it remained a prop for the regular series of lectures that Turner continued to give until the early 1830s, apparently with the aid of Garnett's lecture-notes.[8] It was only when the apparatus room disappeared to make way for a new auditorium in 1859 that the collection fell into disuse, the victim of the diminishing vogue for experimental demonstrations. Although some of Garnett's instruments seem to have found their way to the town's College of Physical Science, a precursor of Newcastle University, they can no longer be identified.

The proposal to publish Garnett's last course of medical lectures in the form he had delivered them at Tom's Coffee House, and to devote the profits to support his children, was a mark of the esteem in which he was held. Barely a month after his death, the RI's managers formally endorsed the project, agreeing to a request from Thomas Parker, as an executor of Garnett's Will, that William Savage, printer and clerk to the RI, should be authorized to print the work on the Institution's in-house press and publish it by subscription.[9] Swayed by compassion and perhaps guilt at the way Garnett had been treated, the managers immediately subscribed £50, a procedure, subsequently deemed irregular, that they eventually replaced with an agreement to cover the cost of printing and production in return for a contribution of £66 from the trustees appointed to manage the subscriptions.[10]

The call for subscribers got off to a brisk start. Individually signed copies of a printed appeal urging compassion for Garnett's two daughters were sent to proprietors and other subscribers to the RI, 'who so often witnessed the peculiar Talents and Virtues of the Doctor; and, collectively, as well as individually, expressed the high Opinion of his Worth'.[11] The targeted publicity was boosted, too, by announcements in the periodical press that spoke warmly of Garnett's merits and legacy: as both the *European Magazine* and the *Monthly Magazine* had it, 'there is not a class which has not been in some manner benefited by the labours of this lamented philosopher'.[12] By the time the lectures appeared, as *Popular Lectures on Zoonomia* in 1804, the list of subscribers stood at over 1,000.[13] Most of the subscriptions were for a guinea, corresponding to a single copy of the book. But many donors subscribed for larger sums. Among sixty-two proprietors on the list were several past and current managers (though conspicuously not Rumford): Sir Joseph Banks, Henry Cavendish, Sir John Coxe Hippisley, Sir Richard Sullivan, Charles Hatchett and the Earl of Egremont subscribed for either 5 or 10 guineas. Shute Barrington, Bishop of Durham (10 guineas), Thomas Bernard (5 guineas), and the reforming M.P. Samuel Thornton (1 guinea), all of them visitors as well as proprietors, also subscribed. So too, for 10 guineas, did Frederick Accum, appointed as chemical assistant to Davy soon after Davy's arrival.

Those who had witnessed Garnett's sadness at close quarters, including Davy and Young (each a subscriber for 5 guineas), could hardly fail to be moved. But the subscriptions attest to an appreciation of Garnett extending far beyond Albemarle Street, albeit not as far as the Andersonian, where the trustees declined, on financial grounds, to join the benefit fund's committee of patrons.[14] Institutional subscribers included the Lincoln Medical Society Literary Fund (£30), the Royal College of Physicians (£20), the Society of Arts (5 guineas) and one of the RI's bankers, Messrs Hoare (20 guineas), probably in reality the ailing senior partner of the bank, Harry Hoare; a founding proprietor, Hoare, had bought his Surrey country house, Mitcham Grove, from Garnett's patron

Alexander Wedderburn in 1786 and may well have taken the Harrogate waters.[15] Also prominent among individual subscribers were several leading figures in British science: Edward Jenner, the London instrument-makers Edward Nairne and George Adams, the Oxford medical professors Christopher Pegge and Martin Wall, Garnett's protégé and successor in Glasgow, George Birkbeck (soon, in August 1804, to move on from the chair) and, from the Edinburgh Medical School, Alexander Monro secundus and both Andrew Duncan and his father Andrew Duncan, the elder.

Most of the names, however, were far less well known. They included admirers in Garnett's home area (including physicians and surgeons from Lancaster, Kirkby Lonsdale and Kendal), friends from his days in Bradford and Harrogate, and a strikingly large number of clergymen. There is evidence, too, of a following in and around the British merchant community in St Petersburg, which seventeen subscribers gave as their address. Garnett's work may have been known there through the son of Thomas Percival, the late Revd Thomas Bassnet Percival, who had lived in St Petersburg from 1792 until his death in 1798 as chaplain to the British Embassy and Company of British Merchants. Perhaps also through the same Alexander Crichton whom Rumford had engaged to lecture during Garnett's indisposition in March 1801: Crichton, a subscriber for 2 guineas, was a known figure in the Russian Academy of Science and at court, where his links culminated, in 1804, in his appointment as physician-in-ordinary to Tsar Alexander and a prominence in court-related positions in St Petersburg that were to last for another fifteen years.[16]

In all, the subscriptions amounted to more than £2,000, ample to cover the contribution of £66 towards the cost of publishing *Zoonomia* and provide significant help for Louisa and Catherine, now settled in Barbon, as Garnett intended, with the devoted Mary Worboys. But the book did more than raise funds. As a testament to Garnett's medical principles and practice, it was an eloquent source. The title itself bore an unmissable message, and we can be sure that it was chosen knowingly, either by the unidentified editor of the volume or by Garnett himself. As Garnett would certainly have wished, it evoked the modern-minded cast of Erasmus Darwin's *Zoonomia* of 1794–6 and, through Darwin, associated the work with some of the most advanced strains of Enlightenment thought about the human body. So too did the subtitle, *The Laws of Animal Life, in Health and Disease*, intentionally reminiscent of Darwin's subtitle, *The Laws of Organic Life*.

In style and structure, Garnett's *Zoonomia* had an oral quality, and the division into fourteen chapters probably corresponded to the structure of the course as he had delivered it at Tom's. The content was also geared to the mainstream medical interests of the students for whom the lectures were mainly intended, as well as Garnett's own plans for the broadly based practice as a physician to which he hoped to return. Roughly half of the chapters were conventional, devoted to a sober coverage of mainstream aspects of medicine. These included the senses (taste, smell, hearing and, in an especially erudite chapter, Garnett's speciality of vision) and the basic functions of respiration, digestion and the circulation of the blood; there was little in them with which an orthodox physician would have found fault. The remaining chapters, by contrast, revealed Garnett as the unyielding Brunonian he had been since his first exposure to Brown in Edinburgh in the 1780s. The 'laws of animal life' that he presented in two substantial chapters were explicitly those of Brown's system, much as he had expounded them as a student before the Royal Medical Society and, later, in his *Lecture on the Preservation of Health* (from which several passages were extracted verbatim).[17] These chapters contained more clinical detail than his earlier statements had done. But they remained rooted in the Brunonian principle that life depended on an interaction between the matter of the body and the 'external powers' acting upon it, and that 'living functions' would cease and decay would set in as soon as such stimuli were withdrawn. Their treatment of disease was likewise straightforwardly Brunonian, encapsulated in the redrawn version of the 'Table of excitement and excitability' from the 1795 edition of Brown's *Elements of Medicine* reproduced in Figure 2.1.

Garnett followed a pattern common among even the loyalest Brunonians in criticizing certain of Brown's teachings and expressing disapproval of the 'arrogance and profligacy' that had done so much to undermine his reputation and hence the spread of his ideas.[18] Nevertheless, his own belief in the 'grand outlines' of the system remained 'unshaken': in providing medicine with the 'rational theory ... founded on nature, and on fact' that it had always lacked, Brown had ensured that, 'like the Newtonian philosophy', his teachings would 'last for ever'.[19] This was in contrast with the theories of Stahl, Boerhaave and Cullen, now 'almost forgotten'. It was an extravagant assertion and the mark of a commitment that had already led Garnett to stand firmly with Brown when, some years earlier, the Swiss physician Christoph Girtanner had been accused of plagiarizing Brunonian ideas and passing them off as his own.[20]

Garnett's accompanying statement that Brunonian principles were 'taught in almost all the schools of Europe and America' was bold, too, though not wholly unfounded. Especially in the German-speaking world, the principles continued to be debated into the early nineteenth century with an immediacy that aroused passionate exchanges, even physical violence, between Brunonian and anti-Brunonian students.[21] There were significant Brunonians in Italy and France as well.[22] And in America Benjamin Rush maintained a qualified adherence to Brown's teachings alongside other, more conventional medical practices until his death in 1813. In Britain, by 1800, two decades of orthodox suspicion of the Brunonian tide had left a more corrosive mark. But adepts remained plentiful, and they included some whom Garnett would have known personally, none better than the prominent and impeccably connected Robert John Thornton, whom he succeeded as physician to the St Marylebone Dispensary. It was a mark of the far from exhausted strength of the Brunonian tradition that a fourth edition of Thornton's *Philosophy of Medicine*, with strong Brunonian overtones (as well as an edgy interest in Beddoes's pneumatic medicine), appeared during Garnett's time at the RI.[23]

What neither Garnett nor Thornton could foresee, however, was the abruptness with which British interest in Brown would soon enter terminal decline, with inevitable consequences for Garnett's and other Brunonian reputations. As early as 1806, the author of a lengthy, unsigned review of *Zoonomia* may already have caught the gathering mood.[24] The review, largely devoted to a chapter-by-chapter summary of the contents, with extended extracts, was favourable enough. It praised the book's 'judicious author' and its value as a clear account of the 'latest and best theories' of medicine for 'those who are not of the medical profession'. Tellingly, though, Garnett's resolute endorsement of Brown passed unremarked; far from being actively opposed, the Brunonian system seemed not to merit detailed comment. This is not to say that ideas reminiscent of Brown's were doomed to oblivion. Michael Barfoot has observed that they surface, for example, in Wilkie Collins's *The Moonstone* (1868), in which the socially inferior medical assistant Ezra Jennings successfully administers a stimulant (a half glass of champagne) to a feverish patient, against the advice of two senior orthodox doctors who favour the traditional sedative remedy of gruel and barley-water.[25] But, as Barfoot argues, such quasi-Brunonian survivals as lingered into the mid-century did so with diminishing reference to Brown himself. By Collins' time and long before, Brown the man was remembered, if at all, as a disreputable eccentric peddling unwholesome alternative medicine.

While Garnett's loyalty to Brown would not, in itself, have set him beyond the bounds of respectable medical practice, the faltering of Brunonianism after his death led inevitably to a depreciation of his achievements. The troubles that had so visibly burdened him towards the end of his time at the RI had a similar effect, and the resulting connotations of inadequacy have left him as someone it has been easy to overlook. It is one facet of the neglect that his *Tour of the Highlands* has yet to receive the attention it deserves. The reissue of the *Tour* in 1811, reset but with identical pagination and unchanged apart from a new map and the removal of the dedication to Rumford, points to an interest still brisk a decade on. The frequency with which the work is found in libraries today also suggests that both editions sold well, despite a price that, two decades after Garnett's death, had risen to 4 guineas from the original two (which already made it a luxury item, if only for the fifty-two plates by Watts).[26]

In Germany, too, the *Tour* had a following. There, the German public's fascination with the British taste for mountainous terrain and Celtic folklore drew the Lutheran pastor, poet and pioneer of romantic sensibility Ludwig Theoboul Kosegarten to prepare a translation, which he published in full and in two printings only two years after the original English edition.[27] A market buoyed by the inaccessibility of Europe's peripheries in wartime was clearly one incentive. Kosegarten's, though, was more than a purely commercial initiative. The addition of an appendix drawn from Alexander Campbell's account of Highland poetry and music conveyed his literary aim of supporting Campbell's (and Garnett's) acceptance of the authenticity of Ossian's poems. It was an endorsement that Garnett would particularly have appreciated, though he is unlikely to have seen the German edition.

Of all Garnett's achievements, none has been more seriously distorted than his contribution to the launch of the RI. Contemporary accounts of his time as professor speak less of failure than of dedicated, uncomplaining service in the face of Rumford's bullying. The fact is that Garnett played a crucial role in seeing the institution through what would in any circumstances have been a difficult initial period, and he left it firmly established, with a rising number of subscribers and a distinguished clientele, including (as at the Andersonian) a substantial female presence. In private correspondence, even the grudging Rumford did not conceal the pleasure he took, in March 1801, in the presence at Garnett's lectures of 'crowds of the first people', including his close friend Lady Palmerston and her daughters.[28] In this increasingly unhappy second year, Garnett undoubtedly had bad days. But he remained resilient, as eyewitnesses and most notices of his life attest. 'W.', in the *Monthly Magazine*'s obituary, wrote unequivocally of lectures delivered 'during two seasons, to a crowded and brilliant audience', and a report in the *Philosophical Magazine* (probably by its founder and editor Alexander Tilloch) insisted that the lectures did 'equal honour to the institution and professor'.[29] The lack of any mention of diminished performance suggests, at least, the need for a more nuanced interpretation of Garnett's last months in the chair.

Those who knew the inner workings of the RI understood well enough that his difficulties owed far more to the circumstances in which he found himself than it did to shortcomings of his own. The judgement of an anonymous biographical sketch of Rumford published soon after Garnett's departure in 1801 was clear: if the RI had fallen short of its initial aspirations, the fault lay with the 'inefficacy and nullity' of a plan that Rumford had hoped to carry through with the appointment of just one inevitably overburdened professor.[30] For Garnett himself, the man fated to be that one professor, there could be only admiration: 'There are few men in the kingdom who could have been selected perhaps with greater propriety, or who possess more various powers than the gentleman in question.' The tragedy, as the writer put it, lay in tensions with Rumford that had brought 'a man of considerable eminence in the philosophical and literary world' to the 'necessity' of resignation.[31]

Later judgements of Rumford's role in Garnett's unhappiness and departure were, if anything, even more scathing. In 1815, in the always sympathetic *Monthly Magazine,* an unsigned editorial comment on the English translation of Georges Cuvier's admiring obituary of Rumford pulled no punches:

> We feel it proper to state, that the Count assumed the character of absolute controller, as well as projector [of the RI] … and conducted himself with a degree of *hauteur* which disgusted its patrons, and almost broke the heart of our amiable friend and its first professor Dr. Garnett.[32]

Five years on, similarly damning testimony was voiced in the unsigned preface to a reissue of Garnett's study of the Moffat waters. The preface was the work of an unidentified friend who had got to know Garnett during his stay in Moffat during the summer of 1797, while he was still at the Andersonian.[33] The friend, who had known Garnett in London as well, had clearly followed events at the RI and seen the corrosive effect of Garnett's 'unmerciful persecutor, who continued to vex and harass him'.[34]

Given the unhappy end to Garnett's time at the RI, there are elements of both irony and appropriateness in the fact that he is best-known today for what is commonly taken as a depiction of him in the institution's new lecture-theatre. In reality, he could only have lectured there during his last few weeks as professor, even though he may well have contributed significantly to the theatre's semi-circular design (see Figure 6.1).[35] The depiction, in a celebrated etching by James Gillray, shows a central figure administering laughing gas to Sir John Coxe

Figure 6.1 'Scientific Researches! ... New Discoveries in Pneumaticks ... or, an Experimental Lecture on the Powers of Air'. Coloured etching by James Gillray, published 23 May 1802 by Hannah Humphrey. The cartoon depicts a lecturer at the Royal Institution administering nitrous oxide to Sir John Coxe Hippisley, with embarrassing results. Such an episode, including its consequences, is recorded in the diary of Elizabeth, Lady Holland as occurring in mid-March 1800, when the lecturer was Garnett. Gillray's is an imaginative reconstruction of this true event, which he sets not in the temporary space in which Garnett would have given the lecture (see Figure 5.2) but in the new lecture-theatre, inaugurated a year later. He also portrays Humphry Davy, holding the bellows, as the lecturer's assistant, although it was another year before Davy arrived at the RI. Courtesy of Getty Images.

Hippisley, with the unmistakable figure of Davy assisting. The episode resembles one that had taken place and been much talked about during Garnett's first year as professor. As the society hostess Elizabeth, Lady Holland recorded in her diary on 22 March 1800, Hippisley had suffered embarrassment of precisely the kind shown in the etching a few days before.[36] However, the date on the etching, 23 May 1802 (almost a year after Garnett had left), means that we cannot be sure of the identity of the lecturer. In 1800, it would certainly have been Garnett who administered the gas. But at that time, he would have been lecturing in the room that served for lectures before the theatre in the etching was built; he would also have lectured without the assistance of Davy, who had not yet arrived. It seems inconceivable that Hippisley would have subjected himself to a second public inhalation, with the same consequence, in the spring of 1802, and we have no evidence of such a repetition. What the etching appears to portray, therefore, is an imaginative reconstruction of a true event of two years earlier transposed to a later time and setting with which Gillray (an annual subscriber to the RI from April 1800) would have been familiar.[37] At all events, whoever the lecturer in Gillray's etching may have been (and to my eyes his face is, if anything, more reminiscent of Young than of Garnett), the scene conveys the excitement that Garnett's lecturing and demonstrations aroused at the peak of his celebrity. In that sense, the lecturer drawn by Gillray 'was' Garnett, and the event was the one witnessed by Lady Holland in March 1800.

In 1821, Garnett's fiercely loyal, and now adult, daughter Catherine was under no illusion when she dismissed the unsigned contention, in an otherwise sympathetic biographical sketch in the *Lonsdale Magazine*, that her father had arrived from Glasgow 'inadequate to the task' and that his lectures at the RI had been poorly received.[38] She was right to do so. By the time she wrote, however, supporting testimonies were becoming rare and giving way to the stereotype of an inconsequential figure, a placeholder whose modest contributions had been deservedly eclipsed by the great names that followed. Regional pride, evident in an extended notice in George Atkinson's *Worthies of Westmorland* in 1850, did something to perpetuate Garnett's reputation locally.[39] But the biographies of Davy in the 1830s and George Peacock's *Life of Thomas Young* in 1855 played into an entrenched canonical view of the origins of the RI that found little place for him. Unsurprisingly, in 1871 George Ellis' laudatory biography of Rumford barely mentioned Garnett in a chapter that treated the contributions of Davy and Young in detail and presented the 'conception and plan' of the institution as 'exclusively' Rumford's own.[40] Writing in the same year, in *The Royal Institution: Its Founder and its First Professors*, the honorary secretary of the RI, Henry Bence Jones, was more generous. He devoted several pages to Garnett's life, drawn from the biographical sketch prefaced to *Zoonomia* and from correspondence in the RI's archives.[41] The 'founder', though, was still Rumford, and the key landmarks in the institution's subsequent rise to prominence in the metropolis and beyond were the appointments of Davy and Jones' particular favourite, Michael Faraday. Garnett was judged to have had 'comparatively little influence', and his tenure of the first chair came across as, at best, an uncertain stepping-stone on the way to the institution's true flowering.[42] And so it remained into the more recent literature. Even Morris Berman, in his reappraisal of what he saw as Rumford's exaggerated contribution to the founding of the RI, had no reason to draw Garnett from the margins.[43]

By the time S. G. E. Lythe set to giving substance to his 'somewhat shadowy' subject in the 1980s, he was faced with an elusive quarry.[44] The membership of societies and other bodies that Garnett liked to display on the title pages of his publications demonstrated the respect he enjoyed as a man of science, and multiple sources pointed to a seriousness and modesty of demeanour that won him friends and admirers. The posthumous appeal for subscriptions to *Zoonomia* indulged in a conventional extravagance of language in referring to the 'most flattering testimonies' of all who had witnessed 'the peculiar Talents and Virtues of the Doctor', but the generosity of the response amply endorsed the sentiment behind the call. If Garnett, despite the acclaim, never quite penetrated the very highest reaches of the nation's scientific community, metropolitan or provincial, one explanation lies in his early death. A streak of impetuousness and vulnerability to low spirits, which Garnett's self-diagnosis ascribed to a persistent level of Brunonian excitement 'above the point of health', did not help either.[45] Yet even the passage of time may not have wholly undone the consequences of the personal misfortunes and stresses he had to endure. And it is certainly hard to imagine that he would ever have achieved the balance of self-confidence, determination and deftness in personal relations that helped Davy, with whose remote provincial origins and early career there are so many parallels, to climb higher and more quickly than he managed to do.

Behind the vulnerabilities and unrealized promise, however, there remains a career, begun and completed in the short space of barely two decades, that I have described as exemplary. It was a career fashioned amid the profound transformations of the 1780s and 1790s and moulded by the changes – social, economic, political and cultural – of those turbulent years. Along the way, Garnett saw much of the disruption and pain of the age. The accelerating transformation of the yeoman world of his Westmorland childhood, the suffering associated with the early Highland clearances and the tensions that made for uneasy lives in the new manufacturing towns all disturbed him and helped to give reform and improvement an ineradicable centrality among his guiding ideals. But, like any son of the Enlightenment, he knew that change could also breed opportunity and profit, especially for someone with his profile of scientific and medical knowledge and gifts as a communicator of science to audiences across the social spectrum. If, as Samuel Johnson observed, learning had become a 'trade', with 'the multitude' as its customers, Garnett was supremely equipped to feed the market.[46]

Garnett's skills, allied to a striking accumulation of book-learning, made their mark across the whole range of his activities. In science, he was an acknowledged leader in the analysis of Britain's northern waters; in medicine, he endorsed the theoretical turn pioneered by Erasmus Darwin and, through his thriving practice, did much to advance Harrogate in the hierarchy of British spa towns; and in his tour of the Highlands and Western Isles he combined reason and objectivity with the aesthetic sensibilities of a mind attuned since childhood to the inspiration of mountain grandeur. Yet it was arguably as a lecturer and teacher in the dawning age of the professional academic that he left his most enduring legacy. The passage from the eighteenth-century world of society lecturing in which he took his first steps was to be long and complex. But from his early successes at the Andersonian, it is not hard to trace a lineage, via his evening lectures for 'instruction' at the RI and the initiatives of his protégé George Birkbeck in the mechanics' institute movement, to the university-level programmes that had come to point the way forward in higher and technical education within half a century of his death. In his three years in Glasgow and more briefly in London, he had unwittingly glimpsed something of the new order and, in certain respects, notably in his insistence on the admission of women, ventured into areas that even the new order was to find challenging. It was one of the multiple tragedies of his life that he did not survive long enough to see beyond the watershed in science-based career-making that was to come and that his own career had presaged. More than two centuries on, we can only speculate on what his educational vision might have yielded had he lived beyond his thirty-six years.

Notes

1. Both the day and the year are engraved incorrectly. Garnett died on 28 June and was buried on 2 July, and the year was 1802. I am grateful to David Thomas for drawing this discovery to my attention. On the excavation, in which the coffin plate was also discovered, see https://www.hs2.org.uk/building-hs2/archaeology/uncovering-london-euston/.
2. *Lancaster Gazetteer*, 10 July 1802.
3. 'Deaths', *Gent. Mag.*, 72, part 2 (July 1802), 690, with a brief additional notice, ibid., 72, part 2 (August 1802), 777–8; 'Some account of Thomas Garnett, M.D. &c.', *Eur. Mag.*, 42 (July 1802), 5–6; 'W.', 'Some account of the late Dr. Garnett', *Monthly Mag.*, 14 (Aug. 1802), 48–50; *Ann. Reg.* for 1802 (London, 1803), 512.
4. PROB 1/1388/95, Probate Registers, National Archives, Kew; see Bibliography of MSS. My thanks to David Thomas for allowing me to see his annotated transcription of the Will.

5   C. G. G., 'Dr. Garnett. To the Editor', *Lonsdale Mag.*, 2 (January 1821), 20–2 (20).
6   Bigge, *Expediency of Establishing a Lectureship*. After being read to the society on 4 May 1801, Bigge's proposal was passed to a committee and implemented promptly, though with signs of some members' unease that the lectureship might become unduly independent and a drain on the society's resources.
7   Watson, *Literary and Philosophical Society of Newcastle-upon-Tyne*, 215–16. See also Turner, *General Introductory Discourse*, 17–18 and *Address Delivered at the First Meeting of the Literary & Philosophical Society of Newcastle upon Tyne*, 12–13.
8   On Turner's acquisition of Garnett's notes, which he must have consulted even if he did not use them in his lectures, see Orange, 'Rational dissent and provincial science', 214.
9   RI MM, vol. 3, ff. 55–6 (2 August 1802).
10 RI MM, vol. 3, ff. 321–2 (6 August 1804).
11 A typical recipient was John Soane. The copy he received, dated 18 January 1803 and signed by William C. Cuppage, a subscriber (for 2 guineas) and secretary to the committee appointed to conduct the appeal, is in the Research Library of Sir John Soane's Museum, Lincoln's Inn Fields, London. I am grateful to David Duff for drawing this rare document to my attention. Soane, though one of the RI's proprietors, did not subscribe.
12 *Eur. Mag.* 42 (October 1802), 42 and *Monthly Mag.*, 14 (November 1802), 342.
13 Garnett, *Zoonomia*, 307–21 with (in most copies) a supplementary list on 323–5.
14 And. MM, vol. 2, ff. 48–51 (22 December 1802). A proposal to accept the invitation, moved by Duncan Macfarlan, Minister in the Church of Scotland and the future principal of the University of Glasgow, failed to find a seconder and was not mentioned again.
15 Hutchings, *Mess[rs] Hoare Bankers*, 94.
16 Tansey, 'Life and works of Sir Alexander Crichton'; Appleby, 'Sir Alexander Crichton'; and *ODNB*.
17 Garnett, *Zoonomia*, 169–212.
18 Ibid., 210 and 215.
19 Ibid., 214–15.
20 Garnett, *Preservation of Health*, 1797 edn., iv; 1800 edn., vi. Garnett was responding to the absence of any mention of Brown in Girtanner's 'Mémoires sur l'irritabilité', *Obs. Phys.*, 36 (January 1790), 422–40 and 37 (August 1790), 139–54.
21 On the continuing interest in Brunonianism in German-speaking Europe, see the report of confrontations, amounting to physical violence, in German universities, in Anon., 'Violent disputes, between the Brunonians and anti-Brunonians'. Also Risse, 'History of John Brown's medical system' and 'A frustrated reform'.
22 Chappey, 'Idéologie et perspectives européennes'.

23 [Thornton], *Philosophy of Medicine* (1799–1800), vol. 1, esp. 128–92. For Thornton, writing under a thin veil of anonymity as 'A friend to improvements', Brown was nothing less than 'the father of the true science of medicine' (p. 128).
24 *Brit. Crit.*, 28 (1806), 619–29; reproduced in *Monthly Rep.*, 2 (1807), 176–87.
25 Barfoot, 'Brunonianism under the bed'.
26 *London Catalogue of Books ... to October 1822* (London, 1822), 52. Cf. the advertisement and price for the original edition in *Glasgow Courier*, 2 April 1799.
27 Garnett, *Reise durch dir schottischen Hochlande*.
28 Rumford to his daughter, 2 March 1801, in Jones, *Royal Institution*, 70.
29 W., in *Monthly Mag.*, 14 (August 1802), 49 and the slightly edited reissue of the text in the unpaginated entry on Garnett in John Mason Good, et al., *Pantologia*, vol. 5 (London, 1813 and 1819); and Anon., 'Royal Institute [sic] of Great Britain', *Phil. Mag.*, 9 (1801), 281.
30 Anon., 'Sir Benjamin Thompson, Count of Rumford', 337–8 and 338n.
31 Ibid., 338n.
32 Cuvier, 'Eulogy on Count Rumford', 328n. The comment was probably the work of the magazine's radical founder Sir Richard Phillips.
33 See ch. 4, 93 and ch. 5, 107.
34 Garnett, *Observations on Moffat* (1820), vi.
35 See ch. 4, 97–8.
36 Holland, *Journal*, vol. 2, 60–1. For a firm identification of Garnett as the lecturer, see June Z. Fullmer's letter to the editor of the *Scientific American* (August 1960). Cf. Mary Dorothy George's inclination to see Young as the lecturer, in George, *Catalogue of Political and Personal Satires in the British Museum*, vol. 8, 112–14. My reading of the cartoon seeks to bridge the two positions.
37 On Gillray's election, proposed by Hippisley, see RI MM, vol. 2, f.49 (7 April 1800).
38 C. G. G., 'Dr. Garnett. To the Editor of the Lonsdale Magazine', 20–1, responding in January 1821 to the 'Memoir of Thomas Garnett, M.D.', *Lonsdale Mag.*, 1 (Nov. 1820), 482. Though unsigned, the 'Memoir' was probably by the magazine's editor John Briggs.
39 'Thomas Garnett', in Atkinson, *Worthies of Westmorland*, vol. 2, 205–16.
40 Ellis, *Memoir of Sir Benjamin Thompson*, 378–450.
41 Jones, *Royal Institution*, 141–79.
42 Ibid., v.
43 Berman, *Social Change and Scientific Organization*, 20–5.
44 Lythe, *Thomas Garnett*, 1–3.
45 Garnett, *Zoonomia*, 283–5. In Brunonian terms, Garnett saw his condition as a classic case of indirect debility. See ch. 2, 34 and 37.
46 For Johnson's comment, see ch. 4, 77.

Epilogue
The Garnett heritage

With Garnett's Will proved, his daughters arrived back in Barbon by post chaise, accompanied by his sister Margaret (who seems to have been helping in Great Marlborough Street) and Mary Worboys, in April 1803.[1] There Worboys, thirty and unmarried, settled into the role of mother and sole parent that she was to fulfil throughout Louisa and Catherine's childhood. Despite Garnett's limited estate, she and the two other executors he appointed to administer his Will and act as trustees for his daughters until they reached the age of maturity took their responsibilities seriously.[2] Over the years, the profits from the subscriptions to *Zoonomia* were augmented by a legacy of almost £500 to Louisa from her grandfather John Garnett, and she and Catherine shared land and property, including a house in Barbon, left by a great-uncle, another Thomas Garnett, who died intestate and without living heirs in Newby, Yorkshire in 1818.[3] With an extended Garnett family to take an interest in them in and around Barbon and a continuing contact with their mother's family in the south, the sisters were by no means abandoned.

Following their quiet upbringing, Louisa and Catherine might have been expected to marry within the area, as Garnetts had done for generations.[4] But introductions, in all probability through the Clevelands, paved the way to married lives of a very different kind. Crucial to both their marriages were contacts with medical men employed by or close to the East India Company. One of their mother's older brothers, John Cleveland, is known to have been working as an East India Company doctor in about 1780, and William, his younger brother, contemplated a similar career before opting for practice as a surgeon and apothecary in London. It may well have been through William, who also served in the Kent militia, and his wife Sarah that Louisa met Henry Philip Lovelace, a lieutenant in a light cavalry regiment, the 16th (Queen's) Lancers, then under service with the Company.[5] Apparently already engaged to Lovelace, she embarked for India, along with almost four hundred officers and men (including Lovelace himself), in June 1822. Her ship, an East India Company vessel, arrived in Calcutta five months later.[6] A marriage settlement, signed there on 8 April 1823, made provision for her to receive the income from her properties in England through four specially appointed executors, and she and Lovelace were married on the same day in St George's Anglican Cathedral in Madras.[7]

The Lovelaces lived on in India until 1826, when Lovelace took a year's leave, in readiness for retirement on half pay in London.[8] Their time in India was anything but tranquil. By the early nineteenth century, the EIC had become far more than the vehicle for trade in the East Indies and beyond to which Elizabeth I had granted a royal charter in 1600. Alongside its activities as a joint-stock company with interests primarily in India and China, it had increasingly assumed the role of a territorial and political power, with ships and its own standing army of over a quarter of a million men, twice the size of the British army by the early nineteenth century. For the EIC's employees in India, the constant threat of disorder, rebellion and cholera made for an uneasy existence, and Lovelace himself saw active service, notably in his regiment's celebrated storming of the fortress of Bhurtpore in January 1826.[9] After such experiences, England offered what must have been welcome relief. But of Louisa's later life, we know only that she and her husband lived in London and that she was in Tuscany in 1832, possibly travelling for her health. It was there that she died, probably in Pistoia, in a fire on 15 August 1832; she is buried in the protestant 'English cemetery' in Florence.[10]

Catherine's contacts with the East India Company seem to have dated from the same time as her sister's, and they almost certainly had the same Cleveland family origins. When Louisa left for Calcutta, she travelled on sureties of £200 provided by two surgeons, Thomas Godwin and William Taylor, both of whom had close connexions with the Company. Godwin is known to have been serving as a surgeon, or more probably a surgeon's mate, on an EIC vessel engaged on voyages to Bombay and China in 1816,[11] while Taylor, an Edinburgh M.D. (1817), had entered the Indian Medical Service in Bombay as an assistant surgeon (subsequently surgeon) in 1819.[12] By the early 1820s, Godwin was back in London as a surgeon in Dowgate Hill, the same street where William Cleveland, Catherine's uncle, also lived and practised. It was Godwin whom Catherine married at St Pancras Old Church, on 11 August 1824. Thereafter, she spent her married life with him back in Barbon, living at Burnside Cottage, a Garnett property she had inherited through the family, until her death on 5 May 1845.

Despite a retiring disposition and the ill health, notably back pain, that she suffered in her later years, Catherine seems to have travelled extensively with

Godwin. Her leisured existence also left time for her to become an accomplished artist. However, it was as a dedicated and productive poet and author that she earned an entry in the *ODNB*. Her work bore evidence of wide reading and a particular familiarity with the Lake District, where her husband seems to have owned or rented a property close to William Wordsworth's home at Rydal Mount and was 'much respected' in the Wordsworth family.[13] But she also evoked continental Europe, in prose and poetry, in terms that suggest a first-hand knowledge of France, Switzerland, Italy, perhaps even of Corfu.[14] Her first steps as a poet were inauspicious. Caught up, like her father, in the Ossianic legends, she wrote a metrical version of the poems of Ossian at the age of fifteen; but, dissatisfied with the results and perhaps mindful of growing scepticism about the poems' authenticity, she burned what she had done. With maturity, though, she gained in confidence, and her adult poetry was taken seriously, not least by the Scottish writers Joanna Baillie and John Wilson (the 'Christopher North' of *Blackwood's Edinburgh Magazine*) and, among the Lake Poets, by Robert Southey as well as Wordsworth, both of whom Catherine met through Godwin.

Personal friendship cannot be discounted in the attention that Wordsworth, in particular, paid to her work. As Stephen Behrendt has said, Wordsworth's appreciation of women writers could sometimes be 'more polite than fervent'.[15] But his interest in Catherine's poetry appears to have been genuine, and she was understandably heartened by his permission for her to dedicate her second collection of miscellaneous poems, *The Wanderer's Legacy*, to him in 1829. The dedication she composed was conventionally deferential; her anxiety that Wordsworth's name might excite 'expectations in the reader which my humble efforts will fail to gratify' played well with his susceptibility to flattery.[16] In return, Wordsworth paid her the compliment of a letter of detailed commentary on a volume that he had read 'with much pleasure'.[17] The poems, he wrote, were such as 'cannot but do you honour'. Above all, Catherine's 'great command of language', allied to 'moral purpose', 'feeling' and 'that much rarer gift which is the soul of poetry, imagination', was commendable. With the praise, though, came criticism of her 'workmanship'. Her blank verse was 'not sufficiently broken'. And her choice of the Spenserian stanza, that 'most difficult metre', may have been ill-advised: as a verse-form, in Wordsworth's view, it was poorly adapted to communicate the mixture of 'conflicting passions' and vivid narrative that were a hallmark of her poetry.

Wordsworth's response to *The Wanderer's Legacy*, broadly favourable but with an undertow of reservations, had parallels in the literary press's reception of the collection. The notice in *The Ladies' Monthly Museum* associated admiration for 'a great happiness of expression and a most fertile fancy' with the view that Catherine's poems were 'unduly metaphysical'; in 'straining after effect', she had sacrificed simplicity and not heeded 'the suggestions of her own good sense'. Yet there was no shortage of unqualified praise as well. The *London Literary Gazette* recognized 'a depth of thought, and a strength of feeling, which indicate a mind of a very superior order', and a lengthy article in *The Athenaeum* spoke warmly of the author's 'original powers': in a period not lacking in good poetry, 'we have met with none for a long time that has given us as much pleasure as this volume of Mrs. Godwin'.[18] There was more than enough in the such evaluations to encourage Catherine to continue as a poet.

Five years later, she approached Wordsworth again, asking him, through her husband, for a letter of introduction to his recently acquired publisher Edward Moxon. In Wordsworth's absence (on a visit to his son), it was his sister Dorothy who wrote the letter on his behalf.[19] The idea was that Thomas Godwin would present the letter to Moxon along with the manuscript of Catherine's latest major poem, in forty-four Spenserian stanzas, cast as a pious exhortation to mindfulness of those less fortunate than ourselves. The letter included warm words: 'my Brother thinks highly of Mrs Godwin's powers and attainments' and 'her style, language, and versification <u>appear to me</u> very much superior to those of most of the popular female writers of the present day'. But Dorothy's accompanying insistence that she could not offer 'either advice or opinion' and that Moxon should not allow her comments to sway his judgement left the letter without the unqualified endorsement for which Catherine must have hoped. At all events, it failed to persuade Moxon. When the poem appeared, as *The Reproving Angel. A Vision* in 1835, it was published by Sampson Low, scarcely less prestigious than Moxon but not Catherine's first choice.

It is hard to know how Dorothy's cautious tone should be interpreted. Wordsworth probably did not see Catherine as quite the equal of Felicia Hemans, a visitor, like the Godwins, to Rydal Mount and the most accomplished and best-known of several women writers whom he was encouraging at the time.[20] And Catherine, in turn, may have felt that she could expect little further support from him. Soon, too, tragedy, in the form of Louisa's death, compounded any sense of discouragement and contributed to a personal melancholy that found expression in *The Reproving Angel* and her decision to turn from poetry to prose, in the form of moral tales for children.

As in all her literary and artistic ventures, Catherine continued to receive unwavering support from her husband and family, especially on the Cleveland side. It was Thomas Godwin who ensured her a measure of posthumous visibility by setting aside the considerable sum of £1,200 to finance a sumptuous edition of her collected poetical works that appeared in 1854, two years after his death and nine years after hers. The venture was very much a family affair, led by William Cleveland's grandson, the writer and musician Arthur Cleveland Wigan, who wrote an introductory biographical sketch and appreciation of Catherine's qualities as a poet. Wigan's judgement was generous but not overblown: the reservations implicit in his reflexion that she may have allowed herself to be guided too closely by Wordsworth were at least discretely veiled.[21] Now, though, not all criticisms were as gentle. *The Athenaeum*, so enthusiastic a quarter of a century earlier, pulled no punches: its review described the volume as the 'ponderous mistake of kind but ill-judging friends', and such mild praise for Catherine as it offered was 'for her industry rather than her talent'.[22] Other notices were few and perfunctory at best. One, in the *Literary Gazette*, ventured that the volume contained 'many striking and pleasing pieces', but then did little more than endorse comments from Wordsworth's letter on her *Wanderer's Legacy* collection, as reproduced in Wigan's introduction.[23] More recent criticism has done nothing to retrieve her reputation. As Rosemary Scott states in the *ODNB* entry on her, Catherine's work 'has not survived its period'.[24]

Since neither Louisa nor Catherine had children, the line of direct descent from Garnett came to an end with Catherine's death in 1845, following a long illness and a last, vain attempt to restore her failing health on a continental tour with her husband. She was buried, in accordance with her wishes, beneath the east window of the recently built new church of St John the Baptist in Firbank, close to Sedbergh. Her choice of Firbank rather than Barbon for her burial was significant as a mark not just of an engrained Garnett loyalty to the established church but also of her particular affection for John Garnett, the younger of her father's two brothers, who had held the perpetual curacy of St John's for thirty-five years until his death two years earlier. Godwin, much affected by Catherine's death, lived on at Burnside Cottage, with the still loyal Mary Worboys. When first Worboys and then Godwin died, within six months of each other in 1852, they were buried in the same grave as Catherine, marked by a single tombstone, now fallen.[25] This left only one member of Garnett's family, the older of his brothers, Robert Skyring Garnett, who had known him. And when Robert died, in 1854 at the age of eighty-five, after living for over forty years at Bank House, that last personal bond with Thomas (never, it seems, a close one) was broken.

By now, it was not just memories of Garnett and his immediate family that were fading. So also were the last vestiges of the rural society from which he had emerged. Looking back in his eighties, the geologist Adam Sedgwick, born and raised in Dent, seven miles from Barbon, voiced a well-known lament on the changes that had occurred since his boyhood there in the 1780s.[26] With the nostalgia of old age, he may well have exaggerated the autonomy and dignity of the yeomen, or 'statesmen' as he preferred to call them, whose memory he evoked. But there was no denying that by the mid-nineteenth century little remained of the close-knit community in which Garnett too had spent his early years and to whose ways he remained attached throughout his life. It was not just a matter of the abandonment of agricultural labour in favour of employment in one of the region's larger towns. Although that trend had certainly accelerated, many in small villages such as Barbon still worked the land. But they were now more likely to do so as tenants of large landlords or as employed labourers than as owners or freeholders in their own right. It was in that diminished independence and the inexorable passage of property and freeholds into the hands of often absentee proprietors that Sedgwick perceived the tragedy of the lost world of his childhood.

While Garnett was by no means the first member of a Westmorland yeoman family to venture and succeed beyond his roots, he died at too early a stage in the transformation of rural life to perceive the full magnitude of the changes of which his trajectory was a part. The next generation of Garnetts, however, could be in no doubt that the age-old norms of their community were faltering. The marriages and subsequent lives of Louisa and Catherine were arguably untypical in that they were so powerfully fashioned by their contacts, through the Clevelands, with the East India Company. The lives of Robert Skyring Garnett's two children, though, are revealing of a transition to a more mobile society offering avenues of social and career advancement unimaginable in the world in which Thomas Garnett had had to make his opportunistic way. Robert's daughter broke with the yeoman world of Barbon by marrying a prosperous paper-manufacturer in County Durham, while his son, a younger Thomas Garnett, entered the Anglican priesthood by a route very different from that of his uncle, John.

A non-graduate (like at least half of the ordinands in the north-west), John had probably acquired the necessary command of Latin, Greek and theology at the Queen Elizabeth Grammar School, Kirkby Lonsdale and proceeded to ordination, as deacon in 1797 and priest five years later, by offering personal testimonials as evidence of his moral soundness and the veracity of his 'inward call'.[27] The younger Thomas, by contrast, made the most of the expanding world of educational opportunity by entering the new University of Durham as one of the ablest of the first intake of some forty students in 1833. Unlike John, he took a BA and an MA, both in 'Classical and General Literature', before going on to the one-year License in Theology (L.Th.), a recently introduced qualification favoured by Anglican ordinands.[28] His degrees, followed by ordination as deacon (1840) and priest (1841), positioned him perfectly for a clerical or academic career, and he began strongly with his appointment as one of the two chaplains of University College, the University's first college (1839–41), and election, also in 1839, as one of Durham's first three University Fellows. The fellowship was an especially enviable position, one that Thomas retained (with an annual stipend of £120 and no prescribed duties) for several years, possibly even for the maximum period of ten years allowed by the statutes.

Potentially the scholar of his generation of Garnetts, Thomas was not to fulfil the promise of his years at the university. Three unsigned pamphlets of poetry dating from his Durham days were evidence of pretensions conspicuously at odds with the extreme banality of the verse. By the time he published his collected poems as a slim anonymous volume of *Verses by a Poor Man* in 1842, he was able to add a gushing dedication to Prince Albert, authorized in obscure circumstances but suggesting clerical connexions at a high level.[29] The dedication, though, did nothing for his reputation as a poet. Soon afterwards, he returned to live with his parents at Bank House and spend the rest of his life there, pursuing minor scientific interests and living as a virtual recluse until his death in 1859. It was a sad sequel to a promising start, and part of a diminished Garnett presence in Barbon that took another turn three years later with the death of Thomas's widowed mother, Mary Fleming Garnett, and the sale of Bank House to the Gibson family, owners of the nearby Whelprigg House and Estate. The passage of the property from the Garnetts to the Gibsons was a microcosm of the changed fortunes of a notable Dales family in the new world of the nineteenth century. More significantly, though, it bore witness to the broader decline of a yeoman culture that had combined stability and tradition with scarce but real opportunities of advancement to national prominence for the north's 'hardy progeny' of gifted young men of whom Garnett was such a striking example.

Notes

1 For Worboys's vivid description of the long journey from London, see her letter to Sarah Cleveland, 13 April 1803, in Hardy, *Benenden Letters*, 267–9. The decision to travel in the relative comfort of a private post chaise suggests that the Cleveland family may have contributed to the cost.
2 On the executors, see ch. 6, 133–5.
3 Whelprigg Papers, WD WHELP/2/T51 and WD/WHELP/4/T31.

4   For an account of Catherine's life, with mentions also of Louisa's, see Wigan, 'Memoir of the author'.
5   Graham, *Sixteenth, the Queen's, Light Dragoons*, 68–71.
6   Louisa was among several lady passengers on the *Marchioness of Ely*, one of two East India Company vessels that sailed together for India from Tilbury.
7   *Oriental Mag.*, 1 (1823), 683. The marriage settlement is recorded in WD WHELP/4/T31.
8   *Asiatic J.*, 22 (1826), 343.
9   Graham, *Sixteenth, the Queen's Light Dragoons*, 72–7.
10 The cemetery's records are confusing. Louisa's name is recorded as 'Louise Cleveland Garnett, née Lovelace', and the place of her death appears as Cortona, rather than the more commonly reported Pistoia. See entry sixty-six of the register of burials in the cemetery of the Evangelical Reformed Church of Florence: Swiss Archival Register, 1828–44, online at http://www.florin.ms/18281844.html.
11 The Company chartered the vessel, the *Cumberland*, for service on this route between January and May 1816. See Hackman, *Ships of the East India Company*, 86.
12 Crawford, *Roll of the Indian Medical Service*, 431. Taylor's promotion to the position of surgeon in 1826 suggests that he chose to make his medical career in India. There is no evidence that Godwin ever had a permanent engagement with the IMS.
13 Dorothy Wordsworth to Edward Moxon, 2 October 1834, letter 848 in Wordsworth, *Letters of William and Dorothy Wordsworth*, vol. 5, 743–4.
14 See, for example, Godwin (the married name she used from 1825), *Josephine* (1837). Cf. also the mention of a visit to Corfu 'some years ago' in the Preface to her early prose romance, set in the Balkans, *Reine Canziani* (1825), vi–vii.
15 Behrendt, 'Wordsworth and the women poets', 639.
16 'Dedication. To William Wordsworth, Esq.', in Godwin, *Wanderer's Legacy*, unpaginated.
17 Wordsworth to Catherine Grace Godwin, undated but probably spring 1829. Reproduced in Wigan, 'Memoir of the author', v–vi; also as letter 423 in Wordsworth, *Letters of William and Dorothy Wordsworth*, vol. 5, 57–9.
18 *Lit. Gaz.*, no. 617 (15 November 1828), 721–2 and *Athenaeum*, no. 60 (17 December 1828), 944–6 (944).
19 Dorothy Wordsworth to Moxon, 2 October 1834, cited above, note 13.
20 Behrendt, 'Wordsworth and the women poets', esp. 641–7.
21 Wigan, 'Memoir of the author', vii.
22 *Athenaeum*, no. 1398 (12 August 1854), 990–1.
23 *Lit. Gaz.*, no. 1970 (21 October 1854), 897 and no. 2003 (9 June 1855), 353.
24 Scott, 'Catherine Grace Godwin', ODNB.
25 Mary Worboys died on 21 January 1852 in her eightieth year; *Kendal Mercury*, 31 January 1852. Thomas Godwin died on 12 July; ibid., 17 July 1852.

26 Sedgwick, 'Preface', in Sedgwick, *Memorial by the Trustees of Cowgill Chapel* (1868), vii–xiv.
27 John Garnett was ordained as both deacon and priest in Chester Cathedral. On the preparation of non-graduate ordinands about the turn of the century, see Jones, 'Recruitment, background, and education of the clergy'. Also Slinn, *Education of the Anglican Clergy*, 129–69 on the unique contribution of Westmorland's grammar schools in feeding the supply of ordinands who went on to serve in parishes across the Northern Province.
28 Garnett's university career can be traced through annual editions of *The Durham University Calendar* and files on his undergraduate years in series UND/F1 and UND/CF1, Durham University Records. On his clerical career, see Durham Diocesan Records, DDR/EA/CLO/3/1839/7. Both collections in ASC Durham.
29 The three separately paginated parts that appeared in Durham in 1841 were collected in the following year as *Verses by a Poor Man*, 2nd edn., now with the dedication to Albert. I am grateful to Michael Kingsbury for identifying the author from his own two copies of the collected edition, inscribed with dedications by Garnett to Joseph Gibson and his wife, the future owners of Bank House.

Bibliography

Portraits, Manuscripts, and Printed Sources

(A) Portraits

'Thomas Garnett M.D.' Mezzotint. Garnett, pen in hand, seated next to a Nooth apparatus. Probably early 1790s. Unknown artist, unknown engraver. Reproduced here as Figure 3.3.

Portrait, oil on canvas, sometimes (improbably) attributed to David Wilkie, c.1798–9. University of Strathclyde Collections. Original catalogued as GLAEX A9. Photograph as GB 249 OP/4/5/2. Reproduced here as Frontispiece.

'Thomas Garnett, M.D.' Stipple engraving. Garnett full face. Engraved by James Hopwood the Elder, from an original (location unknown) by John Raphael Smith. Published 25 March 1800 by Cadell & Davies, Strand. Reproduced as frontispiece of Garnett, *A Lecture on the Preservation of Health*, 2nd edn. (London, 1800)

'T. Garnett M.D. Professor of Natural Philosophy in the Royal Institution of Great Britain'. Stipple engraving. Garnett standing with one hand on chamber of a vacuum pump, the other holding a book. From a portrait (location unknown) by Thomas Phillips. Engraved by Samuel Phillips, 18 Tavistock Street, Bedford Square. Published 1 May 1801. Reproduced here as Figure 5.1.

'Thomas Garnett, M.D.' Stipple engraving. Garnett full face, seated before an open book. Drawn by John Raphael Smith, engraved by William Satchwell Leney. 'Published Jan. 1. 1805, by the Executors, for the benefit of his orphan Children'. Printed as frontispiece of Garnett, *Popular Lectures on Zoonomia* (London, 1804).

(B) Manuscripts

American Philosophical Society, Philadelphia, USA
Letter from Erasmus Darwin to Garnett, 14 December 1794.
Archives and Special Collections, Durham University Records, Durham
Durham University Records
UND/F1 and UND/CF1, files on the undergraduate years of the Revd Thomas Garnett.
Durham Diocesan Records
DDR/EA/CLO/3/1839/7, record of the Revd Thomas Garnett's clerical career.

Cumbria Archive Centre, Kendal
Papers relating to the Garnett's daughters and the Gibson family of Whelprigg House, Barbon, Cumbria. Series WD/WHELP/2 and 4.

Dartmouth College, Hanover, NH, USA. Rainer Special Collections Library
Letters from Rumford to Garnett, 26 January 1800 and Rumford to Banks, 30 May 1800. MSS 800126 and 800329.

Edinburgh University Library, Centre for Research Collections
Dissertations and papers read by Garnett before the Royal Physical Society and Natural History Society:
'Pauca de legibus quibus gubernantur corpora viventia. Auctore Thoma Garnett'. Royal Physical Society Dissertations, vol. 10 (1785–8), ff. 494–501. Undated. EUA Da. 67 Phys.
'On the organs of vision in different animals. Read 19 Apr. 1787 by Thomas Garnet [*sic*] of Kirby Lonsdale Westmoreland'. Papers of the Natural History Society, vol. 6 ('From 2d November 1786 to 26 April 1787'), dissertation 235. Read 19 April 1787. EUA Da. 67 Nat.
'Quaedam observationes de strabismo. Auctore T. Garnett'. Royal Physical Society Dissertations, vol. 10 (1785–8), ff. 408–25. Undated but probably read late 1787. EUA Da. 67 Phys.
'A short view of some of the principal laws by which living matter is regulated. Read 17th Jany 1788 by Thomas Garnett of Westmoreland'. Papers of the Natural History Society, vol. 7 ('From 15 November 1787 to 17 April 1788'), dissertation no. 84. EUA Da. 67 Nat.

University matriculation and graduation registers:
Matriculation Register for Medicine, 1783–90, in series 'Matriculation Albums, 1627–1980'. Edinburgh University Special Collections. EUA IN1/ADS/STA/2.
Laureation & Degrees (First Laureation Album), 1587–1809, in series 'Laureation and degrees albums, 1586–1896'. Edinburgh University Special Collections. EUA IN1/ADS/STA/1/1.

Library of Birmingham
James Watt Papers
Copy press letter book, 1797–1803. MS 3219/4.
Correspondence between Garnett, James Watt, and John Carmichael, January–February 1797. MS 3219/4/29/33 and 42.

National Archives, Kew
Records of probate granted in Prerogative Court of Canterbury and related Probate Jurisdictions. Will Registers:
'Will of Thomas Garnett, Doctor of Medicine, Doctor of Physic of Great Marlborough Street, Middlesex'. Dated 26 February 1802. Probate granted 10 March 1803. PROB 11/1388/95.
'Will of Catherine Grace Godwin, Wife of Barton [*sic*] Westmorland'. Probate granted 23 July 1845. PROB 11/2021/95.

'Will of Thomas Godwin of Barbon within Kirkby Lonsdale Westmorland'. Probate granted 31 July 1852. PROB 11/2156/463.

Royal Institution, London

Minutes of Meetings of Managers, vols. 1–3 of 15, RI MS AD/02/B/02/A01-03. Reproduced in facsimile as *The Archives of the Royal Institution of Great Britain in Facsimile. Minutes of Managers' Meetings, 1799-1900*, ed. Frank Greenaway. 7 vols. (Ilkley: Scolar Press, in association with the Royal Institution of Great Britain, 1971–7).

'Autobiography of Thomas Webster, F.G.S. &c. Architect of the Theatre of the Royal Institution of Great Britain. Born 1773; died 26 Decr 1844', with additional miscellaneous correspondence tipped in. RI MS HBJ.

Royal Medical Society, Edinburgh

Dissertations read before the RMS:

James Ford, 'What is the best method of studying medicine?'. Dissertations of the RMS, vol. 11 ('Medical dissertations read before the Medical Society of Edin. Beginning about the Middle of Winter 1778'), ff. 152–9. Signed [f. 159] 'Novr. 78. J. Ford'.

Garnett, 'In what does life consist? How are those variations from health, called diseases, produced? And how shall we best cure them?'. Dissertations of the RMS, vol. 21 ('Questions with the comments of the members of the Royal Medical Society'), dissertation no. XI, ff. 365–87. Signed [f. 387] 'Thomas Garnett. Alumnus Brunonis'. Dissertation undated. Volume dated 1787–8.

Garnett, 'A. B. (aetat. 9) has, for about a fortnight, laboured under symptoms similar to those of a common catarrh … '. Dissertations of the RMS, vol. 22 ('Cases with comments by members of the Royal Medical Society'), case no. X, ff. 1–15. Signed 'Thos Garnett'. Dissertation dated December 1787.

Royal Society Library, London

Diary of Sir Charles Blagden, eight volumes, 1771–1820.

University of Strathclyde Archives and Special Collections, Glasgow

Minutes of Meetings of Managers and Trustees, Anderson's Institution. University of Strathclyde Archives and Special Collections, two volumes: GB 249 OB/1/1/1 (1796–9) and GB 249 OB/1/1/2 (1799–1810). Transcripts at GB 249 OB/1/2/1 and 2.

Thomas Garnett Papers. GB 249 OM/64.

(C) Printed Sources

Aitken, John. *An Address to the Chirurgo-Obstetrical Society, Delivered at Their First Meeting*. Edinburgh: Printed by J. McKenzie, 1786.

Alexander, William [of Harrogate]. *Plain and Easy Directions for the Use of Harrogate Waters*. 2nd edn. Knaresborough and Harrogate: Printed for E. Hargrove, 1780. 1st edn. 1773; 3rd edn. 1783.

Alexander, William [of Halifax]. *The Horley Green Mineral Water: Its New Chemical Analysis and Medicinal Uses*. London: Longman, Orme, Brown, Green, and Longman; Leyland and Son, Halifax, 1840.

Alvin, Christine. 'A Title Acquired without Labour: Dr George Mossman, MD (1763–1824)'. *J. Med. Biog.* 14 (2006): 210–17.

Anderson, John. *Extracts from the Latter Will and Codicil of Professor John Anderson*. Glasgow: Printed in the Courier Office, by W. Reid & Co., 1796.

Anderson, Robert G. W., ed. *Cradle of Chemistry: The Early Years of Chemistry at the University of Edinburgh*. Edinburgh: John Donald, 2015.

Andrews, Malcolm. *The Search for the Picturesque: Landscape Aesthetics and Tourism in Britain, 1760–1800*. Aldershot: Scolar Press, 1989.

Annals of Philosophy, Natural History, Chemistry, Literature, Agriculture, and the Mechanical and Fine Arts. For the Year 1800. By T. Garnett, M.D. F.L.S. … and Other Gentlemen. London: Printed for T. Cadell, Jun. and W. Davies, 1801. Later volumes for 1801 (published 1802) and 1802 (published 1804).

Anon. 'A treatise on the mineral waters of Harrogate … by Thomas Garnett, M.D.'. *Med. Comm. for the Year 1792*, Decade II, 7 (1793): 66–86.

Anon. *A Catalogue of Minerals in the Museum of Anderson's Institution, Glasgow*. Glasgow: Printed in the Courier Office, by W. Reid & Co., 1798.

Anon. 'Doctor Garnet [sic], M.D.'. In *Public Characters of 1799–1800*, 312–20. Dublin: Printed for James Moore, 1799.

Anon. 'Doctor Garnet [sic], M.D.'. In *Public Characters of 1799–1800*, 415–24. London: Printed for Richard Phillips, 1799. Also, significantly amended, in a second printing (same date and place), 405–14.

Anon. 'Observations on a Tour … by … Garnett'. *Crit. Rev.* ser. 2, 29: 1–12 (May 1800) and 416–28 (Aug. 1800).

Anon. 'Lord Loughborough'. In *Public Characters of 1800–1801*, 256–72. London: Printed for Richard Phillips, 1801.

Anon. [Alexander Tilloch?]. 'Royal Institute [sic] of Great Britain', *Phil. Mag.* 9 (Apr. 1801): 281–2.

Anon. 'Sir Benjamin Thompson, Count of Rumford, F.R.S. &c. &c'. In *Public Characters of 1801–1802*, 315–39. London: Printed for Richard Phillips, 1801.

Anon. 'Mr. Dawson, of Sedbergh'. In *Public Characters of 1801–1802*, 364–78. London: Printed for Richard Phillips, 1801.

Anon. 'Some account of Thomas Garnett, M.D. & c'. *Eur. Mag.* 42 (Jul. 1802): 5–6.

Anon. 'Deaths'. *Gent. Mag.* 72, part 2: 690 (Jul. 1802) and 777–78 (Aug. 1802).

Anon. 'Violent disputes, between the Brunonians and anti-Brunonians in Germany', *Monthly Mag.* 14 (Oct. 1802): 215–16.

Anon. [John Briggs?], 'Memoir of Thomas Garnett, M.D.'. *Lonsdale Mag.* 1 (Nov. 1820): 478–82.

Appleby, John H. 'Sir Alexander Crichton, F.R.S. (1763–1856), imperial Russian physician at large', *NRRS* 53 (1999): 219–30.

Aston, Joseph. *Manchester Guide: A Brief Historical Description of the Towns of Manchester & Salford, the Public Buildings, and the Charitable and Literary Institutions*. Manchester: Printed and sold by Joseph Aston, 1804.

Atkinson, George. *Worthies of Westmorland; or, Notable Persons Born in That County since the Reformation*. 2 vols. London: J. Robinson, 1849–50.

Banks, Joseph. *Scientific Correspondence of Joseph Banks, 1795–1820*, ed. Neil Chambers. 7 vols. London: Pickering & Chatto, 2007.

Barfoot, Michael. 'Brunonianism under the Bed: An Alternative to University Medicine in Edinburgh in the 1780s'. In Bynum and Porter, eds., *Brunonianism in Britain and Europe*, 22–45.

Bateman, Wynne. *Philosophorum veterum et sapientum de populari religione sensus, ac theologiae ratio. Concio ad clerum habita in templo Beatae Mariae Cantabrigiae, pridie Kal. Dec. M.DCC.XLV*. Cambridge: J. Bentham, 1746.

Beddoes, Thomas. 'Observations on the Character and Writings of John Brown, M.D'. In Brown, *Elements of Medicine*, xxxiii–clxviii. 1795 edn.

Beddoes, Thomas, and James Watt. *Considerations on the Medicinal Use, and on the Production of Factitious Airs. Part I. By Thomas Beddoes, M.D. Part II. By James Watt, Engineer*. 3rd edn. Bristol: Bulgin & Rosser, for J. Johnson, London, 1796.

Beddoes, Thomas. *A Lecture Introductory to a Course of Popular Instruction on the Constitution and Management of the Human Body*. Bristol: N. Biggs, for Joseph Cottle; sold in London by J. Johnson, 1797.

Behrendt, Stephen. 'Wordsworth and the Women Poets'. *Eur. Rom. Rev.* 23 (2012): 635–50.

Bennett, William. *Observations on the Sulphureous Springs of Harrogate*. London: Henry Renshaw, 1843.

Bergman, Torbern. *Opuscula physica et chemica, pleraque antea seorsim edita*. 6 vols. Stockholm, Uppsala, and Åbo: in officinis librariis Magni Swederi, 1779–90.

Bergman, Torbern. *Physical and Chemical Essays: To which are Added Notes and Illustrations, by the Translator*, trans. Edmund Cullen. 3 vols. London: Printed for J. Murray; and William Creech, Edinburgh, 1784–91.

Berman, Morris. *Social Change and Scientific Organization: The Royal Institution, 1799–1844*. London: Heinemann Educational, 1978.

Bigge, Thomas. *On the Expediency of Establishing, in Newcastle upon Tyne, a Lectureship on Subjects of Natural, and Experimental Philosophy*. Newcastle: Printed by S. Hodgson, 1802. Dated 29 Apr. 1802. Read 4 May 1802.

Birkbeck, George. *Tentamen chemico-physiologicum inaugurale, de sanguine*. Edinburgh: Adam Neill, 1799.

Booth, Christopher C. 'Robert Willan and his kinsmen'. *Med. Hist.* 25 (1981): 181–96.

Booth, Christopher C. *John Haygarth, FRS (1740–1827): A Physician of the Enlightenment* [*Memoirs of the American Philosophical Society*, volume 254]. Philadelphia: American Philosophical Society, 2005.

Boswell, James. *The Journal of a Tour to the Hebrides, with Samuel Johnson, LL.D.* London: Printed by Henry Baldwin, for Charles Dilly, 1785.

Briggs, Asa. *Victorian Cities*. London: Odhams, 1963; and subsequent editions (Penguin).

Briggs, John. *The Remains of John Briggs, Late Editor of 'The Lonsdale Magazine' and of 'The Westmorland Gazette': To which Is added, a Sketch of His Life*. Kirkby Lonsdale: Printed and sold by Arthur Foster, 1825.

Brown, John. *Joannis Brunonis, M.D. De medicina prælectoris, societatis regiæ medicæ edinensis præsidis, Elementa medicinæ*. Edinburgh: Prostant venales apud C Elliot. 1780; revised edition, 1784.

Brown, John. *Observations on the Principles of the Old System of Physic, Exhibiting a Compend of the New Doctrine: By a Gentleman Conversant in the Subject*. Edinburgh: From the Apollo Press, by Martin and McDowall, for the Author, 1787.

Brown, John. *The Elements of Medicine; or, A Translation of the Elementa Medicinae Brunonis: With Large Notes, Illustrations, and Comments. By the Author of the Original Work*. 2 vols. London: J. Johnson, 1788.

Brown, John. *The Elements of Medicine; or, A Translation of the Elementa medicinae Brunonis: With Large Notes, Illustrations, and Comments. By the Author of the Original Work*. Philadelphia: Printed by T. Dobson, 1790. Later editions, 1791, 1793, 1795.

Brown, John. *The Elements of Medicine of John Brown, M.D. Translated from the Latin, with Comments and Illustrations, by the Author: With a Biographical Preface by Thomas Beddoes, M.D. and a Head of the Author*. 2 vols. London: J. Johnson, 1795.

Brown, Sanborn C. *Benjamin Thompson, Count Rumford*. Cambridge, MA and London: MIT Press, 1979.

Buchan, William. *Cautions Concerning Cold Bathing, and Drinking the Mineral Waters: Being an Additional Chapter to the Ninth Edition of His Domestic Medicine*. London: Printed for A. Strahan, T. Cadell, and J. Balfour; and W. Creech, At Edinburgh, 1786.

Buffon, Georges-Louis Leclerc, Comte de. 'Dissertation sur la cause du strabisme ou des yeux louches'. *Mém. Acad. Sci.* (1743): 231–48. Read 19 June 1743.

Burns, James H. 'Twilight of the Enlightenment: James Headrick (1759–1841)'. *Scot. Hist. Rev.* 81 (2002): 186–211.

Butt, John. *John Anderson's Legacy: The University of Strathclyde and Its Antecedents 1796–1996*. East Linton: Tuckwell Press in association with the University of Strathclyde, 1996.

Bynum, William F., and Roy Porter, eds. *Brunonianism in Britain and Europe* [*Med. Hist.* 32, supplement no. 8] 1988.

Calvert, Michael. *An Account of the Knaresbrough Spaw: With an Analysis of the Water, and Some General Observations on Its Medicinal Qualities and Effects*. 2nd edn. Knaresborough: Printed by W. Langdale, 1831.

Campbell, John. 1st Baron. *Lives of the Lord Chancellors and Keepers of the Great Seal of England, from the Earliest Times till the Reign of King George IV*. 7 vols. London: John Murray, 1847.

Cantab, A. 'John Dawson, of Sedburg [sic], Kendal, in Westmoreland. To the Editor of the European Magazine'. *Eur. Mag.* 40 (December 1801): 406–7. Letter dated 'Trinity College, Nov. 9, 1801'.

Carey, George Saville. *The Balnea; or, An Impartial* Description *of All the Popular Watering Places in England*. London: Printed by J. W. Myers, for W. West, et al., 1799.

Caroe, Gwendy. *The Royal Institution: An Informal History*. London: John Murray, 1985.

Chalmers, Alexander, ed. *The General Biographical Dictionary: Containing an Historical and Critical Account of the Lives and Writings of the Most Eminent Persons in Every Nation*. New edn., 32 vols. London: Printed for J. Nichols, et al., 1812–17.

Chalmers, Iain, Ulrich Tröhler, and John Chalmers. '*Medical and Philosophical Commentaries and Its Successors*'. In John Chalmers, ed., *Andrew Duncan Senior*, 36–55. Edinburgh: National Museums of Scotland, 2010.

Chalmers, John, ed. *Andrew Duncan Senior: Physician of the Enlightenment*. Edinburgh: National Museums of Scotland, 2010.

Chalmers, John. 'Andrew Duncan senior (1744–1828): A Biographical Overview'. In John Chalmers, ed., *Andrew Duncan Senior*, 1–35. Edinburgh: National Museums of Scotland, 2010.

Chalmers, John. 'Medical clubs and societies founded by Andrew Duncan'. In John Chalmers, ed., *Andrew Duncan Senior*, 114–33. Edinburgh: National Museums of Scotland, 2010.

Chalmers, John. 'Duncan and the Brunonian society'. In John Chalmers, ed., *Andrew Duncan Senior*, 181–6. Edinburgh: National Museums of Scotland, 2010.

Chambers, Robert, ed., *A Biographical Dictionary of Eminent Scotsmen: Originally edited by Robert Chambers. Revised throughout and continued by the Rev. Thomas Thomson*. 3 vols. London, Glasgow, and Edinburgh: Blackie and Son, 1875.

Chappey, Jean-Luc. 'Idéologie et perspectives européennes de l'idée républicaine sous le Directoire: enjeux politiques et scientifiques de la diffusion des theories médicales de John Brown en Europe (vers 1780–vers 1820)'. In Pierre Serna, ed., *Républiques soeurs: Le Directoire et la Révolution atlantique*, 185–203. Rennes: Presses Universitaires de Rennes, 2009.

Christie, John R. R. '"The Most Perfect Liberty": Professors and Students in the Age of the Chemical Revolution'. In Anderson, ed., *Cradle of Chemistry*, 85–98. Edinburgh: John Donald, 2015.

Clark, John Willis, and Thomas McKenny Hughes. *The Life and Letters of the Reverend Adam Sedgwick*. 2 vols. Cambridge: Cambridge University Press, 1890.

Clarke, Henry Lowther and W. N. Weech. *History of Sedbergh School 1525–1925*. Sedbergh: Jackson & Son, 1925.

Coley, Noel G. 'John Warltire 1738/9-1810: Itinerant Lecturer and Chemist'. *West Mid. Stud.* 3 (1969): 31–44.

Coley, Noel G. 'Physicians and the Chemical Analysis of Mineral Waters in Eighteenth-Century England', *Med. Hist.* 26 (1982): 123–44.

Coley, Noel G. 'Physicians, Chemists and the Analysis of Mineral Waters: "The Most Difficult Part of Chemistry"', *Med. Hist.*, Supplement no. 10 (1990): 56–66.

A Companion to the Watering and Bathing Places of England: Containing Their Amusements, Curiosities, Antiquities, Seats in Their Vicinities, Chief Inns, and Distances from London. London: Printed by D. Brewman for H. D. Symonds, 1800.

Constantine, Mary-Ann, and Nigel Leask, eds. *Enlightenment Travel and British Identities: Thomas Pennant's Tours of Scotland and Wales*. London: Anthem Press, 2017.

Cossic-Péricarpin, Annick, and Patrick Galliou, eds. *Spas in Britain and in France in the Eighteenth and Nineteenth Centuries*. Newcastle: Cambridge Scholars Press, 2006.

Crawford, Dirom Grey. *Roll of the Indian Medical Service 1615–1930*. London: W. Thacker; Calcutta and Simla: Thacker, Spink & Co., 1930.

Cuvier, Georges. 'Eulogy on Count Rumford'. *Monthly Mag.*, 39 (May 1815): 323–39.

Darwin, Erasmus. 'A New Case in Squinting ... communicated by Thomas Astle', *Phil. Trans.* 68 (1778): 86–96.

Darwin, Erasmus. *The Botanic Garden: A Poem in Two Parts; Part I. Containing The Economy of Vegetation. Part II. The Loves of the Plants. With Philosophical Notes*. London: J. Johnson, 1791.

Darwin, Erasmus. *Zoonomia; or, The Laws of Organic Life*. 2 vols. London: J. Johnson, 1794–6.

Darwin, Erasmus. *The Letters of Erasmus Darwin*, ed. Desmond King-Hele. Cambridge: Cambridge University Press, 1981.

Davy, Humphry. 'Experimental essays on Heat, Light, and on the Combinations of Light'. In *Contributions to Physical and Medical Knowledge Principally from the West of England, Collected by Thomas Beddoes, M.D.*, 5–147. Bristol: Biggs and Cottle, 1799. Also in Davy, *Collected Works*, vol. 2, 1–86.

Davy, Humphry. *Researches, Chemical and Philosophical: Chiefly Concerning Nitrous Oxide, or Dephlogisticated Nitrous Air, and Its Respiration*. London: Printed by Biggs and Cottle, Bristol, for J. Johnson, 1800.

Davy, Humphry. *A Syllabus of a Course of Lectures on Chemistry, Delivered at the Royal Institution of Great Britain*. London: Press of the Royal Institution of Great Britain, W. Savage, Printer, 1802. Also in Davy, *Collected Works*, vol. 2, 327–436.

Davy, Humphry. *A Discourse, Introductory to a Course of Lectures on Chemistry, Delivered in the Theatre of the Royal Institution on the 21st January, 1802*. London: Press of the Royal Institution of Great Britain, W. Savage, printer: 1802. Also in Davy, *Collected Works*, vol. 2, 307–26.

Davy, Humphry. *The Collected Works of Sir Humphry Davy, Bart. LL.D. F.R.S.*, ed. John Davy. 9 vols. London: Smith, Elder and Co., 1839.

Davy, Humphry. *The Collected Letters of Sir Humphry Davy*, ed. Tim Fulford and Sharon Ruston. 4 vols. Oxford: Oxford University Press, 2020. Also in Oxford Scholarly Editions Online, 2021.

Davy, John. *Memoirs of the Life of Sir Humphry Davy, Bart. LL.D. F.R.S. By His Brother*. 2 vols. London: Smith, Elder and Co., 1836.

Dawson, John. *Four Propositions, &c. Shewing, not only, that the Distance of the Sun, as attempted to be determined from the Theory of Gravity, by a late Author, is, upon his own Principles, erroneous; but also, that it is more than probable that this Capital Question can never be satisfactorily answered by any Calculus of the Kind*. Newcastle: Printed by J. White and T. Saint, for W. Charnley, 1769.

Dawson, John. 'John Dawson to Mr. Urban, Sedbergh, 20 Sept. 1770'. *Gent. Mag.* 40 (Oct. 1770): 452–3.

Dawson, John. *The Doctrine of Philosophical Necessity briefly Invalidated*. London: Printed for Richardson and Urquhart and W. Pennington, Kendal, 1781; 2nd edn. London: Printed for T. Cadell and W. Davies, 1803.

Deane, Edmund. *Spadacrene Anglica; or, The English Spaw Fountaine: Being a Brief Treatise of the Acide, or Tart Fountaine in the Forest of Knaresborow, in the West-Riding of Yorkshire. As also a Relation of other Medicinall Waters in the Said Forest*. London: Printed for John Grismand, 1626.

Denholm, James. *A History of the City of Glasgow and Suburbs: Compiled from Authentic Records and other Respectable Authorities. To which Is Added a Sketch of a Tour to Loch Lomond and the Falls of Clyde*. 2nd edn. Glasgow: Printed by and for R. Chapman, and Stewart and Meikle, 1798. 1st edn. 1797.

Denholm, James. *The History of the City of Glasgow and Suburbs: To which Is added, A Sketch of a Tour to the Principal Scotch and English Lakes*. 3rd edn. Glasgow: Printed by R. Chapman, for A. Macgoun, 1804.

Devine, T. M., and Gordon Jackson, eds. *Glasgow. Volume I: Beginnings to 1830*. Manchester and New York: Manchester University Press, 1995.

Diderot, Denis. *Le Rêve de d'Alembert*, ed. Jean Varloot. Paris: Éditions du Peuple, 1971.

Dobson, Jessie, 'The College Criminals: 2. Eugene Aram'. *Ann. R. Coll. Surg.* 10 (1952), 267–75.

Dodd, Charles R. *The Annual Biography: Being Lives of Eminent or Remarkable Persons, Who Have Died within the Year, MDCCCXLII*. London: Chapman and Hall, 1843.

Duncan, Alexander. *Memorials of the Faculty of Physicians and Surgeons of Glasgow 1599–1850*. Glasgow: James Maclehose and Sons, 1896.

Duncan, Andrew. 'Conclusion of the clinical lectures at Edinburgh, 26th July 1776'. *Med. Phil. Comm.* 4, part 1 (1776): 101–5.

Eddy, Matthew D. *The Language of Mineralogy: John Walker, Chemistry and the Edinburgh Medical School, 1750–1800*. Farnham: Ashgate, 2008.

Edmonds, Fiona, and Sarah A. Rose, eds. *The Victoria History of the Counties of England: A History of the County of Westmorland*, vol. I. Martlesham: Boydell & Brewer, forthcoming.

Edwards, Nicholas. 'Some correspondence of Thomas Webster (circa 1772–1844), Concerning the Royal Institution'. *Ann. Sci.* 28, no.1 (1972): 43–60.

Ellis, George E. *Memoir of Sir Benjamin Thompson, Count Rumford, with Notices of His Daughter: Published in Connection with an Edition of Rumford's Complete Works by the American Academy of Arts and Sciences*. Boston: American Academy of Arts and Sciences, 1871.

Emerson, William. *A Short Comment on Sir I. Newton's Principia: Containing Notes upon Some Difficult Places of That Excellent Book*. London: Printed for J. Nourse, 1770.

Ewan, Joseph, and Nesta Dunn Ewan. *Benjamin Smith Barton: Naturalist and Physician in Jeffersonian America*. St Louis: Missouri Botanical Garden, 2007.

Falconer, William. *An Essay on the Bath Waters, in Four Parts*. London: Printed for T. Lowndes, 1772.

Falconer, William. *A Practical Dissertation on the Medicinal Effects of the Bath Waters*. Bath: Printed by R. Cruttwell, for G. G. J. and J. Robinson, 1790.

Farington, Joseph. *The Farington Diary*, ed. James Greig. 8 vols. London: Hutchinson, 1922–28.

Farish, William. *A Plan of a Course of Lectures on Arts and Manufactures, More Particularly Such as Relate to Chemistry*. 2nd edn. Cambridge: Printed by J. Burges, 1796.

Fullmer, June Z. 'Letter to the Editor'. *Sci. Am.* 203, 2 (Aug. 1960): 12–14.

G. [Thomas Garnett?]. 'An account of the Discovery, Progress, and Present State of Galvanism'. *Annals of Philosophy … for the Year 1800* 1 (1820): 3–25.

C. G. G. [Garnett, Catherine Grace]. 'Dr. Garnett. To the Editor of the Lonsdale Magazine'. *Lonsdale Mag.* 2 (Jan. 1821): 20–2.

Garnett, Catharine [*sic*] Grace. *The Night before the Bridal, a Spanish Tale; Sappho, a Dramatic Sketch; and other Poems*. London: Printed for Longman, Hurst, Rees, Orme, Brown, and Green, 1824.

Garnett, Catherine Grace. *Reine Canziani: A Tale of Modern Greece*. 2 vols. London: Printed for Hurst, Robinson, and Co.; and A. Constable and Co., Edinburgh, 1825.

See also Godwin, Catherine Grace

Garnett, Emmeline. 'Interim Draft History of Barbon', Cumbria County History Trust (2014). https://www.cumbriacountyhistory.org.uk/township/barbon.

Garnett, Thomas. *Dissertatio physica inauguralis, De visu. Quam annuente summo numine, Ex Auctoritate Reverendi admodum Viri, D. GULIELMI ROBERTSON, S.S. T.P. Academiae Edinburgenae Praefecti*. Edinburgh: Balfour and Smellie, Academiae Typographos, 1788.

Garnett, Thomas, 'Account of a Suppuration of the Liver, terminating Successfully'. *Med. Comm., for the Year 1788* Decade II, 3 (1789): 303–7.

Garnett, Thomas. *Experiments and Observations on the Horley-Green Spaw, Near Halifax: To which Is Added a Short Account of Two Other Mineral Waters, in Yorkshire*. Bradford: Printed for the author, by George Nicholson; sold by T. Knott, London, 1790.

Garnett, Thomas. 'History of a case of dropsy, cured by the use of *Infusum Nicotianae*'. *Med. Comm., for the Year 1791* Decade II, 6 (1792): 271–3.

Garnett, Thomas. 'Letter to Andrew Duncan'. *Med. Comm., for the Year 1791* Decade II, 6 (1792): 401–3.

Garnett, Thomas. *A Short Statement of Facts, Relative to the Late Conduct of Mr. William Thackwray of the Queen's Head, Harrogate*. Printed on three sides, signed 'T. Garnett', and dated 'Harrogate, July 20, 1792'. Only copy identified: BL CUP.21.g.44/73(a-b).

Garnett, Thomas. *Experiments and Observations on the Crescent Water at Harrogate.* Leeds: Printed by Thomas Gill. Sold By J. Johnson and T. Knott London; and E. Hargrove, Harrogate, 1791.

Garnett, Thomas. 'Letter to Andrew Duncan on the beneficial effects of kali sulfuratum (potassium sulphide)'. *Med. Comm., for the Year 1795* Decade II, 10 (1795): 368–70.

Garnett, Thomas. *A Treatise on the Mineral Waters of Harrogate: Containing the History of these Waters, Their Chemical Analysis, Medicinal Properties, and Plain Directions for Their Use.* Sold By J. Johnson and T. Knott, London; G. Mudie,Edinburgh; and E. Hargrove, Harrogate, 1792. Subsequent editions, with slightly modified subtitles: 2nd (1794); 3rd (1799); 4th (1804); 5th (1810); 6th (1816); 7th (1822); 8th (1829).

Garnett, Thomas. 'Meteorological Observations made on different parts of the western coast of Great Britain'. *Mem. MLPS* 4, pt. 1 (1793): 234–72. Read 8 Mar. 1793.

Garnett, Thomas. 'Observations on rain gages [sic]'. *Trans. R. Ir. Acad.* 5 (1794): 257–63. Dated Harrogate, 10 Dec. 1793. Read 25 Jan. 1794.

Garnett, Thomas. 'A Case of Petechiae unaccompanied with Fever, with observations on the same'. *Mem. Med. Soc. London.* 4 (1795): 233–46. Read 18 Feb. 1793.

Garnett, Thomas. 'Meteorological Observations, Collected and arranged by Thomas Garnett, M.D. physician at Harrogate'. *Mem. MLPS* 4, pt. 2 (1796): 517–640. Read 27 Mar. 1795.

Garnett, Thomas. *Outlines of a Course of Lectures on Natural & Experimental Philosophy.* Glasgow: Printed in the Courier Office, by W. Reid & Co., 1796.

Garnett, Thomas. 'Observations on the Wigglesworth Water'. *Mem. Med. Soc. London* 5 (1799): 119–22. Letter To J. C. Lettsom, 19 Dec. 1793. Read 25 May 1795.

Garnett, Thomas. 'Observations on the Nature and Virtues of the Harrogate Waters'. *Mem. Med. Soc. London* 5 (1799): 123–31. Read 27 May 1793.

Garnett, Thomas. *Outlines of a Course of Lectures on Chemistry.* Liverpool: Printed by J. M'Creery; sold by Cadell and Davies, London,1797.

Garnett, Thomas. *A Lecture on the Preservation of Health.* Liverpool: Printed by J. M'Creery and sold by Cadell and Davies, London, 1797. 2nd edn. London: Printed for T. Cadell, Junior, and W. Davies, 1800.

Garnett, Thomas. *Observations on a Tour through the Highlands and Part of the Western Isles of Scotland, Particularly Staffa and Icolmkill: To which are Added, a Description of the Falls of the Clyde, of the Country round Moffat, and an Analysis of Its Mineral Waters.* 2 vols. London: Printed by Luke Hansard for T. Cadell, Junior & W. Davies, 1800. 2nd edn. 2 vols. London: Printed for John Stockdale, 1811.

Garnett, Thomas. *Observations on Moffat, and Its Mineral Waters.* London: Printed by Luke Hansard for the Author, 1800.

Garnett, Thomas. *Observations on Moffat, and Its Mineral Waters: With Notes and Additions, by the Editor.* Edinburgh: Reprinted by John Orphoot, 1820.

Garnett, Thomas. *Outlines of a Course of Lectures on Chemistry.* London: Printed by G. Woodfall, for T. Cadell, Junior and W. Davies, 1801.

Garnett, Thomas. *Reise durch die Schottischen Hochlande und einen Theil der Hebriden. Aus dem Englischen übersetzt und mit Alexander Campbells Abhandlung über die Dicht- und Tonkunst der Hochländer wie auch über die Aechtheit der dem Ossian zugeschriebenen Gesänge vermehrt von Ludwig Theoboul Kosegarten*. 2 vols. Lübeck and Leipzig: Friedrich Bohn, 1802.

Garnett, Thomas. *Popular Lectures on Zoonomia, or the Laws of Animal Life in Health and Disease*. London: Press of the Royal Institution of Great Britain. W. Savage, printer, 1804.

Garnett, Revd Thomas. *Verses by a Poor Man: Part the Second*. Durham: F. Andrews, Saddler-Street; Whittaker and Co., London; Oliver and Boyd, Edinburgh; Curry and Co., Dublin, 1841.

Garnett, Revd Thomas. *Verses by a Poor Man: Dedicated by Express Permission, to His Royal Highness Prince Albert*. 2nd edn., corrected, with additional pieces. London: William Edward Painter; sold by F. Andrews, Durham, 1842.

George, Mary Dorothy. *Catalogue of Political and Personal Satires preserved in the Department of Prints and Drawings in the British Museum*. vol. 8 [1801–1810]. London: By Order of the Trustees, 1947.

Gilpin, William. *Observations, Relative Chiefly to Picturesque Beauty, Made in the Year 1776, on Several Parts of Great Britain: Particularly the High-Lands of Scotland*. 2 vols. London: Printed for R. Blamire, 1789.

Gilpin, William. *Three Essays: On Picturesque Beauty; On Picturesque Landscape; and On Sketching Landscape*. London: Printed for R. Blamire, 1792.

Girtanner, Christoph. 'Mémoires sur l'irritabilité, considérée comme principe de vie dans la nature organisée', *Obs. Phys.* 36 (Jan. 1790): 422–40 and 37 (Aug. 1790): 139–54.

Godwin, Catherine Grace. *Reine Canziani: A Tale of Modern Greece*. 2 vols. London: Printed for Hurst, Robinson, and Co.; and A. Constable and Co., Edinburgh, 1825.

Godwin, Catherine Grace. *The Wanderer's Legacy: A Collection of Poems, on Various Subjects*. London: Samuel Maunder, 1829.

Godwin, Catherine Grace. *Josephine; or, Early Trials*. London: John W. Parker, 1837.

Godwin, Catherine Grace. *Louisa Seymour; or, Hasty Impressions*. London: John W. Parker, 1837.

Godwin, Catherine Grace. *Alicia Grey; or, To be Useful Is to be Happy*. London: John W. Parker, 1837.

Godwin, Catherine Grace. *The Poetical Works of the Late Catherine Grace Godwin edited, with a Sketch of Her Life, by A. Cleveland Wigan*. London: Chapman and Hall, 1854.

See also Garnett, Catherine Grace

Golinski, Jan. *Science as Public Culture: Chemistry and Enlightenment in Britain, 1760–1820*. Cambridge: Cambridge University Press, 1992.

Golinski, Jan. *The Experimental Self: Humphry Davy and the Making of a Man of Science*. Chicago and London: University of Chicago Press, 2016.

Good, John Mason, Olinthus Gregory, and Newton Bosworth. *Pantologia: A New Cabinet Cyclopaedia, Comprehending a Complete Series of Essays, Treatises, and Systems, Alphabetically Arranged*. London: Printed for G. Kearsley et al., 1813. Reissued, unchanged,1819.

Graham, Henry. *History of the Sixteenth, The Queen's, Light Dragoons (Lancers), 1759 to 1912*. Devizes: Privately Printed, George Simpson, Printer, 1912.

Grainge, William. *The History and Topography of Harrogate, and the Forest of Knaresborough*. London: John Russell Smith; Pateley Bridge: Thos. Thorpe, 1871.

Granvile, Augustus Bozzi. *The Spas of England, and Principal Sea-Bathing Places. Northern Spas*. London: Henry Colburn, 1841.

Gray, James A. *History of the Royal Medical Society 1737–1937*, ed. Douglas Guthrie. Edinburgh: Edinburgh University Press, 1952.

Gray, James A. 'The Royal Medical and Medico-Chirurgical Societies'. In John Chalmers, ed., *Andrew Duncan Senior*, 134–55. Edinburgh: National Museums of Scotland, 2010.

Haakonssen, Lisbeth. *Medicine and Morals in the Enlightenment: John Gregory, Thomas Percival and Benjamin Rush*. Amsterdam and Atlanta, GA: Rodolpi, 1997. Also Clio Medica Online, vol. 44.

Hackman, Rowan. *Ships of the East India Company*. Gravesend: World Ship Society, 2001.

Hailstone, Samuel. *A Dose for the Doctor; or, A Bitter Pill for George Mossman: Containing an Account of His Life*. London, 1796.

Hailstone, Samuel. *The Dose Repeated; or, Another Pill for George Mossman*. London, 1796.

Hamilton, William. *Letters Concerning the Northern Coast of the County of Antrim: Containing a Natural History of Its Basaltes*. London: Printed by George Bonham, for Luke White, 1786.

Hamlin, Christopher. *A Science of Impurity: Water Analysis in Nineteenth-Century Britain*. Berkeley, CA: University of California Press, 1990.

Hamlin, Christopher. 'Chemistry, Medicine, and the Legitimization of English Spas, 1740–1840'. *Med. Hist.*, supplement no. 10 (1990): 67–81.

Hardy, Charles Frederick. *Benenden Letters: London, Country, and Abroad, 1753–1821*. London: J. M. Dent & Co., 1901.

Hardy, Charles Frederick. *The Hardys of Barbon and Some Other Westmorland Statesmen: Their Kith Kin and Childer*. London: Constable, 1913.

Hargrove, Ely. *The History of the Castle and Town of Knaresbrough: With Remarks on Spofforth. Rippon, Aldborough, Boroughbridge, Ribston, &c*. Knaresborough: Printed for and sold by E. Hargrove, 1769.

Hargrove, Ely. *The History of the Castle, Town, and Forest of Knaresbrough; with Harrogate, and Its Medicinal Waters. The Antiquities and Remarkable Places to be seen in the Neighbourhood, Eminent for Their Situation, and Celebrated in Ancient History*. 2nd edn. York: Printed for and Sold By E. Hargrove, Bookseller, at his shops in Knaresborough and Harrogate, 1775. Subsequent editions, with slightly modified titles and publication details: 3rd edn. (1782); 4th edn. (1789); 5th edn. (1798); 6th edn. (1809; reissued 1821).

Harley, David. 'Ethics and Dispute Behavior in the Career of Henry Bracken of Lancaster: Surgeon, Physician and Manmidwife'. In Robert Baker, Dorothy Porter, and Roy Porter, eds., *The Codification of Medical Morality*, 47–71. Dordrecht and London: Kluwer Academic, 1993.

Harrison, David. 'Thomas Garnett, the Lodge of Lights, and the Radical Enlightenment'. *Philalethes. The Journal of Masonic Research & Letters* 72, 4 (2019): 147–51. Also in

Harrison, David. *Masonic Mosaic: Foundations of a World under Construction*, 95–110. Masonica: Oviedo, 2020.

Harrison, John Anthony. 'Blind Henry Moyes: An "Excellent Lecturer in Philosophy"'. *Ann. Soc.* 13 (1957): 109–25.

Heald, William Margetson, under alias 'Julius Juniper'. *The Brunoniad: An Heroic Poem. In Six Cantos. Containing a Solemn Detail of Certain Commotions which Have, of Late, Divided the Kingdom of Physic against Itself.* London: Printed for G. Kearsley, 1789.

Hembry, Phyllis. *The English Spa 1560–1815: A Social History*. London: Athlone Press, 1990.

Hodgson, Harry Roberts. *The Society of Friends in Bradford: A Record of 270 Years*. Bradford: Percy Lund, Humphries & Co., Ltd. and The Country Press, 1926.

Hodgson, John. 'Westmorland as it was'. Briggs, *Remains of John Briggs* 1: 201–10. First part also in *Lonsdale Mag.* 3 (1822): 248–54.

Hofmann, August Wilhelm. *Harrogate and Its Resources: Chemical Analysis of Its Medicinal Waters; Report addressed to the Chairman of the Harrogate Water Committee. With an Appendix, on the Modes of Their Administration.* London: Printed by S. Galon, 1854.

Holland, Elizabeth, Lady. *The Journal of Elizabeth, Lady Holland (1791–1811)*, ed. Earl of Ilchester. 2 vols. London: Longmans, Green, and Co., 1908.

Horsley, Samuel. 'On the computation of the sun's distance from the earth, by the theory of gravity: in a letter to Mathew Maty M.D. Sec. R.S. from the Rev. Mr. Horsley F.R.S'. *Phil. Trans.* 59 (1769): 153–4. Dated Oxford 5 May1769. Read 1 June 1769.

Hume, Abraham. *The Learned Societies and Printing Clubs of the United Kingdom: Being an Account of Their Respective Origin, History, Objects, and Constitution*. London: G. Willis, 1853.

Hussey, Christopher. *The Picturesque: Studies in a Point of View*. 2nd edn. London: Frank Cass, 1967.

Hutchings, Victoria. *Messrs Hoare Bankers: A History of the Hoare Banking Dynasty*. London: Constable, 2005.

Hutton, Charles. *Miscellanea Mathematica: Consisting of a Large Collection of Curious Mathematical Problems, and Their Solutions. Together with Many Other Important Disquisitions in Various Branches of Mathematics. Being the Literary Correspondence of Several Eminent Mathematicians*. London: Printed for G. Robinson and R. Baldwin, 1775.

Hutton, Charles. *The Correspondence of Charles Hutton: Mathematical Networks in Georgian Britain*, ed. Benjamin Wardhaugh. Oxford: Oxford University Press, 2017.

Inkster, Ian, and Jack Morrell, eds. *Metropolis and Province: Science in British Culture, 1780–1850*. London: Hutchinson, 1983.

Ishizuka, Hirao. *Fiber, Medicine, and Culture in the British Enlightenment*. New York: Springer, 2016.

Israel, Jonathan. *Radical Enlightenment: Philosophy and the Making of Modernity 1650–1750*. Oxford: Oxford University Press, 2001.

Jacob, Margaret C. *The Radical Enlightenment: Pantheists, Freemasons and Republicans*. London: Allen & Unwin, 1981. New edition, Lafayette, LA: Cornerstone Book Publishers, 2006.

James, Frank A. J. L. 'Constructing Humphry Davy's Biographical Image'. *Ambix* 66 (2019): 214–38.

James, Frank A. J. L., and Anthony Peers. 'Constructing Space for Science at the Royal Institution of Great Britain'. *Phys. Persp.* 9 (2007): 130–85.

James, John. *The History and Topography of Bradford, (in the County of York,) with Topographical Notices of Its Parish*. London: Longman, Brown, Green, and Longmans; Charles Stanfield, Bradford, 1841.

Jay, Mike. *The Atmosphere of Heaven: The Unnatural Experiments of Dr Beddoes and His Sons of Genius*. New Haven and London: Yale University Press, 2009.

Jenkinson, Jacqueline. *Scottish Medical Societies 1731–1939: Their History and Records*. Edinburgh: Edinburgh University Press, 1993.

Jennings, Bernard, ed. *A History of Harrogate & Knaresborough: Written by the Harrogate W.E.A. Local History Group*. Huddersfield: Advertiser Press, 1970.

Johnson, Samuel. *A Journey to the Western Islands of Scotland*. London: Printed for W. Strahan and T. Cadell, 1775.

Johnston, Dorothy B. 'All Honourable Men? The Award of Irregular Degrees in King's College and Marischal College in the Eighteenth Century'. In Jennifer J. Carter and Joan H. Pittock, eds., *Aberdeen and the Enlightenment: Proceedings of a Conference Held at the University of Aberdeen*, 136–45. Aberdeen: Aberdeen University Press, 1987.

Jones, David Albert. 'Recruitment, Background, and Education of the Clergy'. In W. M. Jacob, ed., *The Clerical Profession in the Long Eighteenth Century*, 31–63. Oxford: Oxford University Press, 2007.

Jones, Henry Bence. *The Royal Institution: Its Founder and Its First Professors*. London: Longman's, Green, & Co., 1871.

Jones, Peter M. *Industrial Enlightenment: Science, Technology and Culture in Birmingham and the West Midlands*. Manchester: Manchester University Press, 2008.

Jordanova, Ludmilla. *Defining Features: Scientific and Medical Portraits, 1660–2000*. London: National Portrait Gallery, 2000.

Juniper, Julius. *See* Heald, William Margetson

Kaufman, Matthew H. 'John Aitken (d. 1790) – Grinder or Scholar', *J. Med. Biog.* 11 (2003): 199–205.

Kelly, Thomas. *George Birkbeck: Pioneer of Adult Education*. Liverpool: Liverpool University Press, 1957.

Kett, Joseph F. 'Provincial Medical Practice in England 1730–1815'. *J. Hist. Med.* 19 (1964): 17–29.

Knight, David M. *Humphry Davy: Science and Power*. Oxford: Blackwell, 1992.

Knox, John. *View of the British Empire, More Especially Scotland: With Some Proposals for the Improvement of That Country, the Extension of Its Fisheries, and the Relief of the People*. London: Printed for J. Walter, 1784.

Landen, John. *Animadversions on Dr. Stewart's Computation of the Sun's Distance from the Earth*. London: Printed for the author, by George Bigg; sold by J. Nourse, 1771.

Langford, Paul. *A Polite and Commercial People: England 1727–1783*. Oxford: Clarendon Press, 1989.

Lawrence, Susan C. *Charitable Knowledge: Hospital Pupils and Practitioners in Eighteenth-Century London*. Cambridge: Cambridge University Press, 1996.

Laws and Lists of Members of the Royal Society of Medicine of Edinburgh. Edinburgh: Printed by William Smellie for the Society, 1788.

The Laws and Regulations of the Royal Physical Society, instituted at Edinburgh, July 2, 1771 and confirmed by Royal Charter, May 5. 1788. Edinburgh, 1788.

Laws of the Society, instituted at Edinburgh, M.DCC.LXXXII for the Investigation of Natural History. Edinburgh, 1788.

Leask, Nigel. *Stepping Westward: Writing the Highland Tour c.1720–1830*. Oxford: Oxford University Press, 2020.

Lillywhite, Bryant. *London Coffee Houses: A Reference Book of Coffee Houses of the Seventeenth, Eighteenth, and Nineteenth Centuries*. London: Allen and Unwin, 1963.

List of Members, Laws, and Library Catalogue of the Medical Society in Edinburgh. Edinburgh: Printed for the Society, 1820.

List of the Graduates in Medicine in the University of Edinburgh from MDCCV to MDLCCCVI. Edinburgh: Printed by Neill & Company, 1867.

The London Catalogue of Books, with their Sizes, Prices, and Publishers: Containing the Books published in London, and those altered in Size, or Price, since the Year 1800 to October 1822. London: William Bent, 1822.

Lythe, S. G. E. *Thomas Garnett (1766–1802): Highland Tourist*. Glasgow: Polpress, 1984.

Mackenzie, Allan. *History of the Lodge Canongate Kilwinning, No. 2: Compiled from the Records 1677–1888*. Edinburgh: Printed for the Lodge by Brother James Hogg, 1888.

Marshall, J. D. 'Some Aspects of the Social History of 19th-Century Cumbria: (I) Migration and Literacy'. *Trans. CWAAS* ser. 2, 69 (1969): 280–307.

Marshall, J. D. *Old Lakeland: Some Cumbrian Social History*. Newton Abbot: David and Charles, 1971.

Marshall, J. D. '"Statesmen" in Cumbria: The Vicissitudes of an Expression'. *Trans. CWAAS* new ser., 72 (1972): 248–73.

Martin, Benjamin. *A Course of Lectures in Natural and Experimental Philosophy, Geography and Astronomy: In which the Properties, Affections, and Phaenomena of Natural Bodies, hitherto discover'd, are exhibited and explain'd on the Principles of the Newtonian Philosophy*. Reading: Printed and sold by J. Newbery and C. Micklewright, 1743.

Martin, Thomas. 'Origins of the Royal Institution'. *Br. J. Hist. Sci.* 1 (1962–3): 49–63.

Martin, Thomas. 'Early Years of the Royal Institution'. *Br. J. Hist. Sci.* 2 (1964–5): 99–115.

McElroy, Davis D. *Scotland's Age of Improvement: A Survey of Eighteenth-Century Literary Clubs and Societies*. Pullman: Washington State University Press, 1969.

Mee, Jon, and Jennifer Wilkes. 'Transpennine Enlightenment: The Literary and Philosophical Societies and Knowledge Networks in the North, 1781–1830'. *J. 18th-Cent Stud.* 38 (2015): 599–612.

Merrill, Jane. *Sex and the Scientist: The Indecent Life of Benjamin Thompson, Count Rumford (1753–1814)*. Jefferson, NC: McFarland & Company, 2018.

Metcalf, John. *The Life of John Metcalf, commonly Called Blind Jack of Knaresborough: With Many Entertaining Anecdotes of His Exploits in Hunting, Card-Playing, &c. ....* York: Printed and sold by E. and R. Peck, 1795.

Morton, Alan Q., and Jane A. Wess. *Public & Private Science: The King George III Collection*. Oxford: Oxford University Press in association with the Science Museum, 1993.

Muir, James. *John Anderson, Pioneer of Technical Education, and the College He Founded*, ed. James M. Macaulay. Glasgow: John Smith & Son, 1950.

Musson, A. E., and Eric Robinson. *Science and Technology in the Industrial Revolution*. Manchester: Manchester University Press, 1969.

Neesam, Malcolm G. *Harrogate Great Chronicle, 1332–1841 in Two Parts. Part One: 'Early Harrogate, 1331–1841'*. Lancaster: Carnegie Publishing, 2005.

Nichols, John. *Illustrations of the Literary History of the Eighteenth Century: Consisting of Authentic Memoirs and Original Letters of Eminent Persons*. 8 vols. London: Printed for the author by John Nichols and Son, 1817–58.

Nicholson, Cornelius. *The Annals of Kendal: Being a Historical and Descriptive Account of Kendal and the Neighbourhood; With Biographical Sketches of Many Eminent Personages connected with the Town*. 2nd edn. London: Whitaker & Co.; and Kendal: T. Wilson, T. Atkinson, W. Fisher, J. Robinson, 1861.

Nomina eorum, qui gradum medicinae doctoris in academia Jacobi Sexti Scotorum Regis, quae Edinburgi est, adepti sunt. Ab anno MDCCV. Ad annum MDCCCXLV Edinburgh: Neill and Company, 1846.

Orange, A. Derek. 'Rational dissent and provincial science'. In Inkster and Morrell, eds., *Metropolis and Province*, 205–30. London: Hutchinson, 1983.

Paris, John Ayrton. *The Life of Sir Humphry Davy, Bart., LL.D., Late President of the Royal Society, Foreign Associate of the Institute of France, &c. &c. &c.* 2 vols. London: Henry Colburn and Richard Bentley, 1831.

Peacock, George. *Life of Thomas Young, M.D., F.R.S., &c.* London: John Murray, 1855.

Pennant, Thomas. *A Tour in Scotland: MDCCLXIX.* Chester: Printed by John Monk, 1771.

Pennant, Thomas. *A Tour in Scotland, and Voyage to the Hebrides: MDCCLXXII.* Chester: Printed by John Monk, 1774. Reissued in two parts, London: Printed for Benj. White, 1776.

Perrin, Carleton E. 'A Reluctant Catalyst: Joseph Black and the Edinburgh Reception of Lavoisier's Chemistry'. *Ambix* 29 (1982): 141–76.

Pigott, G. West. *The Harrogate Spas with an Introductory Essay.* London: T. C. Newby; and Harrogate: W. Dawson, 1853.

Platt, A. E. *The History of the Parish and Grammar School of Sedbergh.* London: Longmans Green, 1876.

Playfair, John. 'Account of Matthew Stewart, D.D.'. *Trans. Roy. Soc. Ed.* 1 (1788): 57–76. Read 2 Apr. 1786.

Playfair, John. 'Biographical account of the late John Robison, LL.D. F.R.S.Edin. and Professor of Natural Philosophy in the University of Edinburgh'. *Trans. Roy. Soc. Ed.* 7 (1815): 495–539. Also in *The Works of John Playfair, Esq.*, 4 vols. Edinburgh: Printed for Archibald Constable & Co. Edinburgh, and Hurst, Robinson, and Co. London, 1822, vol. 4, 121–78.

Pococke, Richard. *Richard Pococke's Irish Tours*, ed. John Mcveigh. Dublin: Irish Academic Press, 1995.

Porter, Roy, and George S. Rousseau. *Gout: The Patrician Malady.* New Haven and London: Yale University Press, 1998.

Porterfield, William. *A Treatise on the Eye, the Manner and Phaenomena of Vision.* 2 vols. Edinburgh: Printed for A. Miller, London and for G. Hamilton and J. Balfour, Edinburgh, 1779.

Priestley, Joseph. *The History and Present State of Discoveries Relating to Vision, Light, and Colours.* London: Printed for J. Johnson, 1772.

Priestley, Joseph. *An Examination of Dr. Reid's Inquiry into the Human Mind on the Principles of Common Sense, Dr. Beattie's Essay on the Nature and Immutability of Truth, and Dr. Oswald's Appeal to Common Sense in Behalf of Religion.* 2nd edn. London: Printed for J. Johnson, 1775.

Priestley, Joseph. *Disquisitions Relating to Matter and Spirit.* London: Printed for J. Johnson, 1777.

Priestley, Joseph. *The Doctrine of Philosophical Necessity Illustrated: Being an Appendix to the Disquisitions Relating to Matter and Spirit.* London: Printed for J. Johnson, 1777.

Priestley, Joseph, and Richard Price. *A Free Discussion of the Doctrines of Materialism, and Philosophical Necessity, in a Correspondence between Dr. Price, and Dr. Priestley.* London: Printed for J. Johnson and T. Cadell, 1778.

Prospectus of the Royal Institution of Great Britain, Incorporated by Charter MDCCC: Patron the King; With a Copy of the Charter, and a List of the Subscribers.

London: Printed for the Royal Institution, By W. Bulmer and Co. Sold By Cadell and Davies. Dated Albemarle Street, 21 Jan. 1800. List of subscribers dated Jan. 1800.

The Prospectus, Charter, Ordinances and Bye-Laws, of the Royal Institution of Great Britain: Together with Lists of the Proprietors and Subscribers; and an Appendix. London: Printed for the Royal Institution, By W. Bulmer and Co. Sold By Cadell and Davies, 1800. List of subscribers dated 1 May 1800. Also in Rumford, *Complete Works*, vol. 4, 771–85; and *Collected Works*, vol. 5, 471–85.

Pryme, George. *Autobiographic Recollections of George Pryme, Esq. M.A., Edited by His Daughter*. Cambridge: Deighton, Bell, and Co.; and London: Bell and Daldy, 1870.

Raine, James. *A Memoir of the Rev. John Hodgson*. 2 vols. London: Longman, Brown, Green, Longmans, and Roberts, 1857–8.

Reid, Thomas [philosopher]. *An Inquiry into the Human Mind, on the Principles of Common Sense*. 2nd edn. Edinburgh: Printed for A. Millar, London, and Kincaid and J. Bell, Edinburgh, 1765.

Reid, Thomas [physician]. *Directions for Warm and Cold Sea-Bathing: With Observations on Their Application and Effects in Different Diseases*. London: Sold by T. Cadell, and W. Davies; and at Ramsgate, by P. Burgess, 1795.

Report by the Managers to the Trustees, on the Property, Affairs, and Increased Means of Anderson's University of Glasgow. Glasgow: Printed in the Chronicle Office, n. d. (1832?).

Richardson, Edgar P. 'The Athens of America 1800–1825'. In Russell Frank Weigley, ed., *Philadelphia: A 300-Year History*, 208–57. New York and London: W. W. Norton, 1982.

Richmond, D. C. 'On a proposed system of grouping schools in the County of Westmorland'. In *Schools Inquiry Commission: Vol. IX; General Reports by Assistant Commissioners, Northern Counties*, 901–11. London: Printed by George E. Eyre and William Spottiswoode, for Her Majesty's Stationery Office, 1868.

Risse, Guenter B. 'The history of John Brown's medical system in Germany during the years 1790–1806'. PhD diss., University of Chicago, 1971.

Risse, Guenter B. 'A frustrated reform: Brunonianism in Romantic Germany'. Unpublished paper, 1982, available on the ResearchGate open access platform.

Risse, Guenter B. *New Medical Challenges during the Scottish Enlightenment*. Amsterdam; New York: Rodopi, 2005. Also Clio Medica Online, vol. 78.

Risse, Guenter B. 'Explaining Brunonianism: A Biography of Edinburgh's Master of Conviviality, John Brown, MD (1745–1788)'. Edited September 2020. Available on the Academia.edu and ResearchGate open access platforms.

Robinet, Jean-Baptiste. *De la Nature*. Amsterdam: E. van Harrevelt, 1761.

Robinson, W. Andrew. *The Last Man Who Knew Everything: Thomas Young, the Anonymous Polymath Who Proved Newton Wrong, Explained How We See, Cured the Sick, and Deciphered the Rosetta Stone, Among Other Feats of Genius*. Oxford: Oneworld, 2006.

Rosner, Lisa. *Andrew Duncan M.D., F.R.S.E. (1744–1828)*. Edinburgh: History of Medicine and Science Unit, University of Edinburgh, 1981.

Rosner, Lisa. *Medical Education in the Age of Improvement: Edinburgh Students and Apprentices, 1760–1826*. Edinburgh: Edinburgh University Press, 1991.

Rosner, Lisa. 'Eighteenth-Century Medical Education and the Didactic Model of Experiment'. In Peter Dear, ed., *The Literary Structure of Scientific Argument: Historical Studies*, 182–94. Philadelphia: University of Pennsylvania Press, 1991.

Rumford, Count [Benjamin Thompson], *Proposals for Forming by Subscription, in the Metropolis of the British Empire, a Public Institution for Diffusing the Knowledge and Facilitating the General Introduction of Useful Mechanical Inventions and Improvements, and for Teaching, by Courses of Philosophical Lectures and Experiments, the Application of Science to the Common Purposes of Life*. Signed by Rumford Brompton-Row, 4 Mar. 1799. Also in Rumford, *Complete Works*, vol. 4, 739–70; Rumford, *Collected Works*, vol. 5, 439–70; and Jones, *Royal Institution*, 121–34.

Rumford, Count [Benjamin Thompson]. *The Complete Works of Count Rumford*. 4 vols. Boston: American Academy of Arts and Sciences, 1870–5.

Rumford, Count [Benjamin Thompson]. *Collected Works of Count Rumford*, ed. Sanborn C. Brown. 5 vols. Cambridge, MA: Belknap Press of Harvard University Press, 1968–70.

Rush, Benjamin. *Letters of Benjamin Rush*, ed. L. H. Butterfield. 2 vols. Princeton, NJ: Princeton University Press for the American Philosophical Society, 1951.

Ruston, Sharon. 'Shelley's links to the Midlands Enlightenment: James Lind and Adam Walker'. *J. 18th-Cent. Stud.* 30 (2007): 227–41.

Ruston, Sharon. *Creating Romanticism: Case Studies in the Literature, Science and Medicine of the 1790s*. Basingstoke: Palgrave Macmillan, 2013.

Saunders, William. *A Treatise on the Chemical History and Medical Powers of Some of the Most Celebrated Mineral Waters; with Practical Remarks on the Aqueous Regimen. To which are added, Observations on the Use of Cold and Warm Bathing*. London: Printed and sold by William Phillips, 1800.

The Sedbergh School Register 1546 to 1909. Leeds: Richard Jackson, 1909.

Sedgwick, Adam. *A Memorial by the Trustees of Cowgill Chapel*. Cambridge: Cambridge University Press, 1868.

Sedgwick, Adam. *Supplement to the Memorial of the Trustees of Cowgill Chapel*. Cambridge: Cambridge University Press, 1870.

Shepherd, Thomas Hosmer. *Modern Athens! Displayed in a Series of Views; or, Edinburgh in the Nineteenth century: Exhibiting the Whole of the New Buildings, Modern Improvements, Antiquities, and Picturesque Scenery, of the Scottish Metropolis and its Environs, from Original Drawings, by Mr. Thomas H. Shepherd. With Historical, Topographical, and Critical Illustrations*. London: Jones & Co., 1831.

Sher, Richard B. 'Commerce, Religion and the Enlightenment in Eighteenth-Century Glasgow'. In Devine and Jackson, eds., *Glasgow. Volume I*, 312–59. Manchester and New York: Manchester University Press, 1995.

Short, Thomas. *The Natural, Experimental, and Medicinal History of the Mineral Waters of Derbyshire, Lincolnshire, and Yorkshire, Particularly Those of Scarborough*. London: Printed for the author, and sold by F. Gyles, 1734

Short, Thomas. *An Essay towards a Natural, Experimental, and Medicinal History of the Principle [sic] Mineral Waters of Cumberland, Westmoreland ... Particularly Those of Neville Holt, Cheltenham, Weatherslack, Hartlepool, Astrope, Cartmall &c*. Sheffield: printed for the author, by John Garnet, 1740.

Short, Thomas. *A General Treatise on Various Cold Mineral Waters in England, but More Particularly on those at Harrogate, Thorp-Arch, Dorst-Hill, Wigglesworth, Nevill-Holt, and Others of Like Nature. With their Principles, Virtues and Uses. Also a Short Discourse on Solvents of the Stone in the Kidneys and Bladder*. London: Printed for the author; and Sold By A. Millar, W. Owen, and W. Johnston, 1765.

Simpson, William. *Observations on Cold Bathing*. Leeds: Printed by Thomas Gill, 1791.

Sinclair, Sir John. *Address to the Society for the Improvement of British Wool: Constituted at Edinburgh, on Monday, January 31, 1791*. London: Printed for T. Cadell, 1791.

Sinclair, Sir John. *The Statistical Account of Scotland: Drawn up from the Communications of the Ministers of the Different Parishes*. 21 vols. Edinburgh: Printed and sold by William Creech; also sold by J. Donaldson et al., 1791–9.

Slinn, Sara. *The Education of the Anglican Clergy 1780–1839*. Woodbridge: Boydell Press, 2017.

Smith, John. *General View of the Agriculture of the County of Argyll: With Observations on the Means of Its Improvement*. Edinburgh: Printed for Mundell & Son and J. Mundell, College, Glasgow, 1798.

Smith, Robert. *A Compleat System of Opticks in Four Books, viz. a Popular, a Mathematical, a Mechanical, and a Philosophical Treatise: To which are Added Remarks upon the Whole*. 2 vols. continuously paginated. Cambridge: Printed for the author, 1738.

Smith, Sarah J. 'Retaking the Register: Women's Higher Education in Glasgow and beyond, c. 1796–1845'. *Gender Hist*. 13 (2000): 310–36.

Smollett, Tobias. *The Expedition of Humphry Clinker. By the Author of Rodrick Random*. 2nd edn. 3 vols. London: Printed for W. Johnston; and B. Collins, Salisbury, 1771.

Steinke, Hubert. *Irritating Experiments: Haller's Concept and the European Controversy on Irritability and Sensibility, 1750–90*. Amsterdam and New York: Rodopi, 2005. Also Clio Medica Online, vol. 76.

Stewart, Matthew. *The Distance of the Sun from the Earth Determined, by the Theory of Gravity: Together with Several Other Things Relative to the Same Subject*. Edinburgh: Printed for A. Millar, J. Nourse, and D. Wilson, London; and W. Sands, and A. Kincaid & J. Bell, Edinburgh, 1763.

Stroud, William. 'History of the Medical Society of Edinburgh'. In *List of Members ... of the Medical Society in Edinburgh*, iii–ci. Edinburgh: Printed for the Society, 1820

Tansey, E. M. 'The life and works of Sir Alexander Crichton, F.R.S. (1763–1856): A Scottish physician to the Imperial Russian Court'. *NRRS* 53 (1999): 219–30.

Thackray, Arnold. 'Natural Knowledge in Cultural Context: The Manchester Model'. *Am. Hist. Rev.* 79 (1974): 672–709.

Thom, William. *Works of the Rev. William Thom, Late Minister of Govan*. Glasgow: Printed for James Dymock, 1799.

Thompson, William. *Sedbergh, Garsdale, and Dent: Peeps at the Past History and Present Condition of Some Picturesque Yorkshire Dales*. Leeds: Richard Jackson, 1892.

Thomson, James. *The Seasons. By Mr. Thomson*. London: Printed in the year MDCCXXX.

Thomson, John. *An Account of the Life, Lectures, and Writings of William Cullen, M.D.* 2 vols. Edinburgh and London: William Blackwood and Sons, 1859.

Thornton, Robert John. Signed 'A friend to improvements'. *The Philosophy of Medicine; or, Medical Extracts on the Nature of Health and Disease, Including the Laws of the Animal Oeconomy, and the Doctrines of Pneumatic Medicine*, 4th edn., 5 vols. London: Printed by C. Whittingham for T. Cox, et al., 1799–1800.

Thorpe, J. *Thorpe's Visitor's Hand-Book for Harrogate, and Stranger's Companion to all Objects of Interest in the District: Together with a Popular Description of the Mineral Waters, and a Map of Harrogate and Ten Miles round*. 3rd edn. Harrogate: R. Ackrill, 1859.

Topham, Jonathan R. 'Anthologizing the Book of Nature: The Origins of the Scientific Method and Circulation of Knowledge in late Georgian Britain'. In Bernard Lightman, Gordon McOuat, and Larry Stewart, eds., *The Circulation of Knowledge between Britain, India and China*, 119–52. Leiden: Brill, 2013.

Turner, Revd William. *A General Introductory Discourse. (Delivered, on Tuesday, Nov. 16, 1802) on the Objects, Advantages, and Intended Plan of the New Institution for Public Lectures on Natural Philosophy, in Newcastle-upon-Tyne ... to which is Added, a List of the Donations and Annual Subscriptions hitherto received*. Newcastle, 1802.

Turner, Revd William. *An Address delivered at the First Meeting of the Literary & Philosophical Society of Newcastle upon Tyne, held in Its New Apartments, Sept. VI. MDCCCXXV*. Newcastle, 1825.

Vernon, K. D. C. 'The foundation and early years of the Royal Institution'. *Proc. R. Inst.* 39 (1962–63): 364–402.

Volta, Alessandro. 'On the electricity excited by the mere contact of conducting substances of different kinds, in a letter from Mr. Alexander Volta, F. R. S. Professor of Natural Philosophy in the University of Pavia, to the Rt. Hon. Sir Joseph Banks, Bart. K.B. P.R.S'. *Phil. Trans.*, 90 (1800): 403–32. Read 26 June 1800.

W. [W. H. Watts?]. 'Some account of the late Dr. Garnett'. *Monthly Mag.* 14 (Aug. 1802): 48–50.

Wade, Nicholas J. 'Porterfield and Wells on the motions of our eyes'. *Perception* 29 (2000): 221–39.

Wakefield, Gilbert. *Memoirs of the Life of Gilbert Wakefield, B.A. Late Fellow of Jesus College, Cambridge. Written by Himself*. London: Printed by E. Hodson; and sold by J. Deighton, 1792. New edition, 2 vols., 1804.

Walker, Adam. *Syllabus of a Course of Lectures on Natural and Experimental Philosophy.* Manchester, 1771. Reissued 1772, 1790.

Walker, Adam. *A System of Familiar Philosophy, in Twelve Lectures: Being the Course Usually Read by Mr. A. Walker.* London: Printed for the author, 1799.

Walker, Joshua. *Dissertatio chemica inauguralis, de aqua sulphurea Harrowgatensi.* Edinburgh: Printed by Balfour, Auld, and Smellie, 1770.

Walker, Joshua. *An Essay on the Waters of Harrogate and Thorp-Arch in Yorkshire; containing Some Directions for their Use in Diseases. To which are Prefixed, Observations on Mineral Waters in General, and the Method of Analysing them.* London: Printed for J. Johnson; J. Wallis; J. Fielding; E. Hargrove, Knaresborough and Harrogate; and J. Binns, Leeds, 1784.

Wardhaugh, Benjamin. *Gunpowder and Geometry: The Life of Charles Hutton. Pit Boy, Mathematician and Scientific Rebel.* London: William Collins, 2019.

Watson, Robert Spence. *The History of the Literary and Philosophical Society of Newcastle-upon-Tyne (1793–1896).* London: Walter Scott Ltd., 1897.

Watts, Iain. 'Current events: galvanism and the world of scientific news, 1790–1830'. PhD thesis, Princeton University, 2015.

Westheimer, Gerald. 'Law of Equal Innervation of both Eyes: Thomas Reid preceded Hering by a century. An Historical Note'. *Vis. Res.* 101 (2014): 32–3.

Whiting, Charles Edwin. *The University of Durham 1832–1932.* London: Sheldon Press, 1932.

Wigan, Arthur Cleveland. 'Memoir of the author'. In Godwin, *Poetical Works*, i–viii. London: Chapman and Hall, 1854

Wilkes, Jennifer. 'Transpennine Enlightenment: Literary and Philosophical Societies in the north of England, 1780–1800'. PhD thesis, University of York, 2017.

Willan, Robert. *Experiments and Observations on the Sulphur-Water, at Croft and Harowgate, in Yorkshire.* London: Printed for J. Johnson, and W. Browne, 1782. 2nd edn., 1786.

Wilson, Thomas. *Miscellanies: Being a Selection from the Poems and Correspondence of the Rev. Thomas Wilson, with Memoirs of His Life*, ed. F. R. Raines. Manchester: Chetham Society, 1857.

Withers, Charles W. J. 'Geography, Natural History and the eighteenth-Century Enlightenment: putting the world in place'. *HWJ* 39 (1995): 136–63.

Wolfe, Jessica. 'Gorgonick Spirits: Myth, Figuration, and Mineral Vivency in the writings of Thomas Browne'. In Miriam Emma Jacobson, and Julie Park, eds., *Organic Supplements: Bodies and Things of the Natural World, 1580–1790*, 103–27. Charlottesville: University of Virginia Press, 2020.

Wordsworth, William, and Dorothy Wordsworth. *The Letters of William and Dorothy Wordsworth. Volume 5. The Later Years. Part II. 1829–1834*, ed. Ernest De Selincourt and Alan G. Hill. 2nd edn. Oxford: Oxford University Press, 1979. Also Oxford Scholarly Editions online, 2015.

Young, Thomas. *A Syllabus of a Course of Lectures on Natural and Experimental Philosophy*. London: Press of the Royal Institution: W. Savage, printer. Sold at the house of the Royal Institution, Albemarle Street; and by Cadell and Davies, 1802.

Young, Thomas. *A Course of Lectures on Natural Philosophy and the Mechanical Arts*. 2 vols. London: Printed by William Savage for Joseph Johnson, 1807.

Youngson, A. J. *The Making of Classical Edinburgh: 1750–1840*. Edinburgh: Edinburgh University Press, 1966.

Youngson, A. J. *Beyond the Highland Line: Three Journals of Travel in Eighteenth-Century Scotland. Burt, Pennant, Thornton*. London: Collins, 1974.

Index

Aberdeen 62, 73 n.56
Accum, Frederick 135
Adair, James Makittrick 73 n.54
Adams, George 111, 136
Aitken, John 29
Albert, Prince 153
Alexander, Tsar 136
Alexander, William 57–8
Allanby, William 23 n.30
Allen, John 128 n.19
Allen, Joseph 17, 20
America
    American Philosophical Society 70, 131 n.82
    American Revolution 52, 69–70, 96, 108
    American students at Edinburgh 27, 69
    Garnett's plans for emigration 4, 71, 77–9, 81
analyses
    gases 59–61, 73 n.49
    waters 1, 4, 50–1, 52, 57, 59–62, 73 n.46, 79, 120, 136, 140
Andersonian Institution, Glasgow 1, 4–6, 81–90, 107, 111–12, 114, 117, 135, 140, 144
    audiences 85–8, 99
    Garnett as professor 1, 4–6, 81–9, 98–100, 111–12, 117, 140, 144
    Garnett's loyalty 89, 100
    lectures 5, 84–7, 98
    premises 84–6, 97–8
    trustees, managers, and visitors 82–3, 98
Anderson, John 81–2, 98
    lectures 83, 85
    university career 81–3
    Will and Codicil 82–3, 87
Anderson's University. *See* Andersonian Institution, Glasgow
Annals of Philosophy 126
apothecaries 3, 14–15, 20–1, 32, 50–1, 54, 57, 62–3, 79, 147

Aram, Eugene 62, 73 n.53
Argyll agriculture 95
Aikin, Arthur 126
Aikin, Charles Rochemont 126
The Athenaeum 151
Athol, Duke of 91–2
Atkinson, George, *Worthies of Westmorland* 142
Auvergne 94

Baillie, Joanna 149
Banks, Sir Joseph 93, 109, 113, 118–19, 121–2, 135
Barbon 1, 3, 111, 119–20, 133–4, 136, 147–8, 151–3
    Bank (High Bank) House 10–12, 14, 22 n.2, 89, 151, 153, 155 n.29
    Burnside Cottage 148
    chapel of ease 13, 22 n.10
    Garnett's affection for 6, 21, 111–12, 119, 133–4, 147, 152
    Garnett's childhood in 9–15, 22 n.2, 22 n.10, 40, 143
    population 14
Barfoot, Michael 138
Barrington, Shute 108, 135
Barton, Benjamin Smith 44 n.7, 69
Bateman, Wynne 14, 23 n.15, 23 n.17
Bath 55, 57
Bavaria, Prince Elector of 108
Beddoes, Thomas 40, 45 n.24, 121, 138
Behrendt, Stephen 149
Bergman, Torbern 59–61
    Opuscula physica et chemica 59, 73 n.46
Berkeley, Bishop George 41
Berman, Morris 142
    Social Change and Scientific Organization 127 n.1, 129 n.35
Bernard, Thomas 108, 117, 135
Bettering Society 108–9

Bigge, Thomas 134
  *Expediency of Establishing a
    Lectureship* 145 n.6
Birkbeck, George 111, 128 n.19, 129 n.34,
    136, 144
Birmingham 50, 87–8, 157
Black, Joseph 26
  on magnesia alba 38
Blagden, Charles 118
Boerhaave, Hermann 38, 137
Boyle, Robert 59
Bracken, Henry 16
Bradford
  cultural elite 52
  Garnett in 4, 6, 49–52, 71 n.8, 77–8, 136
  social unrest 52, 78
Bramble, Matthew 55
Briggs, John 146 n.38
Brown, James 83
Brown, John 4, 88, 146 n.23
  character 31, 45 n.24, 137, 138
  critic of medical establishment 30–6,
    45 n.27
  education 31
  *Elements of Medicine/Elementa
    medicinae* 31, 33–6, 45 n.24,
    45 n.26, 70, 137
  lectures 1, 30–1
  masonic affiliation 42
  Old System of Physic 31, 45 n.27
  philosopher 40–1
Brown, Sanborn C., *Benjamin Thompson*
    129 n.35
Brunonianism/Brunonian principles 1, 4–5,
    30–9, 51, 67, 88, 137–8, 145 n.21
  Brunoniad 32
  Garnett as Brunonian 1, 30–41, 88,
    102 n.52, 137–8
  debility, direct and indirect 34, 37, 138,
    146 n.45
  decline and rejection 137–8
  excitement/excitability 32–4, 37, 137, 143
  following in Germany 137–8, 145 n.21
  scale of sickness and health 33–4, 137
Brunton, Deborah 24 n.37
Buchanan, George 44 n.7
Buffon, Georges 38
Burke, Edmund 91
Bury Grammar School 80
Buxton 57

Cadell and Davies, publishers 109
Campbell, Alexander 139
carbonated water 66, 79
Carey, George Saville 55–6, 72 n.31
Carlisle, Anthony 118
Carmichael, John 88
Casterton 10–11
Cavendish, Henry 118, 135
Celtic folklore/traditions 93–4, 96, 139
Chaptal, Jean-Antoine 59
Charlotte, Queen 26
chemical nomenclature 58–9, 86–7
Chester 21
Chirurgo-Obstetrical Society 29
Christian theism 18
Christie, John R. R. 44 n.9, 128 n.30
classical education 12–13, 119–20
Cleveland (Garnett), Catherine Grace (wife
    of TG) See Garnett (Cleveland),
    Catherine Grace (wife of TG)
Cleveland, John 67, 147
Cleveland (Ward), Sarah 70, 78
Cleveland, William 67, 99, 147–8, 151
Coleridge, Samuel Taylor 121
Collins, Wilkie, *The Moonstone* 138
Constantine, Mary-Ann 103 n.62
Copland, Alexander 79
Corsi, Pietro 46 n.34
Craig, James 25
Crescent Inn, Harrogate 53
Crescent water 53–4, 59–60
Crichton, Alexander 122, 136
Critical Review, reputation of 119
Crowther, James 51
Cullen, William 26, 30, 32, 36, 45 n.27,
    137
Cuppage, William C. 145 n.11
'Curious Travellers' project 103 n.62
Currie, James 78, 100 n.2
Cuvier, Georges 140

Dale, David 97
Dalton, John 3
Darwin, Erasmus 38, 93, 144
  The Botanic Garden 68
  evolutionary ideas 99–100
  Garnett's respect for 6, 58, 68–9,
    72 n.44, 74 n.74, 136
  respect for Garnett 68–9, 84
  scientific medicine 58, 144

Zoonomia; or, the Laws of Organic Life 58, 136
Davy, Humphry 130 n.51, 135, 141–2
  parallels with Garnett's career 3–4, 143
  professor at Royal Institution 121–5, 130 n.51
  relations with Garnett 122, 124–5, 135
Dawson, John 111
  Garnett's debt to 2–3, 14–19
  honours 20, 24 n.35
  mathematical career 18–20, 23 n.32
  medical career 15–16, 20–1, 43–4
  morality and religion 18–19, 23 n.27
  portrait and memorial 17, 20
  provincial roots 14–20
  success as teacher 3, 15–18
Deane, Edmund 54–5
  Spadacrene Anglica 72 n.23
de la Hire, Philippe 38
Dent 21
Dessert, Nicolas 94
Diderot, Denis, *Le Rêve de d'Alembert* 35
dispensaries
  Edinburgh 29
  St Marylebone 5, 127, 138
Drake, James 52
duelling/duels 6, 36, 51, 63, 74 n.60
Duff, David x, 145 n.11
Duncan, Andrew 29–30, 36, 39, 42, 68, 74 n.71, 84, 136
  Medical (and Philosophical) Commentaries 30
Durham 19, 153, 155 nn.28–9

Eaglesfield 3
Eason, Alexander 79, 83–4
East India Company (EIC) 147–8, 152
Edinburgh (University of) 1, 3, 16, 21, 51, 56, 68, 80, 88, 111, 120–1
  American students 27, 69
  curriculum 25–30
  examination procedures 38–9, 47 n.46
  extramural lectures 29–31, 128 n.19
  Garnett at 25–47
  Garnett's dissertations 27–9, 35–8, 40, 42, 102 n.52, 157–8
  Garnett's graduation 38–9
  medical school 57, 69, 88, 136
  professors 25–32
  Public Dispensary 29
  student societies 26–9, 35, 39–40, 51, 69
Edinburgh Evening Post 36
Elizabeth I 148
Ellis, George 142
Emerson, William 19, 23 n.32
emigration 71, 77–9, 81, 95
enclosures 64–7, 72 n.29
Encyclopaedia Britannica 43
English cemetery, Florence 148
Enlightenment 136, 143
  European 50
  Garnett, 'son' of 143
  'Industrial' 50
  moderate and radical 40
  Scottish 40, 64, 81–2
  'Transpennine' 50
Ewbank, Jane 114

Faculty of Physicians and Surgeons, Glasgow 89, 134
Falconer, William 57
Faraday, Michael 142
Farish, William 110, 118
Faujas de Saint Fond, Barthélemy 94
Fingal's Cave 93–4
Ford, James 26, 44 n.6
Fort Montague 54
Fothergill, John 50
Fourcroy, Antoine-François de 59
Freemasonry 6, 39–44
  Brown as Freemason 42
  Garnett as Freemason 41–4
  James Thomson as Freemason 42–3
  Scottish 41–2, 47 nn.59–60
  United Grand Lodge of England 42
French chemistry 58–9, 86–7
French Revolution 84

galvanism 118–19, 122, 126
Gardenstone, Lord 31
Garnett, Alice 11, 80
Garnett (Cleveland), Catherine Grace (wife of TG) 67–8, 70–1, 78, 80, 97–9, 107
Garnett, Edward 10
Garnett, Elizabeth 10–11
Garnett, Emmeline 22 n.10
Garnett (Godwin), Catherine Grace (daughter of TG) 119, 133–4, 136

birth and baptism 98–9, 107, 112
death and burial 151
defence of father 142
poetry 149–52
Wordsworth's opinion of 149–50, 154 n.17
Garnett, Georgiana Kendal 11, 152
Garnett, John (father of TG) 10–11, 147
Garnett (Lovelace), Louisa Cleveland 80, 119, 133, 136, 151, 152
  death 150, 154 n.10
  marriage 147–8, 154 n.6
  voyage to India 147–8, 154 n.6
Garnett, Margaret 10, 67, 133, 147
Garnett, Mary Fleming 11, 153
Garnett, Revd John (brother of TG) 10–11, 151–2, 155 n.27
Garnett, Robert Skyring 10, 151–2
Garnett, Thomas 3, 7, 21, 43–4, 49, 51, 56–7, 71 n.8, 71 n.14, 74 n.59, 74 n.74, 147, 152
  ambition 20, 68–9, 79
  at Andersonian 1, 4–6, 81–9, 98–100, 111–12, 117, 140, 144
  childhood 9–15, 22 n.2, 22 n.10, 40, 143
  classical languages, on 119–20
  Dawson as mentor 2–3, 14–19
  death and burial 5, 127, 133, 144 n.1
  depression 4, 5, 7, 68, 99, 119–21, 143
  De visu 19, 23 n.30, 24 n.35, 38–9, 41, 46 n.42, 74 n.71
  dissertations 27–9, 35–8, 40, 42, 102 n.52, 157–8
  Edinburgh, studies at 25–39, 44 n.7, 46 nn.47–8
  emigration, plans for 4, 71, 77–9, 81
  family tree 11, 22 n.2
  female education 5, 79, 85–6, 116–17, 144
  Highland tour 1, 5, 89–98, 102 n.41, 119–20, 139, 144 (*see also* Observations on a Tour through the Highlands)
  as independent lecturer 4, 77–81, 84, 125–7, 133–4
  instruments, cabinet of 98, 111–12, 134
  Lecture on the Preservation of Health 72 n.44, 88, 102 n.52, 137, 145 n.20
  lecturing style 5, 7, 77, 86–7, 112–14
  The Life of John Metcalf 54, 72 n.21
  masonic affiliation 41–4
  moderation 40, 81
  natural history, interest in 52, 89, 93, 98–100, 125–6
  'Optics' 43, 47 n.55
  Outlines of a Course of Lectures on Chemistry 124–5, 130 n.49
  Outlines of a Course of Lectures on Natural & Experimental Philosophy 86, 102 n.45, 120, 130 n.49
  patronage by Wedderburn 6, 63–7, 135–6
  political views 40, 52, 81, 100, 105 n.104
  Popular Lectures on Zoonomia. See Zoonomia, Popular Lectures on (Garnett)
  portraits 66, 115, 156
  Reid, influence of 19, 38
  religious views 18–19, 40–3, 151
  resignation from Andersonian 100, 111
  resignation from Royal Institution 115, 121–3, 140
  at Royal Institution 1, 100, 107–26, 140–2
  Rumford, relations with 5–6, 112–13, 117–19, 122–3, 140
  tombstone and coffin plate 133, 144 n.1
  Treatise on the Mineral Waters of Harrogate 58–60, 64–5, 68, 74 n.66
  on vision 37–8, 41, 137 (*see also* Garnett, Thomas, *De visu*)
  Will 133–5, 147
Garnett, Thomas (grandfather of TG) 10–11, 22 n.1
Garnett, Thomas (great-uncle of TG) 11, 147
Garnett, Revd Thomas (nephew of TG) 11, 152, 155 nn. 28–9
Garsdale 15–16, 21
George III 27, 108
Gibson family, Whelprigg 12, 153, 155 n.29
Giddy, Davies 131 n.73
Gillray, James 140, 142
Gilpin, William 91, 92
Girdler, William 70–1
Girtanner, Christoph 137
Glasgow 1, 4–5, 87, 89–90, 100, 111, 113, 142, 144. *See also* Andersonian Institution, Glasgow

Faculty of Physicians and Surgeons 89, 134
Flesh Market 97
Grammar School building 83, 98
'New Town' 85
prosperity 96–8, 107
Royal Infirmary 98
Trades Hall 85, 98, 102 n.36
Gleig, George 47 n.66
Godwin, Catherine Grace. *See* Garnett (Godwin), Catherine Grace (daughter of TG)
Godwin, Thomas 148–51
Golinski, Jan 4, 124, 131 n.75
Gordon, Francis 31
Gough, John 3, 79
gout 56–7, 64
grammar schools
Bampton 12–13
Bury 80
classical curriculum 11–13, 152–3
Glasgow 83, 98
Kirkby Lonsdale 11–12, 14, 152
Sedbergh 14, 50
Westmorland 13, 155 n.27
Great Marlborough Street house and lectures 125–7, 133–4
Green, William 92
Gregory, James 26, 30
Gregory, John 29

Hailstone, Samuel 52, 71 n.8
Halifax 52, 54
Haller, Albrecht von 32
Hall-Stevenson, John 55
Hamilton, Alexander 26
Hamilton, William 94
Hare Hatch House 70
Hargrove, Ely 54, 56, 67
Harrison, Margaret 10, 22 n.1
Harrogate 1, 72 n.34, 77, 93, 99, 120. *See also* Garnett, Thomas, *Treatise on the Mineral Waters of Harrogate*
female visitors 56, 67–8
Garnett in 4, 57–71, 74 n.70, 112
growth and improvement 49–50, 52–7, 64–7, 144
inns 55–6, 60, 67
spa society 72 n.31, 112
waters, variety and analyses of 1, 53–4, 57, 59, 61–2, 79, 120, 136

Hastings exhibitions, Oxford 23 n.17
Hatchett, Charles 135
Haygarth, John 21
Headrick, James 84
Heald, William Margetson ('Julius Juniper') 32
The Brunoniad 32
Hebridean islands 94–5
Hemans, Felicia 150
Henry, Thomas 79
High Bank House (formerly Bank House) 10, 12, 14, 22 n.2, 89, 151, 153, 155 n.29
Highlands and islands, Scottish 1, 89–100
Garnett's tour 1, 5, 89–98, 102 n.41, 119–20, 139, 144
hardship 94–6
Highland Clearances 95, 143
music and poetry 96, 139
sheep-farming 96, 104 n.86
tours and tourism 89–94, 103 n.61
Hippisley, Sir John Coxe 110, 116–17, 135, 140–2
Hippocratic aphorisms 28, 39
Hoare, Harry (Messrs Hoare Bank) 135–6
Hodgson, John 12–13
Hoffmann, Friedrich 59
Hofmann, August Wilhelm 60
Holland, Elizabeth, Lady 141–2
Home, Francis 26
Hope, John 26
Hope, Thomas Charles 121
Horley Green Spa 52–4, 59
Howard, Luke 118
Hull, Christopher 14, 23 n.17
Hume, David 41
Hutcheson, Francis 82
Hutchinson, Thomas 59–63, 73 nn.53–4, 73 n.56
Hutton, Charles 20, 24 n.34

India
East India Company 147–8, 152
Indian Medical Service 148
Louisa Cleveland Garnett in 147–8, 154 n.6
industrialization and urbanization 1–2, 20, 77, 108
infirmaries
Edinburgh 29
Glasgow 98

Leeds 51, 57
Manchester 80
Israel, Jonathan 40

Jacobite rising 96–7
Jacob, Margaret 40
Jacques, John 54
James, Frank A. J. L. ix, 102 n.49, 127 n.1, 127 n.6
Jenner, Edward 136
Jennings, Ezra 138
Johnson, Samuel 77, 96, 143
Jones, Henry Bence, *The Royal Institution: Its Founder and its First Professors* 142
Jones, Peter 50
Jones, Robert 36
Jurin, Jean 38

Keir, James 121
Kendal 3, 21, 79
Kingsbury, Michael x, 12, 22 n.2, 155 n.29
Kirkby Lonsdale 9–11, 14, 112, 152
Knaresborough 54, 58, 62–4, 73 n.53, 111
knowledge, 'marketplace' for 78–81
Knox, John, *View of the British Empire* 94
Kosegarten, Ludwig Theoboul 139

The Ladies' Monthly Museum 149
Lancaster 15–16, 21, 64, 80, 136
Langford, Paul 2
Lavoisier, Antoine 58–9, 87
learning, a 'trade' 77, 143
Leask, Nigel 103 n.62
lectures, vogue for public 2, 4–5, 43, 78–81, 87–8, 123–6
Leeds General Infirmary 51, 57
Leiden 16, 26
Leigh, Robert Holt 19
Lincoln Medical Society Literary Fund 135
Linnaeus, Carl 93
Litterdale 17
Liverpool 4, 78–9, 88
Lodge of Lights, Warrington 42
The London Literary Gazette 150–1
Lonsdale Magazine 142, 146 n.38
Lord Loughborough. *See* Wedderburn, Alexander
Lord Provost of Glasgow 82
Lothian, Robert 87

Lovelace, Henry Philip 147–8
Lovelace, Louisa. *See* Garnett (Lovelace), Louisa Cleveland
Low, Sampson, publisher 150
Lythe, S. G. E. 5, 93, 143

Macfarlan, Duncan 145 n.14
Macpherson, James 96
Manchester 78–81, 85–6
  Garnett's lectures in 4, 78–9
  Literary and Philosophical Society 3, 20, 68, 79–81, 83–4
  'Manchester model' 3, 49
  'shock city' 3
Marchioness of Ely 154 n.6
'marketplace' for knowledge 78–81
Martin, Benjamin 2
Maskelyne, Nevil 118, 129 n.37
Mathematical Tripos, Cambridge 3, 13, 16
Maud, Timothy 50
Maud, William 50–1
Mayfair, Garnett in 100, 107–31
McDonald, Patrick 104 n.84
mechanics' institute movement 144
Medical Society of London 68
Mee, Jon 50
Meikleham, William 83
Mellish, William 109, 127 n.6
Metcalf, Blind Jack 54, 72 n.21
mineralogy 89, 125
Moffat 93, 103 n.72, 107, 140
Monro, Alexander 136
Monthly Magazine 133, 135, 139–40
Morning Chronicle 89, 119
Morning Post 89
Mossman, George
  attacked by Gernett 51–2, 62
  attacked by Hailstone 52
Moxon, Edward, publisher 150
Moyes, Henry 69, 81, 114
Munro secundus, Alexander 26

Nairne, Edward 136
Natural History Society (NHS), Edinburgh 27, 35–8, 40–2, 44 n.7, 69
Newcastle 24 n.34, 50, 98, 100
  Literary and Philosophical Society 98, 134
New Lanark 97
Newton, Sir Isaac, and Newtonianism

affinities with Brunonianism 4–5, 32, 41, 137
masonic tradition 42–3
precession of equinoxes 19
Nichols, John, *Literary History of the Eighteenth Century* 73 n.53
Nicholson, William 118
Nooth, John Mervin 66

Observations on a Tour through the Highlands (Garnett) 1, 5, 89–99
critical review 119–20
German translation 1, 139
illustrations 89–90, 92, 119, 139
Ortt, Richard 80, 99
Ossian 93–4
poetry of 96, 104 n.91, 119, 139, 149
Owen, Robert 97

Paine, Thomas 52
Palmerston, Lady 139
Parker, James Cadwallader 133
Parker, Thomas 133, 135
Parsell, John 86
Parsons, Guglielma Maria Grace 67
patronage 6, 63–7, 77, 136
Peacock, George, *Life of Thomas Young* 142
Pearson, George 130 n.48
Pegge, Christopher 136
Pennant, Thomas 90–1, 93, 103 n.62
Percival, Thomas 6, 79, 84, 136
Percival, Thomas Bassnet 136
Philadelphia 69–70, 75 n.75
Phillips, Simon 115
Phillips, Thomas 114
physician as philosopher 26, 41
physicians 2, 6, 49, 54, 57, 60, 68, 77, 137
status of 26–7, 41, 62, 126–7
Pictet, Marc-Auguste 117
Platt, A. E., *Parish and Grammar School of Sedbergh* 22 n.17
Playfair, John 20
pneumatic medicine 121, 138, 141
poetry 32, 42, 153
Catherine Grace Godwin 149–52
Highland 96, 139
Ossian 96, 104 n.91, 119, 139, 149
Revd Thomas Garnett's 152–3, 155 nn.28–9
romantic 139

Porterfield, William 38, 41
Porter, Roy 56
Price, Richard 23 n.26
Priestley, Joseph 18–19, 38, 40, 69, 81
Protestant Hanoverian Britain 96
provincial dilemma 1, 19–21, 49–50

Quakers 3, 21, 50–1, 57
Queen Elizabeth School (Kirkby Lonsdale) 11–12, 14, 152
The Queen's College, Oxford, Hastings Exhibitions 23 n.17

Redmire Spaw 51
Reid, Thomas 19, 82
Inquiry into the Human Mind 41
on vision 38
Rendall, Jane 128 n.30
Richardson, Edgar P., 'Athens of America' 70
Richmond, D. C. 11–12
Robinet, Jean-Jacques 35
De la nature 35, 46 n.34
Robinson, Elihu 3
Robinson, Mary 10, 22 n.1
Robison, John 43, 47 n.66
Roscoe, William 78, 100 n.2
Rosner, Lisa 36, 44 n.11
Rotheram, John 134
Rousseau, George 56
Royal College of Chemistry 60
Royal College of Physicians 15, 43, 127, 135
Royal College (Corporation), of Surgeons of Edinburgh 29
Royal Infirmary, Edinburgh 29, 43
Royal Infirmary, Glasgow 98
Royal Institution (RI) 1, 4–6, 100, 107, 140
aims 109–10, 129 n.35
Albemarle Street property 112–18, 127 n.1, 127 n.4
campaign for 108–10
foundation 107–21, 142
Garnett at 1, 100, 107–27, 140
improving philosophy 107–12
Journals 111, 118, 121, 124
lecture-theatre, new 97–8, 118, 141
lecture-theatre, temporary 114–17
promotional literature 108–10

proprietors and subscribers 79, 108–9, 114, 116, 135
Rumford, role of 108–10, 112–13, 117–24, 127 n.4, 140–2
Scientific Committee of Council 118, 121
teaching of artisans 109–10, 117, 129 n.34
Royal Irish Academy, Dublin 68, 80
Royal Medical Society (RMS), Edinburgh 42, 44 n.11, 51, 69, 88, 137
Cullenians and Brunonians 36
Dawson a member 24 n.35
dissertations 28–9, 36, 39, 88
Garnett a member 27–9, 36, 88, 137
Hall of 27, 30
Royal Military Academy, Woolwich 24 n.34
Royal Physical Society (RPS), Edinburgh 24 n.35, 27, 35–8, 44 n.7
Royal Society, London 4, 19, 93, 109, 111, 118–19
Rumford, Count Benjamin 129 n.34, 130 n.48, 136
criticism of 140, 142
Davy, liking for 121–4
hostility to Garnett 5–6, 113, 117–19, 122–3, 140
invitation to Garnett 100, 112–13
Royal Institution, role in foundation and management 108–10, 112–13, 117–24, 127 n.4, 140–2
Rush, Benjamin 70, 138
Russian Academy of Science 136
Rutherford, Daniel 26

Sadler, John and James 120
Savage, William, printer to the Royal Institution 134–5
Scottish identity 96
Scott, Rosemary 151
Scruton, John 84
Sedbergh 3, 14–16, 18–21, 40, 43, 50–1, 151
Sedgwick, Adam 15, 18, 21, 151–2
Shelley, Mary, *Frankenstein* 123
Simpson, Thomas 19, 23 n.32
Simpson, William, *Cold Bathing* 72 n.22
Sinclair, Sir John 94–6, 104 n.87
Statistical (*and New Statistical*) *Account of Scotland* 94–5

Skyring, Elizabeth 10–11
Slinn, Sara, *Education of the Anglican Clergy* 155 n.27
Smith, Adam 82
Smith, John 95
Smith, John Raphael 156
Smith, Robert 41
Smollett, Tobias, *Expedition of Humphry Clinker* 55
Soane, John 145 n.11
Society for Bettering the Condition and Increasing the Comforts of the Poor. *See* Bettering Society
Society of Arts 135
Southey, Robert 121, 149
spa treatments. *See also* analyses; Bergman, Torbern; Garnett, Thomas, *Treatise on the Mineral Waters of Harrogate*
procedures 53–4, 61
science of 1, 4, 50–2, 57–63, 73 n.46, 79, 140
vogue for 2, 4–6, 49, 52–7, 63–8, 120, 143–4
squinting 38
Staffa 93–4
St Andrews 51–2, 62, 73 n.56, 134
St Andrew's Church, Sedbergh 20
statesmen 10, 152
Sterne, Lawrence 55
Stewart, James 100
Stewart, Matthew 18–20
St George's Anglican Cathedral, Madras 148
St John's College, Cambridge 14, 22 n.17
St John's Well, Harrogate 67
St John the Baptist Church, Firbank 151
St Marylebone Dispensary 5, 127, 138
St Mary's Church, Radcliffe 80
St Mary's Church, Wargrave 68
St Pancras Old Church 148
St Petersburg 136
Stray, Harrogate 56, 64, 67
St Robert's Well, Knaresborough 54
Sullivan, Richard 110, 135
surgeons and surgery 3, 14–16, 20, 27, 29–30, 32, 49–51, 54, 63, 84, 147–8, 154 n.12
Surgeons, Corporation of, Edinburgh 29
Surgeons, Corporation of, London 16

Taunton, Lord 11
Taylor, William 148, 154 n.12
Temple, Richard 127
Tewit Well, Harrogate 53–4
Thackray, Arnold 3, 49
    Manchester model 49
Thackwray, William 60, 62
Thomas, Carol and David x, 22 n.2
Thomas, David 22 n.2, 144 n.1
Thompson, Benjamin. *See* Rumford,
    Count Benjamin
Thomson, James (chemist) 121
Thomson, James (poet) 42–3, 121
Thomson, Thomas 126
Thomson, William 83
Thom, William 82
Thoresby, Ralph 54
Thornton, Samuel 135
Thornton, Robert John 127, 138
    Brunonian 138
    Philosophy of Medicine 138, 146 n.23
Tilloch, Alexander 139
Tindall, William 63
Tom's Coffee House 125, 131 n.85, 134, 137
Treaty of Paris (1783) 70
Tuke, William 50
Turner, William 98, 134, 145 n.8

Udal, Charles 15
Underwood, Thomas Richard 121
United Grand Lodge of England 42
universities/university education 13, 16, 25, 144, 153, 155 n.28. *See also* Edinburgh (University of)
    Anderson's (*see* Andersonian Institution, Glasgow)
    Cambridge 3, 13–16, 21, 22 n.17, 43, 110
    Durham 152–3
    Glasgow 5, 81–3, 103 n.62, 145 n.14
    Newcastle 134
    Oxford 22 n.17, 43, 90, 136
    Pennsylvania 69–70

Villiers, Mary, countess of Buckingham 55
Virgil 12
vision 37–8, 41, 137

vivency, mineral 35–6
Volta, Alessandro, electric pile 118–19

Wakefield, Gilbert 13, 52
Walker, Adam 80–1, 101 n.16
Walker, Joshua 57–8
Wall, Martin 136
Wargrave 68, 70
Warltire, John 81
Warrington 42, 80
Watt, James 6, 80, 87–8, 98, 119, 121
Watt, James, Jnr 84
Watts, Iain 129 n.38
Watts, Walter Henry 89–90, 92, 97, 119
Webster, Thomas 112–13, 114, 116, 120, 124, 129 n.34, 130 n.48, 158
Wedderburn, Alexander 6, 63–7, 135–6
    dedicatory plate to 65
Wedderburn House 64, 67, 70, 74 n.66
Westmorland 1–3, 9, 43, 80, 119, 134, 152
    schools and literacy in 2, 11–13, 155 n.27
Wigan, Arthur Cleveland 151
Wilberforce, William 108
Wildbore, Charles 19–20
Wilkes, Jennifer 50
Wilkes, John 52
Willan, Robert 21, 24 n.37, 50
Wilson, John 149
Wilson, Thomas 23 n.27
winds, Darwin and Garnett on 68–9
Wistar, Caspar 69
Wolfe, Jessica 46 n.34
women at lectures 5, 79, 85–6, 116–17, 144
Worboys, Mary 67–8, 99, 111, 119, 133–4, 136, 147, 151, 153 n.1, 154 n.25
Wordsworth, Dorothy 150–1
Wordsworth, William 149–50

yeoman families 3, 10, 15, 67, 143, 152–3
    changing fortunes 7, 10
York 56, 114, 128 n.30
York Cascade 91–2
Young, Thomas 124, 135, 142
    Course of Lectures on Natural Philosophy and the Mechanical Arts 124

Zoonomia; or, the Laws of Organic Life
(Darwin) 58, 136
Zoonomia, Popular Lectures on (Garnett)
41, 46 n.42, 142
Brunonian content 34, 137–8

neglect 5
publication 125–6, 134–5
review 138
subscribers 134–6, 145 n.11, 147

www.ingramcontent.com/pod-product-compliance
Lightning Source LLC
Chambersburg PA
CBHW052119300426
44116CB00010B/1716